Economic Well-being and Household Debt

The growing indebtedness of households reported over the last 30 years and in most developed countries has serious economic and social implications. This book provides insight into the concepts, measures, and determinants of household indebtedness, over-indebtedness, and well-being by integrating theoretical perspectives, adopting recent analytical methods, and using a sample of Polish households.

The authors identified the socio-demographic and economic characteristics of indebted and over-indebted households, as well as the basic characteristics of indebtedness and the differences in its subjective perception among over-indebted households and those that are not over-indebted. They determined the spatial differentiation of over-indebtedness, examining the relationship between economic, social, and behavioural factors and over-indebtedness and the role of over-indebtedness in shaping the economic well-being of households. The results of a questionnaire conducted on a sample of Polish households and econometric modelling served as the basis for assessing the economic well-being of indebted households. This assessment was conducted with the use of a composite well-being indicator developed by the authors. Given the multidimensional nature of the issues being analysed, the authors offer an approach that accounts for two separate but overlapping dimensions of economic well-being, namely, material and financial, and two ways of assessing each of them: objective and subjective.

The book holds appeal for researchers, scholars, and students of economics, finance, consumer economics, and economic psychology and offers practical guidance for policymakers and advisors who deal with consumer affairs.

Agnieszka Wałęga is Assistant Professor in the Department of Statistics at the Cracow University of Economics.

Grzegorz Wałęga is Assistant Professor in the Department of Microeconomics at the Cracow University of Economics.

Ryszard Kowalski is Assistant Professor in the Department of Microeconomics at the Cracow University of Economics.

Routledge Studies in the European Economy

Economic Transformation in Poland and Ukraine
National and Regional Perspectives
Edited by Rafał Wisła and Andrzej Nowosad

Competitiveness and Economic Development in Europe
Prospects and Challenges
Edited by Sławomir I. Bukowski, Alina Hyz and Marzanna B. Lament

Brexit and the Political Economy of Ireland
Creating a New Economic Settlement
Paul Teague

The Economic and Legal Impact of Covid-19
The Case of Poland
Edited by Jerzy Menkes and Magdalena Suska

Brexit and the Future of the European Union
Firm-Level Perspectives
Edited by Marian Gorynia, Barbara Jankowska and Katarzyna Mroczek-Dąbrowska

The Socioeconomic Impact of COVID-19 on Eastern European Countries
Edited by Paweł Dykas and Rafał Wisła

The European Union Digital Single Market
Europe's Digital Transformation
Edited by Łukasz Dawid Dąbrowski and Magdalena Suska

Economic Well-being and Household Debt
Agnieszka Wałęga, Grzegorz Wałęga, and Ryszard Kowalski

For more information about this series, please visit:
www.routledge.com/series/SE0431

Economic Well-being and Household Debt

Agnieszka Wałęga, Grzegorz Wałęga, and Ryszard Kowalski

Translated by Jasper Tilbury

Routledge
Taylor & Francis Group
LONDON AND NEW YORK

First published 2023
by Routledge
4 Park Square, Milton Park, Abingdon, Oxon OX14 4RN

and by Routledge
605 Third Avenue, New York, NY 10158

Routledge is an imprint of the Taylor & Francis Group, an informa business

British Library Cataloguing-in-Publication Data
A catalogue record for this book is available from the British Library

Library of Congress Cataloging-in-Publication Data
A catalog record for this book has been requested

ISBN: 978-1-032-18470-8 (hbk)
ISBN: 978-1-032-18472-2 (pbk)
ISBN: 978-1-003-25470-6 (ebk)

DOI: 10.4324/9781003254706

Typeset in Bembo
by Apex CoVantage, LLC

Contents

List of figures vii
List of tables viii
Preface x
About the authors xii

Introduction 1

1 **Household indebtedness: theories and facts** 5

1.1 Theoretical background of household indebtedness 5
1.2 Data sources and selected findings on the indebtedness of Polish households 11
1.3 Overview of research on the indebtedness of households in Poland 15
1.4 Summary 21
References 22

2 **Household indebtedness: empirical analysis** 29

2.1 Research methodology 29
2.2 Characteristics of indebted households 35
2.3 Subjective assessment of indebtedness 47
2.4 Motives to borrow 52
2.5 Summary 59
References 60

3 **The nature of household over-indebtedness: theory and measurement** 63

3.1 The concept of over-indebtedness 63
3.2 Determinants of over-indebtedness: literature review 66
3.3 Indicators of over-indebtedness 72
3.4 Summary 79
References 80

4 Characteristics of over-indebted households: empirical analysis 88

4.1 The level of over-indebtedness 88
4.2 Cross-sectional analysis of over-indebted households 91
4.3 The spatial differentiation of over-indebtedness 99
4.4 Determinants of over-indebtedness: regression analysis 105
4.5 Summary 114
References 117

5 Household over-indebtedness and well-being 120

5.1 Evolution of the concept of well-being 120
5.2 Definition of economic well-being 126
5.3 The impact of over-indebtedness on well-being: a theoretical framework 130
5.4 Literature review of the well-being of households in Poland 133
5.5 Summary 140
References 142

6 The economic well-being of over-indebted households: own research 152

6.1 A cross-sectional analysis of the economic well-being of over-indebted households 152
6.2 Measuring economic well-being: a composite indicator approach 163
6.3 The impact of over-indebtedness on economic well-being 174
6.4 Summary 178
References 182

Conclusion 186

Index 192

Figures

1.1	Household debt as % of net disposable income (2019)	12
2.1	Sample structure by province (voivodship)	33
2.2	Late, early, and punctual repayment of credits and loans	46
4.1	Over-indebted households – relationships between objective and subjective over-indebtedness	90
4.2	Representation of over-indebted households	98
4.3	Selected characteristics of household debt by voivodship (%)	100
4.4	Results of voivodship grouping by Ward's method according to DSTI30 and SB	102
4.5	Results of voivodship grouping by Ward's method according to BPL and SB	103
4.6	Results of voivodship grouping by Ward's method according to over-indebtedness and its characteristics	104
5.1	Elements of financial well-being	128
5.2	Financial well-being and its determinants	129
6.1	Size distribution of flats and houses occupied by over-indebted and not-over-indebted households (m^2)	154
6.2	Distribution of indicator values for the overall well-being, and for financial and material dimensions of well-being of over-indebted households (left panel) and not-over-indebted households (right panel)	168

Tables

2.1 CATI surveys: basic data (%) 32
2.2 Characteristics of the sample (%) 34
2.3 Structure of indebted households by age (%) 37
2.4 Structure of indebted households by educational level (%) 38
2.5 Structure of indebted households by household size (%) 41
2.6 Structure of indebted households by place of residence (%) 43
2.7 Structure of indebted households by source of income/maintenance (%) 45
2.8 Perceptions of indebtedness as a threat to health by selected socio-demographic characteristics (%) 47
2.9 Perceptions of indebtedness as a threat to health by selected indebtedness characteristics (%) 48
2.10 Safe levels of indebtedness (expressed as a multiple of monthly incomes) in socio-demographic cross section (%) 50
2.11 Safe levels of indebtedness (expressed as a multiple of monthly incomes) by selected characteristics of indebtedness (%) 51
2.12 Motives for borrowing by age range (%) 53
2.13 Motives for indebtedness by educational level (%) 54
2.14 Motives for indebtedness by place of residence (%) 54
2.15 Motives for indebtedness by household monthly income (%) 55
2.16 Motives for indebtedness by DSTI ratio (%) 55
3.1 Indicators of over-indebtedness 73
4.1 Matrix of over-indebtedness indicators (%) 89
4.2 Proportion of over-indebted households broken down according to socio-demographic features, economic features, and debt characteristics (%) 91
4.3 Structure of over-indebted households by selected socio-demographic features, economic features, and debt characteristics (%) 95
4.4 Over-indebted households' reasons for borrowing (%) 99
4.5 Proportion of over-indebted households by voivodship (%) 101
4.6 Average values of variables in each cluster obtained by the *k*-means method 105

4.7	Explanatory variables in the logit model for over-indebted households: economic, social, and behavioural factors	106
4.8	Results of parameter estimation of the logit model for the dependent variables identifying over-indebted households: economic, social, and behavioural factors (models 1–3)	108
4.9	Results of parameter estimation of the logit model for the dependent variables identifying over-indebted households: economic, social, and behavioural factors (models 4–6)	110
5.1	Selected definitions of economic well-being (financial well-being)	127
6.1	Distribution of the monthly income of over-indebted and not-over-indebted households (%)	153
6.2	Over-indebted and not-over-indebted households' subjective assessments of their financial state (%)	153
6.3	Proportion of over-indebted and not-over-indebted households occupying overcrowded dwellings by form of ownership (%)	155
6.4	The subjectively perceived housing conditions of over-indebted and not-over-indebted households (%)	155
6.5	Levels of difficulty in satisfying selected consumption needs (%)	156
6.6	The financial security of households and their budget management skills (%)	158
6.7	The consequences of over-indebtedness: the health and psychological dimensions (%)	159
6.8	Methods used by over-indebted and not-over-indebted households to cope with financial difficulty (%)	160
6.9	Expenditure foregone by over-indebted and not-over-indebted households when in financial difficulty (%)	162
6.10	Baseline variables identifying economic well-being	166
6.11	Basic characteristics of the economic well-being indicator – overall, and in the financial and material dimensions – for over-indebted and not-over-indebted households	169
6.12	Values of the economic well-being indicator – overall, and in the financial and material dimensions – by socio-demographic, economic, and household indebtedness characteristics	170
6.13	Gini coefficient values representing the inequality of the distribution of the economic well-being of over-indebted and not-over-indebted households	173
6.14	Theil index decomposition of the inequality of economic well-being	173
6.15	Parameter estimates for the linear model of the composite indicator of economic well-being	175
6.16	Parameter estimates for the linear model of the composite indicator of overall economic well-being for over-indebted and not-over-indebted households	177

Preface

This book, which is devoted to economic well-being and household indebtedness in Poland, forms the nucleus of a research project titled *The Economic Well-Being of Over-Indebted Households*. The project is funded by the National Science Centre in Poland through grant No. 2015/19/D/HS4/02569. The country's broader integration into the world economy and its civilisational advancement has helped shape the consumption aspirations of Polish households over the past 30 years. The social and economic transformation that began in 1989 not only enabled consumption patterns typical of highly developed countries to penetrate freely but also allowed them to become consolidated through the use of financial products (credits and loans). Thanks to the use of external sources to finance consumption, a society which for decades had been deprived of the freedom to cultivate a consumer culture now had the opportunity to swiftly improve its living conditions and catch up with the households of Western European countries.

Although it seems obvious to state that over-indebtedness has an impact on the situation of individuals (households), the numerous studies of household consumption in Poland have not yet addressed the broader question of the role of debt in the context of indebted households being able to satisfy their wants and – more generally – its role in their well-being.

This lack of interest in the matter of household indebtedness might be explained by the overall level of indebtedness in Poland, which remains comparatively low compared to highly developed countries. Although intense competition and continuous market growth – halted only briefly by the global crisis of 2008 – have ensured uninterrupted growth in household indebtedness, with the value of household credit increasing more than tenfold between 2000 and 2018 (NBP, 2020), the share of household credit in GDP was approximately only 35% in 2018, which was almost twice as low as the EU15 average and one-and-a-half times lower than the EU28 average (IMF, 2020). Furthermore, the rapid increase in both the volume and value of household lending in recent years has, with real and nominal interest rates remaining low, made it possible to avoid serious macroeconomic pressures. Nevertheless, given that we are dealing not only with the macro-scale but also with the micro-scale, where over-indebtedness is always a huge problem that affects all members of a household, the lack of interest in household over-indebtedness is puzzling.

Taking into account the experiences of developed countries, further increases in household indebtedness can be expected in Poland, such that the issues associated with it will undoubtedly begin to gain in importance. Inevitably, when households accumulate debt, there is a greater likelihood that they will face difficulties in servicing it. What is more, as global experience shows, the negative impact of increased lending on the quality of financial institutions' loan portfolios is delayed, so that it is usually several years after the original loans have been taken out that repayment difficulties and 'bad' loans appear. It is also important to note that the exceptionally favourable macroeconomic conditions experienced since 2008 (income growth, low interest rates, rising property prices) will be difficult to sustain in the long run. Where there is a credit boom and a growing economy, over-indebtedness does not place an excessive burden on the financial system as a whole – irrespective of the scale of private indebtedness. The problem becomes worse, however, in periods of economic slowdown.

Noticing these patterns stimulated our interest in household over-indebtedness. By researching over-indebted households, we were able to gain a better understanding of their current situation and to indicate the possible social and economic consequences of over-indebtedness.

This book was originally published in Polish as *Warunki życia nadmiernie zadłużonych gospodarstw domowych* (2021). Although it concerns Polish households, we believe that well-being and household indebtedness are of wider interest to researchers around the world. We also believe that the analysis of both the socio-demographic and economic characteristics of households and the drivers of over-indebtedness makes it possible to draw universal conclusions about their impact on economic well-being.

We are grateful to Professor Czesław Bywalec and to Professor Marek Kośny for their valuable comments and guidance, which gave this book its final shape. We would like to thank Jasper Tilbury, who has done great work in translating our book into English, and the excellent team at Routledge, which has expertly guided us through the production process from beginning to end. Finally, we owe a debt of gratitude to Professor Wojciech Giza, head of the Department of Microeconomics at the Cracow University of Economics, and to Professor Barbara Pawełek, head of the Department of Statistics at the Cracow University of Economics, for their kindness, constant encouragement and words of support, and for creating an atmosphere that inspires academic work.

References

IMF. (2020). *Global Debt Database – Household debt, loans and debt securities*. www.imf.org/external/datamapper/HH_LS@GDD

NBP. (2020). *Dane finansowe sektora bankowego*. Warszawa: Narodowy Bank Polski. www.nbp.pl/home.aspx?f=/statystyka/pieniezna_i_bankowa/naleznosci.html

Wałęga, A., Wałęga, G., & Kowalski, R. (2021). *Warunki życia nadmiernie zadłużonych gospodarstw domowych w Polsce*. Warszawa: Polskie Wydawnictwo Ekonomiczne.

About the authors

Agnieszka Wałęga is an assistant professor in the Department of Statistics at the Cracow University of Economics. She is a member of the Polish Statistical Association, the Polish Economic Society, and the editorial board of *Entrepreneurial Business and Economics Review*. Her academic interests lie in the statistical analysis of household budgets and in issues connected with poverty, the labour force, and household debt. Her output comprises several dozen publications, including co-written monographs and papers published in academic journals in Poland and abroad. She is the author of a monograph titled *Spójność ekonomiczna gospodarstw domowych w Polsce: analiza statystyczna* (Wydawnictwo UEK 2015) and the co-author of textbooks on labour market statistics.

Grzegorz Wałęga is an assistant professor in the Department of Microeconomics at the Cracow University of Economics. He is a Member of the Polish Economic Society and the Polish Statistical Association. As a member of the National Committee of the Economic Knowledge Contest, he is involved in teaching economics to young people. He is the author and co-author of a number of academic and educational publications, including *Kredytowanie gospodarstw domowych* (PWE 2013) and *1000 pytań. Ekonomia, finanse, zarządzanie* (Difin 2019). His academic and research interests are focused on household economics, personal finance, well-being, and microeconomics. He specialises in issues connected with the indebtedness and over-indebtedness of households.

Ryszard Kowalski is an assistant professor in the Department of Microeconomics at the Cracow University of Economics. He is a member of the Polish Economic Society and the National Committee of the Economic Knowledge Contest. A book co-authored by him, *Metaekonomia. Zagadnienia z filozofii nauki* (Copernicus Center Press 2016), won first prize for the best university-level economics textbook published in 2014–2016 in a competition organised by the Polish Economic Society. He is the author of academic publications on the concept of the modern welfare state, welfare economics, and household economics.

Introduction

The ultimate goal of any economic activity is the satisfaction of human wants, so it is unsurprising that well-being has always been one of the main issues of interest to economists.

Well-being can be treated as a multifaceted research category that covers both the material and non-material spheres of life. The former includes the condition of owned real estate, durable goods (e.g. furniture, kitchen utensils) or other tangible resources, and the financial situation of households, while the latter includes health and health protection, the labour market, the sense of security, social integration, and the forms of, and opportunities for, spending leisure time.

Purchasing power determines the satisfaction of human wants and therefore households' well-being. Under developed financial market conditions, consumers can make intertemporal substitutions of consumption. Access to credit and loans[1] means that current consumption can be increased beyond the level of actual income earned. Yet the higher the level of debt, the more likely it is that the full force of its negative impact will reveal itself: in the increasing burden repayments place on household budgets and through the psychological strain of being in debt.

The central aim of the book is to diagnose the economic well-being of over-indebted households in Poland. Given the complexity of this issue and the need for an interdisciplinary approach, a research problem was formulated that embraces three analytical fields related to households: indebtedness, over-indebtedness, and economic well-being. Specific cognitive, methodological, and practical objectives were pursued in each field. The cognitive objectives were as follows:

1) to identify the socio-demographic and economic features of indebted and over-indebted households,
2) to identify the fundamental characteristics of indebtedness and the differences in how indebtedness is subjectively perceived by over-indebted and not-over-indebted households,
3) to identify the motives for borrowing,
4) to identify ways of coping with financial difficulties,

DOI: 10.4324/9781003254706-1

5) to establish the geographical variations in over-indebtedness,
6) to investigate the dependencies between economic, social, and behavioural factors and over-indebtedness,
7) to assess economic well-being and its variations in relation to over-indebted households in the general, material, and financial dimensions,
8) to define the role of over-indebtedness in shaping the economic well-being of households.

The methodological objectives included the following:

1) selection of indicators of over-indebtedness,
2) the use of Ward's hierarchical clustering method to extract groups of voivodships (provinces) that are similar in terms of over-indebtedness,
3) the application of a logit model to identify the determinants of over-indebtedness,
4) the application of a totally fuzzy and relative approach to the construction of a composite indicator for assessing economic well-being,
5) the use of the Gini coefficient to assess inequalities in the distribution of the values of the composite indicator of economic well-being and the decomposition of these inequalities with the aid of the Theil index.

The practical objectives are linked to the cognitive and methodological ones. It can be assumed that vulnerable categories of households (households that are poor, less well educated, or with multiple children) are particularly exposed to the negative consequences of over-indebtedness. Therefore, the obtained research results and conclusions can be used in social policy aimed at mitigating the consequences of over-indebtedness and in the design of solutions to prevent the negative outcomes produced by debt overload, such as household bankruptcies or social exclusion. Moreover, it can be expected that this information can be of benefit in establishing a system of financial education and debt counselling, and also in designing solutions that will make the financial system more stable. The conducted research has also expanded the range of tools that can be applied in studies investigating the well-being of over-indebted households. The book draws upon the literature devoted to the theoretical and empirical aspects of indebtedness, over-indebtedness, and well-being. The results obtained, and conclusions drawn, in the course of the research are enriched by the findings of earlier studies in this field. The statistical methods were selected primarily on the basis of their usefulness in describing, conducting a comparative analysis of, and drawing conclusions from, the indebtedness and economic well-being of households and on the possibility – according to the nature of the data held – of applying them.

By formulating the research objectives and studying the subject literature, it was possible to devise the main research hypothesis, namely, that over-indebted households are characterised by lower economic well-being than not-over-indebted households, but that the impact of over-indebtedness – as captured by various indicators mapped onto the dimensions (areas) of economic well-being – is varied. Due to the multifaceted nature of the subject matter, five specific sub-hypotheses were added to the main research hypothesis:

1 Income is the most important determinant of over-indebtedness and the economic well-being of households.
2 The subjective dimension of over-indebtedness is greater than the objective one – and there is limited overlap between them.
3 Households that are subjectively over-indebted and those that are objectively over-indebted have different reasons for borrowing.
4 Over-indebtedness has a greater influence on economic well-being in the financial dimension than it does in the material dimension.
5 The characteristics of debt are of greater significance for the economic well-being of the over-indebted than for the economic well-being of the not-over-indebted.

The book draws its data from the results of a Poland-wide questionnaire survey conducted by computer-assisted telephone interviewing (CATI). The respondents were selected by the random generation of mobile telephone numbers using a method known as random digit dial (RDD). The initial sample was composed of approximately 35,500 telephone numbers. The population studied was made up of adults aged 18 or above living in Poland and their households. Having at least one loan or credit at the time of the survey was the criterion for admission to the sample. The total sample size was 1,107. All of the statistical calculations and analyses in the study were performed with the aid of the Statistica and Stata software packages.

The substantive section of the book contains six chapters, of which three address theoretical and methodological issues and three are of an analytical and empirical nature and refer to the results of our original research. Each chapter ends with a brief summary of the most important findings to emerge from that section of the work, while the final, overall outcomes of all of the discussions and analyses can be found in the conclusion. Insofar as it does not begin by setting out the theoretical issues before proceeding to the empirical sections, the book is arranged unconventionally. Its triad of three distinct, substantive issues dictated a different structure, whereby each chapter containing a literature review is followed by one presenting the results of our original research. As for the sequence in which the issues appear, Chapters 1 and 2 are devoted to debt, Chapters 3 and 4 to over-indebtedness, and Chapters 5 and 6 to well-being.

Chapter 1 outlines the problem of household indebtedness. Theories explaining the behaviour of households in the credit market, including original and modified versions of life cycle and permanent income theories, and the contributions made by behavioural economics and sociology to explaining increasing indebtedness, are reviewed. The available data sources on the extent of household borrowing and the basic facts about indebtedness in Poland are then set out. To properly contextualise the analyses, a review of existing research into the indebtedness of Polish households at the microeconomic level is presented in the final part of this chapter.

Chapter 2 is devoted to an empirical analysis of indebted households in Poland. After discussing the research methodology and sample selection, and having described the sample itself, it presents a profile of indebted households based on the results of our original research. An overall picture of debt is presented by reference to objective features and subjective evaluations of indebtedness and, in a separate subsection, the reasons households borrow are investigated according to a socio-economic breakdown of them.

Chapter 3, which constitutes a starting point for further discussion and analysis, defines the concept of over-indebtedness and sets out its intrinsic elements. This is followed by a discussion of the micro- and macroeconomic factors contributing to this phenomenon. The discussion of methodological questions associated with research into the over-indebtedness of households is augmented by a review of the indicators used in these kinds of studies.

Chapter 4, which is empirical in nature, is devoted to an analysis of over-indebted households in Poland. Using objective and subjective indicators, it addresses this phenomenon first at the general level and at the level of the relationships between its various dimensions, before moving to a cross-sectional analysis of over-indebted households. In the next part of this chapter, the geographical distribution and the results of grouping voivodships (provinces) in terms of over-indebtedness are presented. This analysis is supplemented by specifying the determinants of over-indebtedness using econometric modelling.

Chapter 5 considers the relationship between well-being and over-indebtedness. It opens with a subsection on the definition of well-being. It then clarifies the idea of economic well-being and examines the possible pathways by which over-indebtedness can impact well-being. It closes with a review of existing research into the well-being of households in Poland, which lays the foundation for the empirical analyses undertaken in the final chapter.

Chapter 6, which is key as regards verification of the main research hypothesis, focuses on evaluating the variation in the economic well-being of over-indebted households. Using the data from our original research, the economic well-being of over-indebted households is described cross-sectionally and, using a composite indicator, in the general, material and financial dimensions. This chapter ends with an assessment of the impact of over-indebtedness on economic well-being.

Note

1 Despite the differences in their meaning according to whether they are applied in law or economics (Wałęga, 2013), the terms 'credit' and 'loan' are used here interchangeably. This is because these differences are not significant from the point of view of the analysis carried out in the book. What is important is the fact, common to both these forms of borrowing money, that a household takes on an obligation (debt).

Reference

Wałęga, G. (2013). *Kredytowanie gospodarstw domowych*. Warszawa: Polskie Wydawnictwo Ekonomiczne.

1 Household indebtedness

Theories and facts

1.1 Theoretical background of household indebtedness

Household indebtedness is a complex phenomenon and thus presents a considerable analytical challenge. Indeed, to understand its essence, it is necessary to extend the field of discussion far beyond the purely economic – or at least to enrich it by consulting the findings of sociology, psychology, and politics. Only in this way can the role that private debt currently plays in the life of society as a whole and in the lives of individual households be understood.

Standard, textbook explanations of why households use credit are based on two theories: the life-cycle hypothesis of saving (LCH), which was formulated by Franco Modigliani and Richard Brumberg (1954, 1980)[1] and elaborated by the former with Albert Ando (1963), and the permanent income hypothesis (PIH) devised by Milton Friedman (1957). Along with the numerous variations they inspired, both are now collectively known as life-cycle models or theories (Browning & Crossley, 2001). There are a number of details in which the two models differ, including terminology, equations used, and methods of estimating household wealth, but the key difference between them is the time horizon for modelling consumption and savings. For Modigliani, it is finite, while PIH assumes an infinitely long life. The permanent income hypothesis therefore de facto ignores the effect of the life cycle with respect to savings. In general terms, the life cycle theory appears to generate a far broader range of implications than the permanent income theory (for more on the differences between LCH and PIH, see Barnett & Solow, 2000; Ferber, 1973; Jappelli, 2005; Szenberg & Ramrattan, 2008). Where the reasons households borrow are concerned, however, it is not the differences between the two theories that are significant but the similarities.

Both theories assume that consumers behave in a fully rational way, so that they are capable of predicting their future incomes – and, in the case of LCH, the lengths of their lives – with utter certainty. With a view to maximising utility under conditions of intertemporal choice, such rational actors are thought to prefer a relatively constant level of consumption over the course of their lives. This level is determined not by current disposable income but by life resources (the term applied in Modigliani's theory), which is understood as

DOI: 10.4324/9781003254706-2

the current value of income from work gained throughout a whole lifetime (increased – possibly – by an inheritance), or by permanent income (Friedman's term). However, current disposable income fluctuates over time, such that a relatively stable level of consumption cannot be maintained. This problem is resolved by the existence of the credit market: borrowing is a rational tool that can be used to make consumption smoother over time. According to the LCH, households in the initial state of the life cycle (when working lives are beginning) usually have a low level of disposable income and high indebtedness in relation to it, which is the result of the need to finance expenditure associated with education or buying a house or flat, for example. As households age, their disposable incomes rise, and from a certain moment this makes it possible not only to finance consumption but also to build up savings which, in the final stage of life, that of economic inactivity, are used to maintain a constant level of consumption in the absence of income from work. Although, for obvious reasons, in the case of PIH there is no direct reference to life stages, here too, borrowing appears as the natural consequence of bridging the gap between the sought-after level of consumption of a fixed portion of permanent income and the current income earned by households.

The assumptions that accompany any theory sooner or later become the subject of heated debate supported by empirical findings, and LCH and PIH are no exception. Where the life-cycle model is concerned, these findings are primarily connected with the powerful impact on consumption of both expected and unexpected changes in income (for reviews of research on this subject see, for instance, Bańbuła, 2006; Beshears et al., 2018; Jappelli & Pistaferri, 2010) and therefore with a phenomenon that deviates from the postulate that households seek optimal outcomes by smoothing their consumption over time. Of the many factors that could serve to explain this irregularity – and which are also relevant to household indebtedness – the key ones would appear to be those that weaken the assumptions made in the LCH and the PIH regarding the existence of a perfect capital market, the absence of uncertainty, and the full rationality of the decision-maker. As it allows analysis to continue within the bounds of the life-cycle model, to undermine the first two assumptions can be seen as an acceptable, and even necessary, correction to Modigliani and Friedman's original findings (Carroll, 1997; Deaton, 2005). It is quite another matter to negate rationality, which would appear to represent a shift to an entirely different research perspective: that of behavioural economics. No matter how revolutionary this perspective is perceived to be, acknowledging the significance of psychological factors in the context of preferences, beliefs, and the decision-making process – to use the typology proposed by DellaVigna (2009) – was a definite spur to the development of the life-cycle model, while the relaxation of certain assumptions accompanying its standard version made it possible to explain many of the 'anomalies' associated with processes of saving and consumption (Attanasio & Weber, 2010).

In a perfect capital market, households face no liquidity or credit constraints or, to put it another way, they have unrestricted access to the credit market.

Households can smooth consumption under these conditions by borrowing in periods when current income prevents them from pursuing the optimum consumption path. In reality, however, at least some potential borrowers face barriers to accessing loan funds and are therefore unable to borrow the optimum amount, which clearly translates into the level of their consumption (see Crook & Hochguertel, 2007; Hall & Mishkin, 1982; Hayashi, 1985; Jappelli, 1990; Zeldes, 1989). The current income, age, and wealth (assets) of a borrower are the most important determinants of access to credit. These results appear to support – or at least not to contradict – the thesis that, at best, life-cycle models adequately describe the situation of the well-educated middle class (Chen & Finke, 1996; Sinha, 1988; Wolff, 1981).[2]

Uncertainty, which is an aspect of many areas of life, including the ability to finance future consumption, is also part of the reality in which households operate. The precautionary motive, which, it is theorised, becomes salient where levels of future income are uncertain, prompts households to accumulate buffer-stock savings to reduce the negative impact of falling income on consumption (Carroll, 1992, 1997; Deaton, 1991). Its impact in the context of household indebtedness is similar to that of liquidity constraints (Bertola et al., 2006; Deaton, 1991). Indeed, the precautionary motive is strongly connected with restrictions of this kind (Carroll & Kimball, 2001; Deaton, 1991; Deidda, 2013; Xu, 1995). It is important to note that consumers whose access to credit is not constrained will, at any given time, still make decisions according to this pattern (as if their access was constrained) – as long as it is possible that constraints will occur in the future. Where there are liquidity constraints and savings are dictated by the precautionary effect, household decisions tend to be described as short-term consumption smoothing (e.g. a few years), which is known as high-frequency smoothing, rather than as long-term smoothing, which is connected with the entire lifespan (Deaton, 2005).

Although including uncertainty or liquidity constraints in the modelling of households' intertemporal choices makes it possible to at least partially explain the empirically observable sensitivity of consumption to changes in income, the life-cycle model has still not discarded the assumption that decision-makers are rational. However, as behavioural economists have indicated, it is far from being the case that households act to smooth consumption over time in their decisions on saving and borrowing, which means that they do not conduct long-term optimisation analyses. Why not? First, a significant proportion of borrowers are highly ignorant of mathematics and do not understand the legal and financial language of loan agreements, which makes it impossible for them to perform complicated dynamic optimisation calculations (Lusardi & Mitchell, 2014; Lusardi & Tufano, 2015; Martin, 2010). Second, there are psychological determinants of decision-making that appear to play a far greater role in explaining disparities in borrowers' financial capabilities than purely informational differences (De Meza et al., 2008). Could it be that this negation of rationality, which is the principal motif of behavioural economics, marks the shift of LCH towards a normative theory – a change of position from performing a descriptive function to performing a prescriptive function? (Deaton, 2005; Shefrin & Thaler, 1988).[3]

People with low incomes, who are the usual customers of entities offering loans at high interest rates, lack many resources, including money, time, and food. It is this predicament that causes them to be focused on solving their most pressing everyday problems and to lose sight of the long-term consequences of their actions. It can therefore be assumed that they take their decisions under conditions of reduced cognitive capacity. These decisions are thus not a matter of adaptive preferences or specific pathological behaviours flowing from a 'culture of poverty', but the result of a psychology of poverty fuelled by resource scarcity (Mani et al., 2013; Mullainathan & Shafir, 2013; Shah et al., 2012).

Personal experience (the availability heuristic) or an aversion to making a choice when there are a large number of possible options (e.g. a proliferation of loan offers) can also lead to non-optimal borrowing decisions (Bertrand et al., 2010; DellaVigna, 2009). A reluctance to borrow (Hirst et al., 1994; Prelec & Loewenstein, 1998) can also derive from mental accounting, that is, a set of cognitive operations individuals perform connected with categorising, evaluating, and controlling their financial activity (Thaler, 1999). Paul Heidhues and Botond Kőszegi (2010) report that borrowers can, to their own detriment, be over-optimistic about their levels of self-control, while as Ari Hyytinen and Hanna Putkuri (2018) show, borrowers' over-optimistic predictions about their financial situations are positively correlated with higher values of the debt-to-income ratio. The propensity to become heavily indebted can also result from the intuitive linearisation of exponential growth functions (exponential growth bias), which leads to underestimation of the costs of a loan commitment (Stango & Zinman, 2009). Decisions about indebtedness and borrowing are also influenced by a particular way of perceiving personal wealth – not through the lens of net worth, but as if the two sides of the balance sheet were entirely separate entities. Consequently, the economic well-being of two different households with the same net worth can be perceived differently depending on the different levels of assets and liabilities that it is composed of (Sussman & Shafir, 2012).

As a result of hyperbolic discounting, the time inconsistency of preferences leads households to submit to the temptation of a quick 'reward' in the form of easily available loan products, which, to the detriment of their long-term well-being, increases their indebtedness (Heidhues & Kőszegi, 2010; Laibson, 1997; Meier & Sprenger, 2010). Hyperbolic discounting, as well as quasi-hyperbolic discounting, also explains why households simultaneously hold high-interest debt on their credit card accounts and low-liquidity assets – offering comparatively low rates of return – in pension funds (Angeletos et al., 2001; Laibson et al., 2003, 2007).[4] In this view, households display impatience (in the short term) and patience (in the long term) at the same time.[5]

Apart, of course, from its purely material dimension, which is associated with the satisfaction of biological needs, consumption also has a social dimension. This means that it can be regarded as a phenomenon stimulated by the social norms and consumption patterns practised by the social group that constitutes a household's reference group.

According to James Duesenberry's relative income hypothesis (1949), the utility a household derives from consumption depends on what is consumed, and in what quantity, by other households in its reference group.[6] The feeling of belonging to a given group can mean that a household takes on debt in order to conform, on the principle of 'keeping up with the Joneses', to 'compulsory' consumption patterns. What is more, attachment to an existing, already-achieved level of consumption explains the short-run rigidity of consumption in recessions when household incomes are falling.

Nowadays, however, it would appear that the principle of keeping up with the Joneses requires some reformulation. While 30 or 40 years ago households sought to emulate their neighbours, who were the people they had regular, direct contact with, now, in an age when television and other electronic media exert an enormous influence, corporate leaders, minor and major stars of show business, and celebrities with excessive consumption patterns have become a significant reference group (Schor, 1999, 2002). The media, in creating new, often unattainable lifestyles, and in the face of growing disproportions between income and aspirations, have become the driving force of a particular civilisational model by which society now functions. This is the new consumerism, which involves living beyond our means, thanks to borrowing from financial markets. Increasing income inequality, and the workplace and television, which became spaces of socialisation and took over that role from neighbourhoods, are two further forces that have underpinned the transition to the new model of consumption. In effect, vertical emulation began to drive out horizontal emulation, and the principle of keeping up with the Joneses gradually gave way to that of keeping up with the Gateses.[7]

Duesenberry's sociological interpretations of the consumption process and Thorstein Veblen's much earlier theory of the leisure class (1899), which stresses the role of conspicuous consumption in marking the social status of the American upper classes in the nineteenth century, lie behind the expenditure cascades hypothesis proposed a few years ago by Robert Frank and his colleagues (2014). According to the expenditure cascades hypothesis, the households in the adjacent, higher-income bracket are the reference points for a household's consumption patterns, which means that we are dealing with upward-looking consumption norms. When the incomes of the richest are growing far faster than those of other subgroups, a cascade of household spending is triggered that can only function through indebtedness: the ninth decile borrows in an attempt to keep up with the consumption of the richest, while the eighth, which takes the consumption level of the ninth as a reference point, does the same, and so on. Thus, rising inequalities become a significant determinant of the process by which households take on debt.

Echoes of Duesenberry's findings also resound from a second, alternative idea that explains household indebtedness in respect of rising income inequalities: the falling wages hypothesis (Barba & Pivetti, 2009; Stockhammer, 2012, 2015).

Here, indebtedness is explained not by a desire to emulate others but as the effect of becoming attached to one's own pattern of consumption followed in previous periods (backward-looking, self-regarding consumption norms) that is threatened by detrimental trends in income from employment. There is no doubt that this trend is exacerbated by the diminished generosity (contraction) of the welfare state.

Indeed, it has been demonstrated empirically that rising income inequalities have been accompanied by an increase in household debt in recent decades (see Barba & Pivetti, 2009; Bertola & Hochguertel, 2007; Coletta et al., 2019; Iacoviello, 2008; Krueger & Perri, 2006; Kumhof et al., 2015). The rise in income inequalities began in the late 1970s and early 1980s, primarily in the United States and the United Kingdom. Yet in the course of a single decade it had become a global phenomenon, affecting a growing number of countries as each year passed (OECD, 2008, 2011, 2015).

Regardless of how adequately the expenditure cascades and falling wages hypotheses explain rising household indebtedness (see Moore & Stockhammer, 2018 for more detail), they only address the question of why households take on debt. Why, though, was such a sharp increase in indebtedness possible at all? It would appear that the changes in economic policy determined by the triumph of neoliberal ideology in the 1980s – in particular the belief that many areas of the economy needed to be deregulated – are largely responsible for this process. It is precisely the political economy perspective, which stresses the significance of the transformations in the contemporary model of capitalism for processes of saving, consumption, and borrowing, which forms the final part of this subsection's brief review of the determinants and theories of household indebtedness.

The structural changes introduced into the economic system in the late 1970s and early 1980s were intended to result in the deregulation of the economy as a whole and to place greater pressure to compete on market participants. The deregulatory trend extended to markets for specific goods, the labour market (in the name of greater flexibility of employment and the need to reduce employment protection), and the financial market (resulting in the growing importance of owners of capital and in the emergence of new financial products offering greater returns). In a sense, and as effected within the terms of the deregulatory paradigm, this represented a coherent set of changes (Amable, 2010).

By creating an appropriate framework for the growth of globalisation and the diffusion of technological change, deregulation induced an increase in income inequality (OECD, 2011), which meant – from the perspective of theories of indebtedness referring to consumption patterns – that households' borrowing needs to be increased. At the same time, as if by magic, deregulation provided access to finance and activated a series of interrelated processes: a policy to increase access to credit for less affluent households – as a result of political pressure exerted by potential borrowers affected by wage stagnation (Rajan, 2010) and by lenders (Mian et al., 2013); the reduction of liquidity constraints as a result of the rising prices of property used as collateral for loans (for a review of empirical studies, see Moore & Stockhammer, 2018; for a modelling approach, see Ryoo, 2016); and financial innovation and new technologies (Dynan & Kohn, 2007; Lapavitsas & dos Santos, 2008; Mian & Sufi, 2009; Purnanandam, 2011).

If, following the Post-Keynesians, we assume that households seek to maintain the net-wealth-to-income ratio at a certain, desired level, then increases in the value of assets (causing the optimum ratio to be exceeded) combined with the inability or reluctance to sell at least a portion of them will lead households to consume 'surplus wealth' by taking on additional debt (Godley & Lavoie, 2007; Stockhammer & Wildauer, 2018; Wildauer, 2016). In this light, deregulation, through its consequences for asset markets (primarily the property and securities markets), produced the conditions under which asset-transaction explanations of household indebtedness assumed importance (Moore & Stockhammer, 2018; Stockhammer & Wildauer, 2018). However, the new role in which households now found themselves, that of investor, which signalled a certain kind of democratisation of finance, did not necessarily have a positive influence on their well-being (Boyer, 2000; Erturk et al., 2007; Montgomerie, 2009).

1.2 Data sources and selected findings on the indebtedness of Polish households

In the main, the sources of information on household indebtedness are the public administration and household budget surveys. Data are collected both incidentally and systematically, and it is the latter which are of particular importance in assessing the dynamics of processes taking place.

In Poland, aggregated data on household indebtedness are collected by the National Bank of Poland (NBP), and also by institutions such as the Polish Financial Supervision Authority (KNF), the Polish Bank Association (ZBB), and the Credit Information Bureau (BIK). The data, which are reported by commercial banks, concern the level of household debt, the type of debt instrument, the term structure of the debt, and the magnitude of any outstanding liabilities.

The monetary statistics kept by NBP provide information about the receivables of credit institutions (banks and credit unions) and, separately, of the banks themselves, in respect of households (strictly speaking, in respect of private individuals – natural persons, businesspeople employing up to nine people, and individual farmers). The receivables are classified according to their purpose (consumer credit and housing loans, for instance), currency (PLN versus a foreign currency), and maturity.[8] Publicly available data cover the period from December 1996. In that month, the value of the receivables was close to PLN 21 billion. By the end of 2019, the nominal value had risen to almost PLN 755 billion (NBP, 2020b). Impressive though this increase may seem, it must be acknowledged that the scale of household indebtedness in Poland is still not significant when compared to (other) highly developed countries (Figure 1.1).

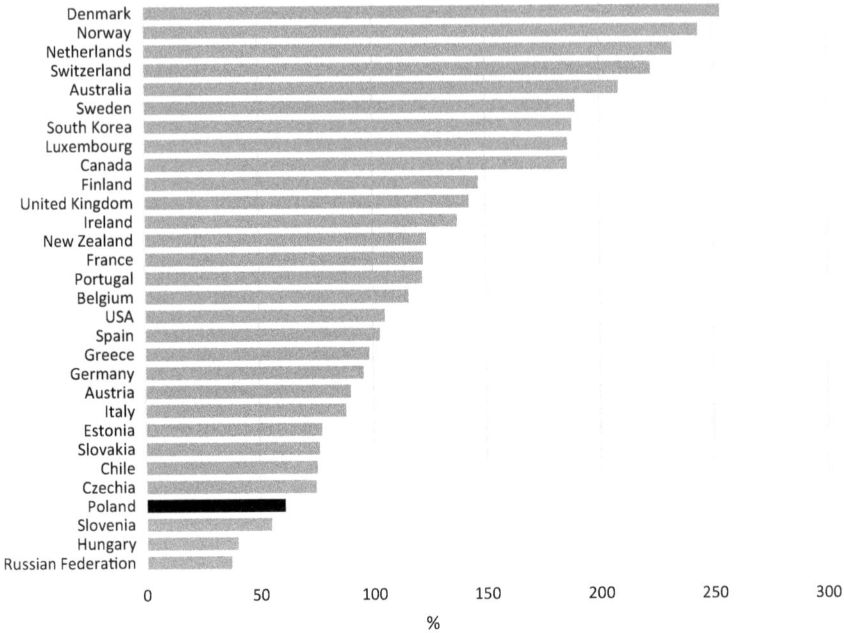

Figure 1.1 Household debt as % of net disposable income (2019)
Source: (OECD, 2021).

At first, consumer credit accounted for approximately 50% of all loans taken by households. In the second half of 1999 and in 2000, the share accounted for by consumer credit rose slightly. In monthly terms, the proportion was 53%–55%. In June 2000, there was a spike to 60%. There then began a gentle, but steady, downward trend. Beginning in the second half of 2011, the share of consumer loans in credit institutions' overall loan receivables from households oscillated between 24% and 27% (December 2019: 27%). While consumer credit was losing ground in relative terms, housing credit was gaining in importance. Whereas in 1996–1997, the latter accounted for only approximately 5% of the value of loans granted to households by credit institutions, its persistent growth meant that, by the very end of 2008, it accounted for over 50% of all loans. A further barrier (60%) was crossed in 2012 and from that time the proportion hovered around 58%–61% (December 2019: 59%). It can therefore be stated that the term structure of debt is close to that of highly developed countries (G. Wałęga, 2013).

Though not fully comparable with the scope of data emerging from monetary statistics, the NBP's financial statistics do constitute a source of additional information on, for example, the quality of the loan portfolio of banks operating in the Polish market, including the quality of loans granted to households.

In December 2019, according to the gross carrying amount, the value of non-performing loans (including impairments) was 2.34% of the value of all housing loans and 10.26% of the value of consumer credit (NBP, 2020a).

The banking sector reports of the Polish Financial Supervision Authority also provide a broad range of data on the quality of the loan portfolio of banks operating in the Polish market, including the quality of loans granted to households. At the end of 2019, the average value of the debt service-to-income (DSTI) ratio[9] for housing loans in the banking sector (in strict terms, this refers to the 27 banks whose housing loan portfolios vis-à-vis households exceeded PLN 100 million) was 30%. It should be noted, however, that over 43% of loans (proportion according to gross carrying amount) had a DSTI ratio greater than 30%. If only loans granted in 2019 are considered, it is worth noting that the share of housing credits with DSTI>30% (measured by nominal value) in the total value of credits of this type granted in 2019 was 56%, while the median debt-to-income (DTI) ratio was in the 3.5–4.0 range. In the case of consumer credit, at the end of 2019, the share of loans with DSTI>30% in the overall value of consumer credit (measured by gross carrying amount) increased in line with the sum of the loan granted: by 36% for loans with a nominal value of up to PLN 8,000, and by as much as 71% for loans worth more than PLN 100,000 (KNF, 2020).

The data published by the Economic Information Bureau (BIG InfoMonitor) in its InfoDebt reports, which have been appearing at regular intervals since 2007 and which are compiled from information in its Debtors' Register and in the database of the Credit Information Bureau (BIK), are of particular relevance to the themes touched on in this book. The reports focus on debtors' late repayments (overdue by at least 30 days) in respect of a wide range of entities, including banks, loan companies, service providers, and local authorities. As well as stating the size and type of late repayments, they also offer debtor profiles and debt breakdowns. Edition No 36 (March 2020), for example, reports that the problem of late repayment affects just under 2.8 million people, whose overdue repayments are worth PLN 77.7 billion (data from 2019). Over 22% of this group has both credit and non-credit arrears. The typical unreliable debtor is a man aged 35–45 living in the Mazowieckie Voivodship or the Śląskie Voivodship (BIG InfoMonitor, 2020).

Direct surveys of households allow for a more detailed analysis of the debt phenomenon from the microeconomic perspective. Household indebtedness can be investigated by consulting the following systematic studies conducted in Poland: *Badanie budżetów gospodarstw domowych* (Household Budget Survey), *Badanie zasobności gospodarstw domowych* (Household Wealth and Debt Survey), and *Diagnoza Społeczna* (Social Diagnosis: Objective and Subjective Quality of Life in Poland).

The Household Budget Survey, which supplies data on income, expenditure, food consumption, the extent to which households are equipped with durables, and housing conditions, has been a Statistics Poland[10] project since 1957. It is a representative survey which, in 2019 as in previous years, covered approximately 36,000 households (GUS, 2020). The data it collects include the amounts of loan and credit repayments. When combined with information on incomes, they make it possible to assess the extent of households' indebtedness. Since 2005, data on debt-servicing expenditure have been available broken down into mortgages, credit card loans, other bank loans, repayment of non-bank loans, and repayment of loans taken from private individuals. In 2018, the Household Budget Survey introduced an additional set of questions on household wealth that covered immovable property and vehicles; mortgages and other loans and credits for a first home and other immovable property; the total value of outstanding credit; and savings and the capacity to save (GUS, 2018; A. Wałęga & Wałęga, 2018b). In 2019, 28% of households were in debt. It was the self-declared view of 45.1% of these households that this was not a significant burden and they made their repayments on time. For 6.6% of them, however, it was a serious strain causing late repayments or their complete cessation. The majority of the households experiencing difficulty in making repayments on time belonged to the first quintile and made up 35.1% of all such households.

The Household Wealth and Debt Survey was piloted in 2014 and repeated in full in 2016. It is conducted jointly by the NBP and Statistics Poland. With a particular focus on the assets they accumulate and the liabilities they incur, it is intended to gather a wide range of data on the financial situation of households. The survey questionnaire is a Polish adaptation of the model version prepared by the Household Finance and Consumption Network (HFCN).[11] The survey conducted in 2016 included just over 12,000 households. Indebtedness was reported by 40.5% of the surveyed households, with 13.9% indebted in respect of housing loans and 32.9% indebted in respect of non-housing credits and loans (NBP, 2017). The results of previous editions of the Household Wealth and Debt Survey have confirmed that the propensity to take on debt is positively correlated with income and education, with young households and those with children also more likely to take on debt. The data collected also allowed inferences to be made about the size of the debt burden in relation to incomes and the options for mitigating – through existing financial buffers – the negative impact of an increase in debt-servicing costs or a fall in income. So it was that, in 2016, the median net DSTI ratio for households with housing loans (in PLN) was 18.3%, while for other debtors it was 12%. Approximately 14% of households with housing loans and 9.2% of households with other types of loans had a DSTI>40%. In the case of PLN-denominated housing loans, 24.4% of households had a DTI>300%. Approximately 40% of all households had the liquid financial assets to repay their total debt (in the case of housing loans, this proportion was 11%), while approximately 9.5% of households possessed no assets. For the latter, any increase in debt-servicing costs would inevitably affect current consumption. In the case of households heavily burdened with debt repayments (DSTI>40%), only a few (0.6%) were unable to repay all of their liabilities with all of their assets (debt to assets (DTA)>100%) and about 1% of indebted households would have found it difficult to repay all of their liabilities (DTA>75%) (NBP, 2017).

Social Diagnosis: Objective and Subjective Quality of Life in Poland was an interdisciplinary project conducted in 2000–2015 designed to capture a broad range of quality-of-life data on households, including income, wealth, savings, and debt. An important feature of the study – which had a positive impact on the quality of the results – was that it was based on panel research and was cyclical in nature (the same households were studied at regular intervals). With regard to the issue of debt, respondents were asked about their use of loans or credit, the institutions they borrowed from, their reasons for borrowing, outstanding debt compared to income, and arrears on housing loans. In 2013, there were questions about the burden of debt repayments on monthly income and the length of the repayment term, while in 2015 there were new questions concerning mortgage repayments, the size of mortgage deposits, and the reasons for borrowing from entities other than banks (A. Wałęga & Wałęga, 2018b). In the last round of the survey, which took place in 2015, 11,740 households participated. At that time, fewer than 34% of respondents said they took advantage of credits or loans. Of these, the vast majority (more than 90% of the households surveyed) looked to banks for this form of expenditure financing. The proportions of all respondents using loan companies or private individuals as the sources of loans were far smaller – at just over 5% for the former and 4% for the latter. The most numerous group of households (almost 40% of all respondents) was formed by those whose debt burdens ranged from 10% to 20% of their monthly incomes, while for approximately 28% of them the DSTI ratio was below 10%. Pensioners, households containing unemployed people, and people who live in small towns were customers of loan companies comparatively more often.[12] The credits and loans were primarily used for durables (over 32% of households), for renovating a house or flat (over 30% of households), and for buying a house or flat (almost 27%) (Panek et al., 2015).

These cyclical research programmes sometimes provide data for other analyses of borrowing by, and lending to, Polish households. What is more, there are also one-off studies in the subject literature that employ different, often original methodology connected with addressing a specific research question. They are discussed in the following subsection.

1.3 Overview of research on the indebtedness of households in Poland

Beata Świecka investigated the insolvency of Polish households using an interview questionnaire on a sample of 581 respondents in the Zachodniopomorskie Voivodship (2008, 2009). Her survey conducted at the turn of June and July 2006 found that insolvent households take on loans exclusively from other non-bank lenders; the loans taken on by insolvent households are used for the purposes of consumption; when they lack funds, insolvent households stop paying credit and loan instalments first of all; and the members of insolvent households have primary or vocational education. Household indebtedness is a function of income, but not of income alone. It is also the product of many other factors, including non-economic ones.

To address the question of what, in an economic crisis, are the sources of household insolvency, Tomasz Zalega (2014) turned his attention to urban households. His survey research was conducted using an interview questionnaire on a sample of 1,135 households between June and August 2012, in eight Polish cities of varying population and size. Of the sampled households, 38.7% took on credits and loans, and the debt of approximately 25% of them exceeded the family's annual income. The majority were in debt to banks (87.5%), loan companies (10.1%), and other non-bank lenders (5.9%). Borrowing from other non-bank lenders was positively correlated with the risk of insolvency, and these institutions were the main source of loan funds for households (relatively few, accounting for 4.3% of the total number of respondents) borrowing to finance current consumption and repay previous debts. In later studies, covering the years 2014–2015, which were conducted on a sample of 2,537 households using an interview questionnaire, Zalega concentrated on urban households of people aged 65+ (2018). In this age group, 46.7% of respondents took out credits and loans, and 20% of these indebted respondents had debts that exceeded their annual income. The surveyed respondents primarily used loan funds offered by banks (93.1% of all those indebted). Just as in the previous study, there emerged a positive correlation between the threat of insolvency and borrowing from other non-bank lenders.

An entirely different research problem was tackled by Piotr Białowolski and his associates (2020), who focused on the role of debt knowledge and debt skills (associated with calculating debt) in shaping attitudes towards indebtedness. Their analysis was based on the results of telephone interviews conducted in November 2017, with a representative sample of adult Polish citizens (N = 1,004). Latent variable (class) analysis was used to identify classes (segments) of respondents, while multinomial regression models were used to assess the relationships between debt literacy – consisting of the debt skills and debt knowledge mentioned earlier – and attitudes towards indebtedness. Although the picture emerging from the analysis is not clear-cut and reinforces the notion that attitudes to indebtedness are complex – with individuals simultaneously showing positive and negative attitudes to indebtedness depending on which aspect of the issue is considered – certain patterns could still be identified. Using a combination of rational and emotional arguments, almost 50% of respondents revealed negative attitudes towards indebtedness. Furthermore, no significant differences were observed between men's and women's attitudes towards indebtedness. Attitudes of indifference were strongly linked to poor debt knowledge and poor debt-calculating skills, while improvements in both areas – especially calculation – were found to be vital to the crystallisation of positive or negative attitudes to indebtedness.

Dominika Maison attempted to identify classes of debtors who had experienced at least one episode with a debt collection agency or with a bank's debt-recovery department (2019). Using cluster analysis, she identified five groups of debtors and found that those she termed Forgetful (27%) and Indebted on Behalf of Others (24%) accounted for the greatest proportions of the research sample (N = 604). The indebtedness of the former was relatively small, and arrears were due to absent-mindedness or even to being unaware of the debt. Of all the groups analysed, however, the latter bore the heaviest debt burden, which stemmed from a desire to satisfy the life needs of their loved ones and meant, for example, borrowing to pay for house repairs or educational fees. For this group, being in arrears was a conscious strategy resulting from specific priorities in debt repayment. While the former group contained the highest proportion of people with tertiary education (of all groups), the latter had the greatest proportion of women, residents of big cities, and people with children. Maison called the remaining, smaller groups Carefree, Lost in Finances, and Avoiders.

The data employed in the present book (see subsection 2.1) were used by Grzegorz Wałęga and Agnieszka Wałęga (2021) to assess over-indebted households, which was achieved by applying the below the poverty line (BPL) measure, and to indicate, with the aid of classification and regression trees (CART), the factors (socio-economic features) that increase the probability of a household being in the group of over-indebted households. As their findings demonstrate, the DSTI ratio, which is a much more popular indicator than BPL, significantly underestimates the extent of over-indebtedness in vulnerable groups, including the youngest and oldest households, households with basic levels of education, low-income households, multi-person households, pensioners, and farmers. While the difference between the DSTI30 and BPL measures of over-indebtedness was almost twofold in relation to the entire sample of households, the difference was much more pronounced for the vulnerable groups mentioned earlier (for instance, among the poorest households, with a net income of up to PLN 1,500, the difference was fourfold). For both indicators analysed (DSTI30 and BPL), the use of classification trees made it possible to identify the net monthly income, the educational level, and the age of the reference person as key variables for distinguishing over-indebted from not-over-indebted households. On the basis of the same data source and using an ordered probit model, Agnieszka Wałęga (2020) analysed the relationship between households' subjective, self assessments of their financial situation and objective indicators of over-indebtedness. In the main, over-indebted households rated their situation as worse than indebted households rated theirs. Importantly, regardless of the size of the debt burden, self-assessments of financial position were better matched to objective measures of debt for households aged under 45. Leaving aside the question of over-indebtedness itself, respondent age and household income were the most significant factors in households' self-assessments of their financial position.

On the basis of data from the Household Budget Survey, Sławomir Zajączkowski and Dawid Żochowski (2007) assessed the distribution of households' debt repayment burden and the debt-servicing capacity of households with bank loans in 1998–2005. In 2005, the proportion of loans taken out by households at high risk of debt repayment difficulties, which the authors defined as those with a negative income buffer, was – depending on the method adopted – in the 12.2–13.5% range. For households repaying mortgages, the proportion was smaller: 7.6–8.3%. What is more, the proportion of loans taken out by households with a negative income buffer fell during the period under review. There was also no significant increase in the average burden of loan repayments (the ratio of total expenditure on debt repayment to total disposable income) falling upon households between 1998 and 2005. In the top quartile of the debt burden ratio (both for the general category of bank loans and for mortgage loans), the value of this ratio was a little over 20%.

The Household Budget Survey was once again employed by Paulina Anioła-Mikołajczak (2016) – in this case to identify determinants of over-indebtedness measured according to negative income buffers. On the basis of an analysis of data for 2011, she concluded that over-indebtedness is strongly determined by age, the education level of the head of the household, socio-economic group, biological type of family, income and, to a lesser extent, place of residence. In a later study using the same dataset (2017), she investigated the influence of the age of the household head on indebtedness and over-indebtedness (measured by the income buffer and DSTI). With regard to indebtedness, the results were consistent with the life-cycle model: households that are indebted are mainly young (almost 40% of households aged 25–44). No relationship between age and over-indebtedness was confirmed for the DSTI ratio – in contrast to the income buffer. The likelihood of over-indebtedness increases with age: 13.6% of households in the 65+ age group had a negative income buffer.

An assessment of the indebtedness of Polish households was also made by Grzegorz Wałęga (2013), using data from the Household Budget Survey covering the years 2000–2011. More than one-third of households were indebted in respect of credits or loans in that period, during which a noticeable trend was developing for households to satisfy their borrowing needs through banks rather than through other non-bank lenders or private finance. The results suggested that income, age, and education played a pivotal role in decisions to take on credit. The typical indebted household was an urban household headed by a well-educated person up to the age of 44, who earned income from paid employment or self-employment. Usually, it was constituted by a relatively high-income married couple with children who had a positive opinion of their material situation. For the majority of indebted households, the debt repayment burden from credits and loans was not great: approximately 75% of them had a DSTI ratio no greater than 20%. The 40% threshold (of repayments in relation to disposable income), which determined excessive indebtedness in the study, was exceeded by 4–6% of all indebted households.

Using data from Social Diagnosis and from the Household Budget Survey (for 2000–2013), Agnieszka Wałęga and Grzegorz Wałęga (2016) applied a logit model to assess the likelihood that a household would take on credits or loans due to its selected socio-economic characteristics. The results of their analysis suggest that income and education have a positive impact on that likelihood, while the age of the household head has a negative impact. In a subsequent paper (A. Wałęga & Wałęga, 2017a), the same authors attempted to assess the influence of households' socio-economic characteristics on debt repayment amounts. On this occasion, the data source was the Household Budget Survey of 2015, and quantile regression models were used in the analysis. As it turned out, the same determinants (socio-demographic characteristics) influenced the repayment amounts with varying force and sometimes in different directions (as regards direction, this primarily concerned the variables of age and livelihood). It was noted that while the influence of variables such as income, household size, and a household's very positive assessment of its material situation grows stronger as household indebtedness increases, the influence of the head of household's marital status grows weaker. The 2015 data mentioned earlier were used again by the authors to find a theoretical model that would best fit the actual distribution of household indebtedness in respect of loans and credits (A. Wałęga & Wałęga, 2017b). Although all of the analysed models – the log-normal distribution, the log-logistic distribution, and the Burr type III distribution – have certain shortcomings within the proposed framework of study, it would appear that the latter offers the closest fit with the real data. Over-indebtedness was the next issue connected with evaluations of the financial situation of Polish households to capture the authors' attention (A. Wałęga & Wałęga, 2018a). A logit model was employed to analyse the factors determining the probability of over-indebtedness – as expressed by a negative income buffer – in Polish households. Referring again to the Household Budget Survey for 2005–2015, it was established that, in the period studied, the proportion of over-indebted households in the total number of indebted households decreased from 14.7% to 9.2%, and that the probability of being classified as a household overburdened with debt repayments was negatively correlated with income and size of residence and positively correlated with the head of household's age. The likelihood of over-indebtedness was also lower in households headed by married men working full-time.

Białowolski (2014, 2019), Białowolski and Węziak-Białowolska (2017), and Białowolski et al. (2019) consulted data from Social Diagnosis to produce multifaceted assessments of indebted households. In the earliest of the cited papers, the author segmented indebted households by using multigroup latent class models and by identifying the key determinants of class membership. Based on data from five editions of Social Diagnosis (2003, 2005, 2007, 2009, 2011), it was possible to conclude that changes in the characteristics of households have little influence on the process that leads them to become indebted. Of the changes that occurred in the debt structure of Polish households, 85% could be explained by factors associated with changes in the Polish credit market, and only 15% could be attributed to the evolution of the socio-economic characteristics of households. However, for mortgage borrowers and the over-indebted, the transformation of the Polish credit market explained only 35% and 65%, respectively, of the change in the size of these groups. The strongest relationship between income and inclusion in a class was observed for households taking out housing loans and, among all classes of borrowers, the effect of age was strongest for – again – households taking on debt to buy a house or flat. Over-indebtedness was primarily a problem for town and city dwellers.

On the basis of data from three editions of Social Diagnosis (2011, 2013, and 2015), Piotr Białowolski (2019) examined the evolution of segments of borrowers (borrowing patterns) using latent class modelling (latent transition). The analysis suggested that households with mortgage obligations, households with no debt at all, and over-indebted households were highly likely to remain in their class. In accordance with the life-cycle pattern, the probability of transitioning to the mortgage borrowers' group was strongly influenced by age, household size, and income. The life cycle also played a significant role in relation to the probability of transitioning to the over-indebted group.

Piotr Białowolski and Dorota Węziak-Białowolska (2017) employed data from two editions of Social Diagnosis to examine the impact of the strong appreciation of the Swiss Franc – at the beginning of 2015 – on the psychological well-being and physical health of borrowers with mortgages denominated in that currency. The authors found that exchange rate changes increase the debt repayment burden on household budgets significantly, but they did not find any impact on the well-being and health of respondents. In a further paper written with Tyler VanderWeele (Białowolski et al., 2019), they drew upon three editions of Social Diagnosis (2011, 2013, and 2015) to assess the impact of debt and savings on physical health, emotional health, and health-seeking behaviours. The study demonstrated that debt, and particularly excessive debt, had a deleterious impact on both the physical and mental health of individuals. Debt lowered people's self-assessment of their health, amplified health concerns and feelings of loneliness, and was detrimental to sleep and life satisfaction scores. It was also a significant driver of suicidal thoughts, which were found to be 49% more likely for those in debt than for those with no debt burden and 139% more likely for those overburdened by debt. It is striking that debt was found to play no significant role in the context of health-seeking behaviours such as taking up sport or cutting down smoking.

The clear conclusion that emerges from this review of available data sources and studies of household debt is that – especially at the microeconomic level – data on indebtedness are collected and processed to a limited extent in Poland. When compared to research conducted in other countries, there is a lack of detailed data on the reasons for using credit, the types of credit broken down by entities and individuals, the initial amounts households borrow and the initial lengths of time they borrow for, amounts outstanding, instalment amounts, interest rates, and late payments and the reasons for them (A. Wałęga & Wałęga, 2018b). This impedes understanding of the way households behave in the financial market – especially when this is only possible by linking it to other information on the social and economic situation of respondents, such as income, consumption, wealth, and economic activity. Quite simply, an in-depth assessment of the economic situation of households and the determinants of their behaviour requires integrated data that are maintained for long enough to allow them to be usefully compared.

1.4 Summary

The theories that seek to explain households' behaviour in credit markets are mainly based on life-cycle models. The desire to increase the explanatory power of models, which is a response to the restrictive assumptions of their original versions, means that theories have been modified to include additional elements such as restrictions to credit-market access and uncertainty. Behavioural economics and experimental economics have made a substantial contribution to explaining irregularities in decisions to take on debt. The inclusion of insights and approaches from psychology has made it possible not only to relax the assumption that market participants behave rationally but also to shed new light on the problems they encounter in the various phases of the loan-taking process. To link them to sociological determinants of the consumption process – reference groups and emulation (imitation) – is a further trajectory in the development of models of household credit behaviour. Furthermore, the microeconomic theory of demand for credit cannot operate in isolation from the environment (system) in which economic entities function. For this reason, when modelling household behaviour on credit markets, it is difficult to ignore the impact of economic policy, deregulation, globalisation, and technological change.

Household indebtedness in Poland has yet to capture the attention of more than a few researchers. There would appear to be three reasons for this state of affairs. First, the indebtedness of Polish households (measured as the ratio of debt to GDP or debt to disposable income) is, as mentioned earlier, still low relative to developed countries, and therefore does not attract much attention. Second, the period of prosperity (unprecedented in Poland's recent history) that prevailed in the first two decades of the twenty-first century did not – despite the temporary disruption caused by the 2008 crisis – result in serious tensions in the retail credit market. Issues that might otherwise have arisen concerning the detrimental outcomes of high credit growth were thus displaced. Third, existing research into the indebtedness of households in Poland at the microeconomic level, and especially research into over-indebtedness, is severely limited by the absence of specialised cyclical surveys of household finance. This restricts the range of themes that can be studied and hampers the in-depth analyses of certain issues such as quality of life.

Notes

1 As Deaton (2005) states, the second of these has acquired the status of a famous unpublished paper. Following the shock caused by the death of his young assistant, Modigliani could not bring himself to revise the extensive manuscript to the standard publication requirements for academic papers. Indeed, it was not until 1980 that it finally appeared – in the second volume of the future Nobel Prize winner's collected works.

2 Even this conclusion may be over-optimistic (see Campbell & Hercowitz, 2019).

3 There is no doubt that the contribution made by behavioural economics is also of considerable practical importance: recognition of the psychological determinants of consumption, saving, and borrowing decisions has created space for policies aimed – on the

one hand – at compelling lenders to provide information that adequately rectifies basic cognitive biases (Bertrand & Morse, 2011; Sunstein, 2006) and – on the other hand – at designing default options in such a way that choices concerning, for example, long-term saving in pension funds make it possible to increase rates of saving.

4 Maintaining high rates of indebtedness in this way can, though, be explained as a perfectly rational action connected with perceptions of the risk of limited access to credit in the future (Druedahl & Jørgensen, 2018; Fulford, 2015; Gorbachev & Luengo-Prado, 2019).

5 The model devised by Thaler and Shefrin (1981), according to which human nature is shaped by two opposing forces – that of the short-sighted, egotistical hedonist and that of the strategic lifespan planner – offers an alternative approach to the problem of self-control.

6 Clearly, from this viewpoint, the preferences of households are treated as interdependent. This is one reason why relative income theory has been very much on the defensive for many years and has only recovered its status as a result, *inter alia*, of the successes of behavioural economics (Frank, 2005; Mason, 2000; McCormick, 2018).

7 Schor (2002, p. 5) is aware that this is something of an exaggeration. As she herself admits, the principle of keeping up with the Gateses might be appropriate for the wealthiest 20% of households, but the *de facto* reference group for the majority is the upper middle class.

8 In the case of maturity, the reference is to loans and other receivables; the latter, however, represent a negligible share of total receivables: less than 1.5% at the end of 2019 (NBP, 2020b).

9 See subsection 3.3 for more detail on the debt service-to-income ratio.

10 Statistics Poland (Główny Urząd Statystyczny) is the main statistical office in Poland.

11 The Household Finance and Consumption Network (HFCN) is a research network dedicated to investigating the financial condition of households: in particular their wealth and indebtedness. It has existed since 2006 and is run by the central banks and central statistical offices of eurozone countries. The National Bank of Poland was granted observer status in this network in 2012 (NBP, 2015).

12 Due, among other things, to the liberal regulatory policy in force after 1989 with respect to this type of business, the data that might make it possible to estimate the size of the non-bank lending market in Poland is highly incomplete. It is estimated that in 2018 the value of loans granted by other non-bank lenders amounted to approximately 7% of the loans and credits granted by the banking sector (Kowalski & Wałęga, 2022).

References

Amable, B. (2010). Crisis in the regulation regime – a new paradigm? *Socio-Economic Review*, *8*(3), 537–541. https://doi.org/10.1093/ser/mwq009

Ando, A., & Modigliani, F. (1963). The "life cycle" hypothesis of saving: Aggregate implications and tests. *American Economic Review*, *53*(1), 55–84.

Angeletos, G.-M., Laibson, D., Repetto, A., Tobacman, J., & Weinberg, S. (2001). The hyperbolic consumption model: Calibration, simulation, and empirical evaluation. *Journal of Economic Perspectives*, *15*(3), 47–68. https://doi.org/10.1257/jep.15.3.47

Anioła-Mikołajczak, P. (2016). Over-indebtedness of households in Poland and its determinants. *Acta Scientiarum Polonorum. Oeconomia*, *15*(4), 17–26.

Anioła-Mikołajczak, P. (2017). The impact of age on Polish households financial behavior – indebtedness and over-indebtedness. *Optimum. Economic Studies*, *1*(85), 106–116.

Attanasio, O. P., & Weber, G. (2010). Consumption and saving: Models of intertemporal allocation and their implications for public policy. *Journal of Economic Literature*, *48*(3), 693–751. https://doi.org/10.1257/jel.48.3.693

Bańbuła, P. (2006). *Oszczędności i wybór międzyokresowy – podejście behawioralne* (Materiały i Studia. Zeszyt nr 208). Warszawa: Narodowy Bank Polski.

Barba, A., & Pivetti, M. (2009). Rising household debt: Its causes and macroeconomic implications – A long-period analysis. *Cambridge Journal of Economics, 33*(1), 113–137. https://doi.org/10.1093/cje/ben030

Barnett, W. A., & Solow, R. (2000). An interview with Franco Modigliani. *Macroeconomic Dynamics, 4*(2), 222–256.

Bertola, G., Disney, C., & Grant, C. (2006). The economics of consumer credit demand and supply. In G. Bertola, R. Disney, & C. Grant (Eds.), *The economics of consumer credit* (pp. 1–26). Cambridge, MA: MIT Press.

Bertola, G., & Hochguertel, S. (2007). Household debt and credit: Economic issues and data problems. *Economic Notes, 36*(2), 115–146. https://doi.org/10.1111/j.1468-0300.2007.00181.x

Bertrand, M., Karlan, D., Mullainathan, S., Shafir, E., & Zinman, J. (2010). What's advertising content worth? Evidence from a consumer credit marketing field experiment. *Quarterly Journal of Economics, 125*(1), 263–306. https://doi.org/10.1162/qjec.2010.125.1.263

Bertrand, M., & Morse, A. (2011). Information disclosure, cognitive biases, and payday borrowing. *The Journal of Finance, 66*(6), 1865–1893. https://doi.org/10.1111/j.1540-6261.2011.01698.x

Beshears, J., Choi, J. J., Laibson, D., & Madrian, B. C. (2018). Behavioral household finance. In B. D. Bernheim, S. DellaVigna, & D. Laibson (Eds.), *Handbook of behavioral economics: Applications and foundations 1* (pp. 177–276). Amsterdam: Elsevier.

Białowolski, P. (2014). Patterns of debt possession among households in Poland – A multi-group latent class approach. *Bank i Kredyt, 45*(2), 79–104.

Białowolski, P. (2019). Patterns and evolution of consumer debt: Evidence from latent transition models. *Quality & Quantity, 53*(1), 389–415. https://doi.org/10.1007/s11135-018-0759-9

Białowolski, P., Cwynar, A., Cwynar, W., & Węziak-Białowolska, D. (2020). Consumer debt attitudes: The role of gender, debt knowledge and skills. *International Journal of Consumer Studies, 44*(3), 191–205. https://doi.org/10.1111/ijcs.12558

Białowolski, P., & Węziak-Białowolska, D. (2017). What does a Swiss franc mortgage cost? The tale of Polish trust for foreign currency denominated mortgages: Implications for well-being and health. *Social Indicators Research, 133*(1), 285–301. https://doi.org/10.1007/s11205-016-1363-9

Białowolski, P., Węziak-Białowolska, D., & VanderWeele, T. J. (2019). The impact of savings and credit on health and health behaviours: An outcome-wide longitudinal approach. *International Journal of Public Health, 64*(4), 573–584. https://doi.org/10.1007/s00038-019-01214-3

BIG InfoMonitor. (2020). *InfoDług. Ogólnopolski raport o zaległym zadłużeniu i niesolidnych dłużnikach*. Warszawa: BIG InfoMonitor.

Boyer, R. (2000). Is a finance-led growth regime a viable alternative to Fordism? A preliminary analysis. *Economy and Society, 29*(1), 111–145. https://doi.org/10.1080/030851400360587

Browning, M., & Crossley, T. F. (2001). The life-cycle model of consumption and saving. *Journal of Economic Perspectives, 15*(3), 3–22. https://doi.org/10.1257/jep.15.3.3

Campbell, J. R., & Hercowitz, Z. (2019). Liquidity constraints of the middle class. *American Economic Journal: Economic Policy, 11*(3), 130–155. https://doi.org/10.1257/pol.20180070

Carroll, C. D. (1992). The buffer-stock theory of saving: Some macroeconomic evidence. *Brookings Papers on Economic Activity, 23*(2), 61–156. https://doi.org/10.2307/2534582

Carroll, C. D. (1997). Buffer-stock saving and the life cycle/permanent income hypothesis. *The Quarterly Journal of Economics, 112*(1), 1–55. https://doi.org/10.1162/003355397555109

Carroll, C. D., & Kimball, M. S. (2001). *Liquidity constraints and precautionary saving* (NBER Working Paper No. 8496). Cambridge, MA: National Bureau of Economic Research. https://doi.org/10.3386/w8496

Chen, P., & Finke, M. S. (1996). Negative net worth and the life cycle hypothesis. *Journal of Financial Counseling and Planning*, 7, 87–96.

Coletta, M., De Bonis, R., & Piermattei, S. (2019). Household debt in OECD countries: The role of supply-side and demand-side factors. *Social Indicators Research*, *143*(3), 1185–1217. https://doi.org/10.1007/s11205-018-2024-y

Crook, J. N., & Hochguertel, S. (2007). *US and European household debt and credit constraints* (Tinbergen Institute Discussion Paper No. 2007–087/3). Amsterdam: Tinbergen Institute. http://doi.org/10.2139/ssrn.1036002

Deaton, A. (1991). Saving and liquidity constraints. *Ecomometrica*, *59*(5), 221–248. https://doi.org/10.2307/2938366

Deaton, A. (2005). Franco Modigliani and the life cycle theory of consumption. *BNL Quarterly Review*, *58*(233–234), 91–107.

Deidda, M. (2013). Precautionary saving, financial risk, and portfolio choice. *Review of Income and Wealth*, *59*(1), 133–156. https://doi.org/10.1111/roiw.12001

DellaVigna, S. (2009). Psychology and economics: Evidence from the field. *Journal of Economic Literature*, *47*(2), 315–372. https://doi.org/10.1257/jel.47.2.315

De Meza, D., Irlenbusch, B., & Reyniers, D. (2008). *Financial capability: A behavioural economics perspective* (Consumer Research No. 69). London: Financial Services Authority.

Druedahl, J., & Jørgensen, C. N. (2018). Precautionary borrowing and the credit card debt puzzle. *Quantitative Economics*, *9*(2), 785–823. https://doi.org/10.3982/QE604

Duesenberry, J. S. (1949). *Income, saving, and the theory of consumer behavior*. Cambridge, MA: Harvard University Press.

Dynan, K. E., & Kohn, D. L. (2007). *The rise in US household indebtedness: Causes and consequences* (FEDS Working Paper No. 2007–37). Washington, DC: Board of Governors of the Federal Reserve System. https://doi.org/10.17016/FEDS.2007.37

Erturk, I., Froud, J., Johal, S., Leaver, A., & Williams, K. (2007). The democratization of finance? Promises, outcomes and conditions. *Review of International Political Economy*, *14*(4), 553–575. https://doi.org/10.1080/09692290701475312

Ferber, R. (1973). Consumer economics, a survey. *Journal of Economic Literature*, *11*(4), 1303–1342.

Frank, R. H. (2005, June 9). The mysterious disappearance of James Duesenberry. *New York Times*.

Frank, R. H., Levine, A. S., & Dijk, O. (2014). Expenditure cascades. *Review of Behavioral Economics*, *1*(1–2), 55–73. https://doi.org/10.1561/105.00000003

Friedman, M. (1957). *A theory of the consumption function*. Princeton, NJ: Princeton University Press.

Fulford, S. L. (2015). How important is variability in consumer credit limits? *Journal of Monetary Economics*, *72*, 42–63. https://doi.org/10.1016/j.jmoneco.2015.01.002

Godley, W., & Lavoie, M. (2007). *Monetary economics: An integrated approach to credit, money, income, production and wealth*. New York: Palgrave Macmillan.

Gorbachev, O., & Luengo-Prado, M. J. (2019). The credit card debt puzzle: The role of preferences, credit access risk, and financial literacy. *The Review of Economics and Statistics*, *101*(2), 294–309. https://doi.org/10.1162/rest_a_00752

GUS. (2018). *Zeszyt metodologiczny. Badanie budżetów gospodarstw domowych*. Warszawa: Główny Urząd Statystyczny.

GUS. (2020). *Budżety gospodarstw domowych w 2019 r.* Warszawa: Główny Urząd Statystyczny.

Hall, R. E., & Mishkin, F. S. (1982). The sensitivity of consumption to transitory income: Estimates from panel data on households. *Econometrica, 50*(2), 461–481. https://doi.org/10.2307/1912638

Hayashi, F. (1985). The effect of liquidity constraints on consumption: A cross-sectional analysis. *The Quarterly Journal of Economics, 100*(1), 183–206. https://doi.org/10.2307/1885741

Heidhues, P., & Kőszegi, B. (2010). Exploiting naïvete about self-control in the credit market. *American Economic Review, 100*(5), 2279–2303. https://doi.org/10.1257/aer.100.5.2279

Hirst, D. E., Joyce, E. J., & Schadewald, M. S. (1994). Mental accounting and outcome contiguity in consumer-borrowing decisions. *Organizational Behavior and Human Decision Processes, 58*(1), 136–152. https://doi.org/10.1006/obhd.1994.1031

Hyytinen, A., & Putkuri, H. (2018). Household optimism and overborrowing. *Journal of Money, Credit and Banking, 50*(1), 55–76. https://doi.org/10.1111/jmcb.12453

Iacoviello, M. (2008). Household debt and income inequality, 1963–2003. *Journal of Money, Credit and Banking, 40*(5), 929–965. https://doi.org/10.1111/j.1538-4616.2008.00142.x

Jappelli, T. (1990). Who is credit constrained in the U.S. economy? *The Quarterly Journal of Economics, 105*(1), 219–234. https://doi.org/10.2307/2937826

Jappelli, T. (2005). The life-cycle hypothesis, fiscal policy and social security. *BNL Quarterly Review, 58*(233–234), 173–186.

Jappelli, T., & Pistaferri, L. (2010). The consumption response to income changes. *Annual Review of Economics, 2*(1), 479–506. https://doi.org/10.1146/annurev.economics.050708.142933

KNF. (2020). *Informacja na temat sytuacji sektora bankowego*. Warszawa: Komisja Nadzoru Finansowego.

Kowalski, R., & Wałęga, G. (2022). Regulation of usury: Justification, consequences, and some lessons from Polish experiences. *Gospodarka Narodowa*, forthcoming.

Krueger, D., & Perri, F. (2006). Does income inequality lead to consumption inequality? Evidence and theory. *Review of Economic Studies, 73*(1), 163–193. https://doi.org/10.1111/j.1467-937X.2006.00373.x

Kumhof, M., Rancière, R., & Winant, P. (2015). Inequality, leverage, and crises. *American Economic Review, 105*(3), 1217–1245. https://doi.org/10.1257/aer.20110683

Laibson, D. (1997). Golden eggs and hyperbolic discounting. *The Quarterly Journal of Economics, 112*(2), 443–478. https://doi.org/10.1162/003355397555253

Laibson, D., Repetto, A., & Tobacman, J. (2003). A debt puzzle. In P. Aghion, R. Frydman, J. Stiglitz, & M. Woodford (Eds.), *Knowledge, information, and expectations in modern economics: In honor of Edmund S. Phelps* (pp. 228–266). Princeton, NJ: Princeton University Press.

Laibson, D., Repetto, A., & Tobacman, J. (2007). *Estimating discount functions with consumption choices over the lifecycle* (NBER Working Paper No. 13314). Cambridge, MA: National Bureau of Economic Research.

Lapavitsas, C., & dos Santos, P. L. (2008). Globalization and contemporary banking: On the impact of new technology. *Contributions to Political Economy, 27*(1), 31–56. https://doi.org/10.1093/cpe/bzn005

Lusardi, A., & Mitchell, O. S. (2014). The economic importance of financial literacy: Theory and evidence. *Journal of Economic Literature, 52*(1), 5–44. https://doi.org/10.1257/jel.52.1.5

Lusardi, A., & Tufano, P. (2015). Debt literacy, financial experiences, and overindebtedness. *Journal of Pension Economics and Finance, 14*(4), 332–368. https://doi.org/10.1017/S1474747215000232

Maison, D. (2019). *The psychology of financial consumer behavior*. Cham: Springer International Publishing. https://doi.org/10.1007/978-3-030-10570-9

Mani, A., Mullainathan, S., Shafir, E., & Zhao, J. (2013). Poverty impedes cognitive function. *Science, 341*(6149), 976–980. https://doi.org/10.1126/science.1238041
Martin, N. (2010). 1,000% interest – good while supplies last: A study of payday loan practices and solutions. *Arizona Law Review, 52*(3), 563–622.
Mason, R. (2000). The social significance of consumption: James Duesenberry's contribution to consumer theory. *Journal of Economic Issues, 34*(3), 553–572. https://doi.org/10.1080/00213624.2000.11506294
McCormick, K. (2018). James Duesenberry as a practitioner of behavioral economics. *Journal of Behavioral Economics for Policy, 2*(1), 13–18.
Meier, S., & Sprenger, C. (2010). Present-biased preferences and credit card borrowing. *American Economic Journal: Applied Economics, 2*(1), 193–210. https://doi.org/10.1257/app.2.1.193
Mian, A., & Sufi, A. (2009). The consequences of mortgage credit expansion: Evidence from the U.S. mortgage default crisis. *Quarterly Journal of Economics, 124*(4), 1449–1496. https://doi.org/10.1162/qjec.2009.124.4.1449
Mian, A., Sufi, A., & Trebbi, F. (2013). The political economy of the subprime mortgage credit expansion. *Quarterly Journal of Political Science, 8*(4), 373–408. https://doi.org/10.1561/100.00012036
Modigliani, F., & Brumberg, R. (1954). Utility analysis and the consumption function: An interpretation of cross-section data. In K. K. Kurihara (Ed.), *Post Keynesian economics* (pp. 388–436). New Brunswick: Rutgers University Press.
Modigliani, F., & Brumberg, R. (1980). Utility analysis and aggregate consumption functions: An attempt at integration. In A. Abel (Ed.), *The collected papers of Franco Modigliani, volume 2: The life cycle hypothesis of saving* (pp. 128–197). Cambridge, MA: The MIT Press.
Montgomerie, J. (2009). The pursuit of (past) happiness? Middle-class indebtedness and American financialisation. *New Political Economy, 14*(1), 1–24. https://doi.org/10.1080/13563460802671196
Moore, G. L., & Stockhammer, E. (2018). The drivers of household indebtedness reconsidered: An empirical evaluation of competing arguments on the macroeconomic determinants of household indebtedness in OECD countries. *Journal of Post Keynesian Economics, 41*(4), 547–577. https://doi.org/10.1080/01603477.2018.1486207
Mullainathan, S., & Shafir, E. (2013). *Scarcity: Why having too little means so much*. London: Allen Lane.
NBP. (2015). *Zasobność gospodarstw domowych w Polsce. Raport z badania pilotażowego 2014 r.* Warszawa: Narodowy Bank Polski.
NBP. (2017). *Zasobność gospodarstw domowych w Polsce. Raport z badania 2016 r.* Warszawa: Narodowy Bank Polski.
NBP. (2020a). *Dane finansowe sektora bankowego*. Warszawa: Narodowy Bank Polski. www.nbp.pl/home.aspx?f=/statystyka/pieniezna_i_bankowa/naleznosci.html
NBP. (2020b). *Należności i zobowiązania monetarnych instytucji finansowych i banków*. Warszawa: Narodowy Bank Polski. www.nbp.pl/home.aspx?f=/statystyka/pieniezna_i_bankowa/nal_zobow.html
OECD. (2008). *Growing unequal?: Income distribution and poverty in OECD countries*. Paris: OECD Publishing. https://doi.org/10.1787/9789264044197-en
OECD. (2011). *Divided we stand: Why inequality keeps rising*. Paris: OECD Publishing. https://doi.org/10.1787/9789264119536-en
OECD. (2015). *In it together: Why less inequality benefits all*. Paris: OECD Publishing. https://doi.org/10.1787/9789264235120-en
OECD. (2021). *Household debt (indicator)*. OECD. https://doi.org/10.1787/f03b6469-en

Panek, T., Białowolski, P., Kotowska, I. E., Czapiński, J., Pytkowska, J., Pawlak, K., & Szumlicz, T. (2015). Warunki życia gospodarstw domowych. Zasobność materialna. Diagnoza Społeczna 2015. Warunki i jakość życia Polaków – Raport. *Contemporary Economics, 9*(4), 54–89. https://doi.org/10.5709/ce.1897-9254.181

Prelec, D., & Loewenstein, G. (1998). The red and the black: Mental accounting of savings and debt. *Marketing Science, 17*(1), 4–28. https://doi.org/10.1287/mksc.17.1.4

Purnanandam, A. (2011). Originate-to-distribute model and the subprime mortgage crisis. *Review of Financial Studies, 24*(6), 1881–1915. https://doi.org/10.1093/rfs/hhq106

Rajan, R. G. (2010). *Fault lines: How hidden fractures still threaten the world economy*. Princeton, NJ: Princeton University Press.

Ryoo, S. (2016). Household debt and housing bubbles: A Minskian approach to boom-bust cycles. *Journal of Evolutionary Economics, 26*(5), 971–1006. https://doi.org/10.1007/s00191-016-0473-5

Schor, J. B. (1999). *The overspent American: Why we want what we don't need*. New York: HarperPerennial.

Schor, J. B. (2002). *Understanding the new consumerism: Inequality, emulation and the erosion of well-being* (PSW-Paper No. 2002/2). Faculteit Politieke en Sociale Wetenschappen, Universiteit Antwerpen.

Shah, A. K., Mullainathan, S., & Shafir, E. (2012). Some consequences of having too little. *Science, 338*(6107), 682–685. https://doi.org/10.1126/science.1222426

Shefrin, H. M., & Thaler, R. H. (1988). The behavioral life-cycle hypothesis. *Economic Inquiry, 26*(4), 609–643. https://doi.org/10.1111/j.1465-7295.1988.tb01520.x

Sinha, T. (1988). Life cycle model of accumulation on trial: An eclectic survey. *Quarterly Journal of Business and Economics, 27*(1), 83–103.

Stango, V., & Zinman, J. (2009). Exponential growth bias and household finance. *The Journal of Finance, 64*(6), 2807–2849. https://doi.org/10.1111/j.1540-6261.2009.01518.x

Stockhammer, E. (2012). Financialization, income distribution and the crisis. *Investigación Económica, 71*(279), 39–70.

Stockhammer, E. (2015). Rising inequality as a cause of the present crisis. *Cambridge Journal of Economics, 39*(3), 935–958. https://doi.org/10.1093/cje/bet052

Stockhammer, E., & Wildauer, R. (2018). Expenditure cascades, low interest rates or property booms? Determinants of household debt in OECD countries. *Review of Behavioral Economics, 5*(2), 85–121. https://doi.org/10.1561/105.00000083

Sunstein, C. R. (2006). Boundedly rational borrowing. *University of Chicago Law Review, 73*(1), 249–270.

Sussman, A. B., & Shafir, E. (2012). On assets and debt in the psychology of perceived wealth. *Psychological Science, 23*(1), 101–108. https://doi.org/10.1177/0956797611421484

Świecka, B. (2008). *Bankructwa gospodarstw domowych: Perspektywa ekonomiczna i społeczna*. Warszawa: Difin.

Świecka, B. (2009). *Niewypłacalność gospodarstw domowych. Przyczyny, skutki, przeciwdziałanie*. Warszawa: Difin.

Szenberg, M., & Ramrattan, L. (2008). *Franco Modigliani: A mind that never rests*. London: Palgrave Macmillan. https://doi.org/10.1057/9780230582439

Thaler, R. H. (1999). Mental accounting matters. *Journal of Behavioral Decision Making, 12*(3), 183–206. https://doi.org/10.1002/(SICI)1099-0771(199909)12:3<183::AID-BDM318>3.0.CO;2-F

Thaler, R. H., & Shefrin, H. M. (1981). An economic theory of self-control. *Journal of Political Economy, 89*(2), 392–406. https://doi.org/10.1086/260971

Veblen, T. (1899). *The theory of the leisure class*. New York: Macmillan.

Wałęga, A. (2020). Indebted households' self-assessment of their financial situation: Evidence from Poland. In B. Ciałowicz (Ed.), *Quantitative methods in the contemporary issues of economics*. Kraków: edu-Libri.

Wałęga, A., & Wałęga, G. (2016). Bogaci i biedni na rynku kredytowym w Polsce. Analiza porównawcza dla lat 2000–2013. *Zeszyty Naukowe Uniwersytetu Ekonomicznego w Krakowie*, *2*(950), 75–92. https://doi.org/10.15678/ZNUEK.2016.0950.0205

Wałęga, A., & Wałęga, G. (2017a). Analiza spłat zadłużenia gospodarstw domowych z zastosowaniem regresji kwantylowej. *Studia i Materiały. Miscellanea Oeconomicae*, *21*(1, t. 1), 71–81.

Wałęga, A., & Wałęga, G. (2017b). Modelling the distribution of loan repayments of households in Poland. In M. Papież & S. Śmiech (Eds.), *The 11th professor Aleksander Zelias international conference on modelling and forecasting of socio-economic phenomena: Conference proceedings* (pp. 437–446). Cracow: Foundation of the Cracow University of Economics.

Wałęga, A., & Wałęga, G. (2018a). Living on the edge: Over-indebted households in Poland. In S. Kapounek & V. Kočiš Krůtilová (Eds.), *21st international scientific conference enterprise and competitive environment: Conference proceedings* (pp. 694–703). Brno: Mendel University in Brno.

Wałęga, A., & Wałęga, G. (2018b). O badaniach zadłużenia gospodarstw domowych w Polsce. *Wiadomości Statystyczne*, *63*(9 (688)), 5–26.

Wałęga, G. (2013). *Kredytowanie gospodarstw domowych*. Warszawa: Polskie Wydawnictwo Ekonomiczne.

Wałęga, G., & Wałęga, A. (2021). Over-indebted households in Poland: Classification tree analysis. *Social Indicators Research*, *153*(2), 561–584. https://doi.org/10.1007/s11205-020-02505-6

Wildauer, R. (2016). *Determinants of US household debt: New evidence from the SCF* (PKSG Working Paper No. 1608; Economics Discussion Papers). Faculty of Arts and Social Sciences, Kingston University.

Wolff, E. N. (1981). The accumulation of household wealth over the life-cycle: A micro-data analysis. *Review of Income and Wealth*, *27*(1), 75–96. https://doi.org/10.1111/j.1475-4991.1981.tb00193.x

Xu, X. (1995). Precautionary saving under liquidity constraints: A decomposition. *International Economic Review*, *36*(3), 675–690. https://doi.org/10.2307/2527366

Zajączkowski, S., & Żochowski, D. (2007). *Obciążenia gospodarstw domowych spłatami długu: Rozkłady i stress testy – na podstawie badań budżetów gospodarstw domowych GUS* (Materiały i Studia No. 221). Warszawa: Narodowy Bank Polski.

Zalega, T. (2014). Upadłość konsumencka a zadłużanie się miejskich gospodarstw domowych w Polsce w okresie kryzysu. *Nierówności Społeczne a Wzrost Gospodarczy*, *2*(38), 152–168.

Zalega, T. (2018). Assessment of the financial situation, determinants and the level of debt of seniors' households. *Nierówności Społeczne a Wzrost Gospodarczy*, *55*, 41–59. https://doi.org/10.15584/nsawg.2018.3.3

Zeldes, S. P. (1989). Consumption and liquidity constraints: An empirical investigation. *Journal of Political Economy*, *97*(2), 305–346. https://doi.org/10.1086/261605

2 Household indebtedness

Empirical analysis

2.1 Research methodology

Reviews of the literature indicate that there is no single, consistent definition of over-indebtedness, and no single method for identifying over-indebted households (these issues are discussed in more depth in subsections 3.1 and 3.3). In this study, we have taken into account the indicators which are most often used in the subject literature and which can also be applied here given the source material collected. This material was, for obvious reasons, the result of a compromise between the wish to do comprehensive research and the constraints of time (length of the interview) and content (avoiding overly specialised, technical language to ensure that the questions were understandable). A detailed description of the indicators can be found in subsection 3.3.

There is likewise no consensus in the subject literature regarding a single, universally applicable definition of economic well-being. Following a literature review, the authors offer their own perspective on this category. It should be noted, too, that there is no unanimity as to which indicators should be included in its analysis. The indicators of economic well-being have therefore been chosen as follows: (1) arbitrarily, (2) based on a review of the subject literature, (3) using formal and statistical criteria, and (4) with the available data in mind.

In their analysis of indebtedness, Anderloni and Vandone (2008) distinguish four main approaches at the level of households: empirical-descriptive, empirical-econometric, qualitative research, and credit scoring.

The first, and most frequent, involves describing the phenomenon of over-indebtedness based on interviews and personal data – including data on human behaviour. The source data used for these kinds of analyses can also take the form of secondary data produced, inter alia, by banks and other financial institutions that collect personal and behavioural data (e.g. the frequency and amount of arrears, and the level and types of consumer spending).

The second approach entails econometric methods (regression and cross-sectional analysis) that enable working hypotheses to be tested on a large number of observations – sometimes using databases created from interviews, personal data, and other macroeconomic or social data.

DOI: 10.4324/9781003254706-3

Qualitative research, the aim of which is to understand the decisions and behaviour of specific people, is the third approach. The data were collected through in-depth interviews, generally with small samples, or came from the case files of institutions involved in questions of indebtedness. In this case, the overall aim was not to generalise the results but to interpret specific situations.

Credit scoring, which is the last of the four approaches, cannot be accomplished without data on loan applicants and loan recipients. The proportion of loans granted that prove to be 'good' or 'bad' risks for lenders can also be investigated using the credit-scoring method.

The present research employs descriptive and statistical-econometric methods. The use of the latter was dictated by the measurement scale applied to the variables analysed. In addition to simple structural indicators, the following were employed:

- qualitative data analysis methods – the subjective views of respondents on indebtedness and economic well-being expressed in interviews were measured on weak scales, which was connected with the choice of appropriate research tools. Correlation analysis methods (Cramér's V coefficient, Spearman's rank correlation coefficient) and statistical tests (chi-squared independence test, Kruskal–Wallis test) were employed;
- regression methods – in order to identify the factors that shape economic well-being and influence the probability of classification as an over-indebted household, the classical approach to regressive modelling (a linear model), and a logit model for the binary variable were applied;
- a composite index based on fuzzy sets theory – in order to study the economic well-being of over-indebted and not-over-indebted households, it is essential to employ comparative analysis. Studies of this kind examine a set of statistical units that are usually described by multiple variables (multiple indicators). In this case, it is necessary to create a composite indicator that expresses the objects being studied numerically – in the same units of measure – so that they can be compared;
- clustering (Ward's method, k-means method) – using the results of the classification obtained by the division into disjoint groups, the objects can be verified, described, and interpreted by comparing the mean values for the subgroups obtained and the intra-group and intergroup variation. It is possible in this way to investigate the internal homogeneity of groups of households, determine the extent to which the obtained clusters differ from each other, and identify the features with the strongest influence on the differentiation of the internal structure of a given cluster;
- measures of inequality – the Gini coefficient and the Theil index were employed to describe variations in economic well-being in and between the groups studied.

Detailed information on how these methods were applied can be found in subsections 2.2, 4.3, 4.4, 6.2, and 6.3. In most cases, the statistical and econometric calculations were performed using the Statistica (version 13.1) and Stata software packages.

Information on the surveyed population of indebted households in Poland was gathered using a standardised research questionnaire completed by means of the computer-assisted telephone interview (CATI) method. The responses obtained during the telephone conversations were recorded in a computer database. The adopted method made it possible to achieve the basic aim of the research: to evaluate the economic well-being of over-indebted households in Poland.

The interviews were conducted by specialist interviewers following a structured script. Specific questions were asked with the aim of collecting in-depth information on the selected topics. One of the questions asked of people who do not settle their debts on time, for example, concerned the reasons for these repayment difficulties. Various ways of asking questions were used in the research tool.

The interview questionnaire contained 19 main questions (closed and semi-open; sometimes developed into detailed questions) and seven socio-demographic questions (size of household, source of income, place of residence, voivodship (province), and the sex, age, and educational level of the household reference person).

The first group of questions in the questionnaire addressed issues of household indebtedness, including the number and forms of loans or credits and monthly debt repayment amounts. Respondents were also asked why they took on debt, how they felt personally about indebtedness, and whether they were able to repay debt from income or savings (assets). Additional and more searching interviews, which enquired, for instance, about the reasons for repayment difficulties, were conducted with respondents who did not settle their debt repayments on time. Questions of how households deal with financial difficulties and what action they take in relation to them were not overlooked in the study.

The second part of the questionnaire was related to objective and subjective factors that shape households' economic well-being. The former included the sizes and forms of ownership of flats, and the capacity to finance a variety of expenses, while the latter included self-assessments of housing conditions, financial situation, possible ways of coping with financial difficulties, and the psychological conditions under which budget management decisions are taken. In this way, the questions in the survey made it possible to identify the over-indebted households in the sample and to evaluate their economic well-being.

The survey was carried out in the second quarter of 2018 as part of a project financed by the National Science Centre (No. 2015/19/D/HS4/02569). The CEM Market and Public Opinion Research Institute, which is one of the oldest private research agencies in Poland, was responsible for the sample selection and the CATI survey. Respondents were selected by Random Digit Dialling (RDD). The initial sample was composed of approximately 35,500 telephone numbers. It was decided to base the research on mobile telephones due to their prevalence – in 2018, 96.7% of households had a mobile phone with an active number (GUS, 2019).

Before the actual survey began, a pilot study was run on a sample of ten indebted households to check the selection, comprehensibility, and communicability of the interview questions. Following the pilot study, and after consulting with CEM specialists, improvements were made to the questionnaire design by replacing certain questions and modifying others.

In accordance with the study's original assumptions, the study population was composed of adults aged 18 and above who were residents in Poland and their households. Individuals were qualified for inclusion in the sample if they had at least one loan or credit at the time of the survey. The survey therefore began with a filter question on the type of debt held. Interviews were terminated if the answer, 'I do not have any credits or loans' was given.

Quota sampling was not employed because the surveyed population was 'unknown' (there are no studies of people in debt that would allow the demographic breakdown of this group to be precisely determined). A statistical error of 3% at a confidence interval of 0.95 was assumed for the entire country. Sampling, which was random, involved selecting a minimum of 1,067 indebted adults resident in Poland who satisfied the inclusion criteria. Given the sample's size and the fact that it was randomly selected, it can be assumed that the data obtained are representative – with the assumed error – of the population of indebted households. The data presented in Table 2.2 confirm that the sample structure did not deviate fundamentally from the structure of indebted households in the Household Budget Survey of 2018 carried out by Statistics Poland.

Additional telephone numbers were sampled where randomly selected individuals did not satisfy the inclusion criteria or withdrew from the survey, and where it was not possible to contact respondents. This procedure continued until sufficient interviews were obtained. The nature of the collected data, which concern a subject widely regarded as sensitive, meant that there were a large number of refusals or instances where the inclusion criteria were not met. On average, it was necessary to make more than 31 calls to complete a single interview. The average duration of the interviews was 14.5 minutes. The resulting sample contained 1,107 people from throughout Poland, which meant a response rate of 3.2% (Table 2.1). The structure of the sample by voivodship is presented in Figure 2.1.

Table 2.1 CATI surveys: basic data (%)

Item	*All contacts (including those not answered)*	*Calls answered*
Response rate (proportion of interviews in total number of contacts)	3.2	7.8
Refusals	26.6	65.7
Did not meet inclusion criterion (no credit or loan declared by respondent)	10.0	24.7

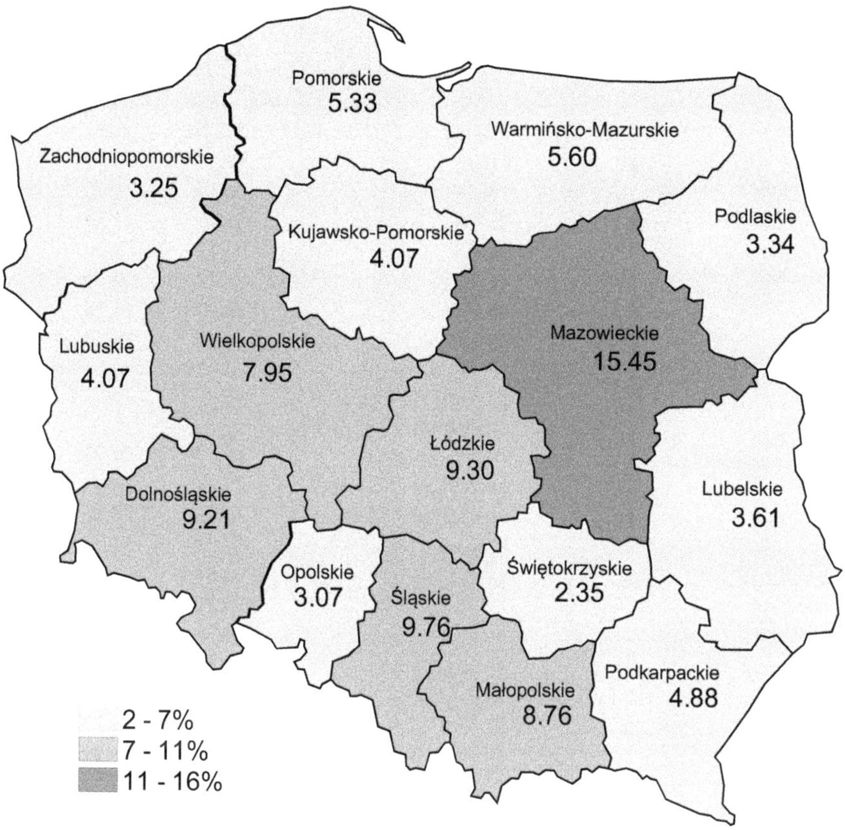

Figure 2.1 Sample structure by province (voivodship)

It should be noted that it was not possible to compare the data collected in this study with other data collected on households in Poland, such as the Household Budget Survey conducted by Statistics Poland or the European Union Statistics on Income and Living Conditions (EU-SILC) because the subject studied here is different: indebted households only.

As stated earlier, in addition to data strictly related to indebtedness and respondents' attitudes towards it, selected socio-demographic data on the characteristics of respondents and their households were also gathered. The basic characteristics of the sample are presented in Table 2.2. For comparison, the table also provides information on the sample structure of indebted households in the Household Budget Survey of 2018.

The demographic variables used to describe respondents representing households were sex, age group, and level of education. Households were described directly by the number of members they had (including children) and by the

Table 2.2 Characteristics of the sample (%)

Variable	*Coding of variable*	*Category*	*Sample structure*	*Structure in Household Budget Survey*[a]
Sex	0	Women	40.83	34.31
	1	Men	59.17	65.69
Age	1	18–24	6.14	1.76
	2	25–34	23.49	17.59
	3	35–44	23.67	28.30
	4	45–54	21.23	20.04
	5	55–64	15.99	17.28
	6	65+	9.49	15.04
Education	1	Lower secondary, primary, no formal education	4.07	8.10
	2	Basic vocational	14.72	26.95
	3	Secondary vocational	25.11	24.08
	4	General secondary	16.71	8.96
	5	Tertiary	39.39	31.92
Number of people in household	1	1	10.84	14.22
	2	2	25.29	27.38
	3	3	27.55	22.93
	4	4	24.66	23.18
	5	5+	11.65	12.28
Number of children in household[b]	0	0	48.15	58.77
	1	1	26.02	21.00
	2	2	20.87	16.10
	3	3	3.88	3.39
	4	4	0.45	0.67
	5	5	0.63	0.08
Monthly income of household (PLN)	1	Up to 2,000	15.36	10.55
	2	(2,000–4,000]	33.00	25.84
	3	(4,000–6,000]	28.05	28.53
	4	(6,000–8,000]	10.60	18.23
	5	Above 8,000	12.98	16.85
Place of residence	1	Rural	25.66	37.54
	2	Town with population up to 50,000[c]	28.65	9.71
	3	Town with population of 50,000–100,000[d]	15.95	18.49
	4	Town with population of 100,000–500,000	16.14	19.15
	5	Town with population above 500,000	13.60	15.11

Variable	*Coding of variable*	*Category*	*Sample structure*	*Structure in Household Budget Survey*[a]
Source of income/ maintenance	1	Own business, self-employed	15.00	9.25
	2	Blue-collar employment	33.06	26.50
	3	White-collar employment	32.43	35.86
	4	Farming	3.25	3.29
	5	Retirement pension	12.83	18.55
	6	Disability pension	1.63	3.59
	7	Benefits and allowances	0.90	2.96
	8	No income	0.36	
	9	Other	0.54	

a – calculation based on anonymised individual data from the Household Budget Survey of 2018;
b – the data from the Household Budget Survey concern children up to the age of 13;
c – Statistics Poland distinguishes a category of towns with a population up to 20,000;
d – Statistics Poland distinguishes a category of towns with a population of 20,000–99,000.

size (population) of the town they lived in. Finally, a household's economic situation was specified based on its net monthly income and its main source of income or maintenance.

2.2 Characteristics of indebted households

This subsection sets out the results of research involving basic measures of household indebtedness in selected socio-demographic cross-sections. Five sources of indebtedness were identified. First, credits or loans from banks or credit unions, that is to say, credits and loans from mainstream financial institutions. Second, given its prevalence in Polish retail outlets, hire purchase was distinguished as a separate type of indebtedness – even though banks and credit unions are, in the majority of cases, the institutions that finance this kind of expenditure. In addition, data were gathered on households' use of other kinds of loans, including, third, those drawn from loan companies and, fourth, from private individuals (family and friends). In the latter case, loans smaller than PLN 500 were not taken into account. Loans taken out from workplaces were the final, fifth, form of indebtedness to be considered. The number of credit and loan agreements held was an additional objective criterion used to define household indebtedness.

The scale of household debt was defined by the nominal debt repayment amounts and the debt service-to-income (DSTI) ratio. Five repayment ranges (up to PLN 200, PLN 200–500, PLN 500–1000, PLN 1,000–2,000, and above PLN 2,000) and four DSTI ranges (up to 10%, 10–20%, 20–30%, and above 30%) were adopted. Another measure used to examine the debt burden was a household's ability to repay it, for which the following three levels were adopted: debt repayment (1) from savings or current income, (2) by selling a proportion of assets, and (3) by selling all assets. Repayment of credits and loans on time was used in the analysis of indebtedness as a supplementary measure of the extent to which households were able to cope with indebtedness.

To provide a detailed portrait of indebted households, the household indebtedness characteristics mentioned earlier were presented by age, size of household (the number of members), education, and place of residence.

Irrespective of age group, respondents took loans or credits most often from banks or credit unions (Table 2.3). Banks were the most common source of loans or credits for those aged 35 and over. For young people (aged 18–34), however, of whom approximately half were indebted in this manner, the primary sources of loans or credits were hire purchase arrangements with shops. Similar observations can be made in respect of loans from loan companies and payday loans, which, although they accounted for only 3.7% of all sources of credit drawn upon by households in all age groups, were the most popular (8.82%) among the youngest age group (18–24 years).

Another source of loan funds for households could be private individuals (family and friends). Here, the highest proportion of loans of this kind was recorded for households in the 18–34 age group and the lowest for those in the 65+ age group. It can be seen from the age-range structure of indebtedness that workplace loans are most popular in the 35–44, 45–54, and 55–64 age groups, which is clearly connected with peak working years.

Approximately 60% of households possessed only one credit or loan. The proportion of households with a large number of credits or loans – three or more – was greatest among the 35–44 and 45–54 age groups. There were variations in the structure of repayment amounts across the age ranges. The debt burden was light, for example, for those in the 18–24 age range, of whom more than 70% allocated no more than PLN 500 to repayments. Larger values were recorded for households of working age, of which 20–35% allocated more than PLN 1,000 to repayments. The relationship between debt repayment amounts and age was confirmed by the chi-squared test of independence[1] ($p<0.001$).

The DSTI ratio is relatively low in Poland. However, as the results of the independence test showed ($p = 0.005$), it is related to the age of the respondent. Depending on the age group, for approximately 60–85% of households, the DTSI ratio did not exceed 20%. Households in the 45–54 and 65+ age groups were most heavily burdened with debt repayments (DSTI>30%).

The analysis of debt repayment capacity showed that, on average, four in ten households could settle their loan obligations from current income or savings, with the value of this indicator being highest for households in the youngest age group (51.47%) and lowest among those aged 55–64 (38.42%). The debt-to-assets burden was heavier in the older age groups, such that for at least 10% of respondents aged 45 and over, the amount of their indebtedness was so great that even selling all of their assets would not allow them to become debt free.

Where education is concerned, the use of loans or credits from banks or credit unions was most frequent in the tertiary group, where approximately three-quarters of respondents borrowed in this way (Table 2.4). Hire purchase

Table 2.3 Structure of indebted households by age (%)

Item	*Age ranges*						*Overall*	*Chi-squared statistic*	*p-value*	*Cramér's V coefficient*
	18–24	*25–34*	*35–44*	*45–54*	*55–64*	*65+*				
Debt type										
Credit or loan from a bank or credit union	41.18	61.92	77.86	70.64	66.67	74.29	68.20	41.53	0.000	0.194
Hire purchase at a retail outlet	48.53	43.85	34.73	32.34	22.60	30.48	34.87	28.10	0.000	0.159
Payday loan or loan from a loan company	8.82	2.31	1.53	2.98	7.34	4.76	3.70	17.15	0.004	0.124
Loans from private individuals	11.76	7.69	4.20	3.83	6.78	1.90	5.60	12.58	0.028	0.107
Workplace loans	2.94	4.23	10.31	20.85	16.38	2.86	10.93	52.74	0.000	0.218
Number of credits and loans										
1	67.65	60.77	55.34	57.87	65.54	65.71	60.52	17.84	0.271	0.073
2	20.59	25.77	28.63	26.38	24.86	30.48	26.56			
3	8.82	8.85	9.92	10.21	6.21	1.90	8.31			
4+	2.94	4.62	6.11	5.53	3.39	1.90	4.61			
Repayment amounts (PLN)										
Up to 200	37.88	20.46	10.77	18.30	26.44	32.69	20.86	74.15	0.000	0.130
(200–500]	36.36	28.96	23.08	28.09	29.31	30.77	28.05			
(500–1,000]	16.67	22.01	30.38	22.98	22.99	24.04	24.23			
(1,000–2,000]	4.55	23.55	25.38	22.98	15.52	8.65	20.04			
Above 2,000	4.55	5.02	10.38	7.66	5.75	3.85	6.83			
DSTI										
Up to 10%	54.84	40.08	33.61	41.04	44.87	32.98	39.72	33.01	0.005	0.105
(10–20%]	29.03	31.82	34.02	24.06	30.77	25.53	29.79			
(20–30%]	6.45	15.70	16.60	14.15	8.33	14.89	13.80			
Above 30%	9.68	12.40	15.77	20.75	16.03	26.60	16.68			
Repayment capacity										
From savings or current income	51.47	40.77	37.79	40.43	38.42	43.81	40.56	5.00	0.416	0.067
By selling a proportion of assets	89.71	80.38	82.44	81.28	84.18	77.14	81.93	6.38	0.271	0.098
By selling all assets	91.18	90.00	93.13	89.36	86.44	86.67	89.79	18.47	0.002	0.304

Table 2.4 Structure of indebted households by educational level (%)

Item	*Education*					*Overall*	*Chi-squared statistic*	*p-value*	*Cramér's V coefficient*
	Lower secondary, primary, no formal education	*Basic vocational*	*Secondary vocational*	*General secondary*	*Tertiary*				
Debt type									
Credit or loan from a bank or credit union	71.11	68.10	65.11	59.46	73.62	68.20	13.83	0.008	0.112
Hire purchase at a retail outlet	35.56	28.22	39.21	40.54	32.11	34.87	9.57	0.048	0.093
Payday loan or loan from a loan company	8.89	6.13	3.24	4.86	2.06	3.70	10.25	0.036	0.096
Loans from private individuals	4.44	9.20	4.68	7.57	4.13	5.60	7.70	0.103	0.083
Workplace loans	0.00	9.82	12.23	5.95	13.76	10.93	14.52	0.006	0.115
Number of credits and loans									
1	68.89	63.19	63.31	63.24	55.73	60.52	16.78	0.158	0.071
2	22.22	28.22	26.62	23.78	27.52	26.56			
3	2.22	5.52	7.55	8.11	10.55	8.31			
4+	6.67	3.07	2.52	4.86	6.19	4.61			
Repayment amounts (PLN)									
Up to 200	38.64	25.15	25.91	25.68	12.21	20.86	98.32	0.000	0.150
(200–500]	31.82	33.74	27.37	32.79	23.96	28.05			
(500–1,000]	15.91	25.15	27.74	20.22	24.19	24.23			
(1,000–2,000]	11.36	15.34	15.33	18.03	26.50	20.04			
Above 2,000	2.27	0.61	3.65	3.28	13.13	6.83			

DSTI									
Up to 10%	39.02	36.77	44.44	37.79	38.76	39.72	16.55	0.167	0.074
(10–20%]	12.20	32.26	27.78	33.72	30.23	29.79			
(20–30%]	14.63	14.84	12.30	13.37	14.47	13.80			
Above 30%	34.15	16.13	15.48	15.12	16.54	16.68			
Repayment capacity									
From savings or current income	26.67	28.83	44.60	39.46	44.27	40.56	17.36	0.002	0.125
By selling a proportion of assets	62.22	71.78	85.25	84.86	84.40	81.93	14.90	0.005	0.150
By selling all assets	66.67	82.21	90.65	91.35	93.81	89.79	16.37	0.003	0.286

arrangements were, in turn, most common among those with vocational or general secondary education, while loans from loan companies and payday loans, which are generally far less common, were chosen most often by those with a lower secondary education and below (8.89%). Meanwhile, respondents with a basic vocational or general secondary education were almost twice as likely to borrow from private individuals than those who completed their education at other levels. It was established that 10–14% of respondents – mainly those with basic vocational, secondary vocational, or tertiary education – took advantage of workplace loans.

The better educated were, in general, more likely to have a greater number of loans – here, 44.27% of those with tertiary education had two or more of them, while, by contrast, 68.89% of those with up to lower secondary education had only one. It is interesting to note, however, that among the least educated the proportion of those with four or more loans was similar to that of respondents with tertiary education: 6.67% and 6.19%, respectively.

As in the case of the number of loans, as the respondent's level of education increased, so did the proportion of households with higher repayment amounts, which was also confirmed by the chi-squared test of independence ($p<0.001$). The frequency of repayment amounts above PLN 1,000 was much greater for the households of respondents with tertiary education, while they did not usually exceed PLN 500 for the households of those with the lowest level of education.

Across all educational levels, the DSTI ratio did not in most cases exceed 10%. However – compared with fewer than one-third of households in the other educational categories – a DSTI ratio above 20% was recorded for almost half of households with the lowest level of education.

Households' capacity to repay their debts from current income and assets increased with educational level. Of households with tertiary education, just a little under 7% would not have been able to pay off their debts by selling all of their assets, whereas as many as one-third of those in the lowest educational category would not have been able to do so.

No matter their size, the vast majority of households turned to banks and credit unions as the basic source of loan funds (Table 2.5). One-person households, which were also to the fore in respect of using the services of non-bank lenders, obtained funds through this channel most often. While one-person households were no more than 7 percentage points ahead of the other categories of households in respect of using bank loans or credits (71.67% compared to the lowest value of 64.34% for greater than four-person households), they borrowed from non-bank lenders more than four times as often than four-person households, which used them least. The proportion of workplace loans used by average-sized households of three or four members was by a distance the highest, while the largest households signed the greatest proportion of hire-purchase agreements and borrowed most frequently from friends and family. The use of hire-purchase agreements was a distinguishing

Table 2.5 Structure of indebted households by household size (%)

Item	*Number of people*					*Overall*	*Chi-squared statistic*	*p-value*	*Cramér's V coefficient*
	1	*2*	*3*	*4*	*5+*				
Debt type									
Credit or loan from a bank or credit union	71.67	66.43	69.18	69.23	64.34	68.20	2.22	0.694	0.045
Hire purchase at a retail outlet	29.17	31.43	37.70	35.16	40.31	34.87	5.95	0.203	0.073
Payday loan or loan from a loan company	7.50	3.93	3.28	1.83	4.65	3.70	8.05	0.090	0.085
Loans from private individuals	5.00	6.79	3.93	5.13	8.53	5.60	4.63	0.327	0.065
Workplace loans	6.67	8.57	15.08	11.72	8.53	10.93	10.18	0.037	0.096
Number of credits and loans									
1	66.67	65.00	56.72	55.68	64.34	60.52	20.26	0.062	0.078
2	25.00	25.71	29.84	26.74	21.71	26.56			
3	8.33	5.71	8.20	10.62	9.30	8.31			
4+	0.00	3.57	5.25	6.96	4.65	4.61			
Repayment amounts (PLN)									
Up to 200	21.85	25.36	18.09	17.04	24.81	20.86	31.72	0.011	0.085
(200–500]	31.93	29.71	24.01	30.00	26.36	28.05			
(500–1,000]	31.09	22.10	28.29	19.63	22.48	24.23			
(1,000–2,000]	12.61	16.30	23.03	24.07	19.38	20.04			
Above 2,000	2.52	6.52	6.58	9.26	6.98	6.83			
DSTI									
Up to 10%	25.66	40.78	38.93	42.86	46.49	39.72	28.71	0.004	0.097
(10–20%]	26.55	32.16	27.86	30.20	31.58	29.79			
(20–30%]	17.70	12.16	15.00	13.47	11.40	13.80			
Above 30%	30.09	14.90	18.21	13.47	10.53	16.68			
Repayment capacity									
From savings or current income	35.00	42.50	44.26	37.73	38.76	40.56	4.79	0.309	0.066
By selling a proportion of assets	72.50	81.43	84.59	81.68	86.05	81.93	8.35	0.079	0.113
By selling all assets	80.83	90.71	91.15	90.11	92.25	89.79	3.38	0.496	0.130

feature of households with three or more members when compared to their smaller counterparts.

The burden of repaying two, three, or four or more, loans and credits affected households of three and four people more often than other households, whereas more than 90% of households of one or two people had no more than two loans or credits. This observation was confirmed by the result of the chi-squared test of independence, which indicated a relationship between the number of credits and household size at a significance level of $p = 0.062$.

For all households, the most frequent amount of monthly loan- and credit-repayment liabilities was in the PLN 200–1,000 range. However, repayments exceeding PLN 1,000 accounted for a significant share of the repayment burden for households of three and four people (29.61% and 33.33%, respectively). A relationship between repayment amounts and household size was confirmed in this case too ($p = 0.011$).

The burden of loan repayments in relation to income was far heavier for one-person households. The DSTI ratio, which was greater than 20% for approximately 48% of these households, exceeded 30% of income for just over 30% of them – very nearly three times the ratio for the largest households. A relationship between household size and the debt repayment burden on the household budget was confirmed by the chi-squared test of independence ($p<0.01$).

One-person households also had the least capacity to pay debts in their entirety. Although the difference in this regard with respect to other households was not especially significant in the case of the ability to repay debts from current income or savings (2.73 percentage points in relation to the second lowest value for other groups of households), there was a clear difference in the case of repayment financed by selling some or all of one's assets, which amounted to 8.93 and 9.28 percentage points, respectively (again taking the second lowest value as the reference point). Here, as many as 27.5% of one-person households were unable to repay their debts by selling some of their assets, and over 19% of them could not do so even by selling all of them.

Place of residence had a bearing on the sources households borrowed from (Table 2.6). For instance, three-quarters of the inhabitants of large towns took on credit from banks and credit unions. By contrast, rural households and those in small- and medium-sized towns were more likely to take advantage of hire-purchase agreements with retail outlets than households in towns with populations greater than 500,000. This variation can be linked primarily to the availability and spatial distribution of banking outlets. It was common in rural areas to borrow from private individuals, while in small towns it was noticeable that a greater than average proportion of borrowers used loan companies. Analysis of the number of loan agreements by place of residence showed no significant differentiation: six out of ten households had one agreement and, on average, every fourth household had two.

Table 2.6 Structure of indebted households by place of residence (%)

Item	*Rural*	*Town and population*			*Overall*	*Chi-squared statistic*	*p-value*	*Cramér's V coefficient*
		Up to 100,000	*100,000–500,000*	*Above 500,000*				
Debt type								
Credit or loan from a bank or credit union	66.78	66.46	69.10	76.00	68.20	5.22	0.156	0.069
Hire purchase at a retail outlet	37.46	35.57	35.96	26.67	34.87	5.47	0.140	0.070
Payday loan or loan from a loan company	2.83	4.07	3.93	3.33	3.70	0.87	0.832	0.028
Loans from private individuals	8.83	3.86	5.06	6.00	5.60	8.52	0.036	0.088
Workplace loans	9.54	11.18	14.04	9.33	10.93	2.75	0.432	0.050
Number of loans and credits								
1	61.13	61.99	56.18	59.33	60.52	6.85	0.652	0.046
2	26.50	26.83	25.28	27.33	26.56			
3	8.13	7.32	11.24	8.67	8.31			
4+	4.24	3.86	7.30	4.67	4.61			
Repayment amounts (PLN)								
Up to 200	24.64	20.00	21.59	15.44	20.86	38.51	0.000	0.108
(200–500]	26.43	30.20	31.25	20.81	28.05			
(500–1,000]	23.21	26.12	23.86	20.81	24.23			
(1,000–2,000]	20.00	19.18	16.48	26.85	20.04			
Above 2,000	5.71	4.49	6.82	16.11	6.83			
DSTI								
Up to 10%	40.77	40.13	40.37	35.82	39.72	7.65	0.570	0.050
(10–20%]	27.69	31.49	27.95	29.85	29.79			
(20–30%]	11.54	14.63	14.29	14.93	13.80			
Above 30%	20.00	13.75	17.39	19.40	16.68			
Repayment capacity								
From savings or current income	40.64	40.65	43.26	37.33	40.56	1.19	0.756	0.033
By selling a proportion of assets	85.51	80.89	82.58	77.33	81.87	4.76	0.190	0.085
By selling all assets	92.93	88.82	88.76	88.00	89.76	2.13	0.545	0.103

In rural areas, and in small- and medium-sized towns, the repayment burden on households was low. For approximately half of them, this meant spending no more than PLN 500 on repayments. However, the repayment burden for households in towns with a population above 500,000, where approximately 43% of households allocated more than PLN 1,000 to repayments each month, was considerably heavier. The results of the chi-squared independence test ($p<0.01$) confirmed a relationship between the amount of monthly debt repayments and place of residence. The DSTI values broken down by place of residence did not reflect these differences in repayment amounts: the percentage of households in large towns with a DSTI ratio greater than 20% was only a few points higher than that of households in the provinces and smaller towns. This leads to the conclusion that the higher nominal repayments of households in large urban centres must be accompanied by higher income.

Broken down by place of residence, no great variation was noted for households in respect of the capacity to repay debts from current assets or savings, or to do so by selling some or all of their assets. It was noticeable, however, that the percentage of 'over-extended' households, that is, households with debts greater than assets, was lower in villages and in the countryside.

Analysis of the types of debt held shows that households behaved differently in terms of where (how) they became indebted depending on their sources of income (Table 2.7). Thus, the self-employed, white-collar employees, retirement pensioners, and disability pensioners relied to the greatest degree on finance from the banking system and from credit unions. Blue-collar employees, for their part, were more likely than other groups to sign hire-purchase agreements with retail outlets. There were considerable differences between groups in respect of payday loans and loans from loan companies, which were used twice as often by those who supported themselves from the remaining sources of income: private farms, benefits and allowances, no income, and 'other'. However, white-collar employees turned to loan companies and payday loans more rarely: the proportion of households of this kind among all those surveyed was only 1.95%. As expected, employees (in both blue-collar and white-collar positions) took advantage of workplace loans most frequently.

Certain variations in the numbers of credits and loans, and in repayment amounts, were also discernible. More than 90% of indebted households of pensioners and those with other sources of income had a maximum of two loans, while among households of employees in white-collar positions, this percentage was lower and amounted to only 83.57%. There was a similar breakdown for credit and loan repayment amounts. Among the households of retirement pensioners, disability pensioners, and employees in blue-collar positions, the biggest group was formed by those repaying low amounts (up to PLN 1,000). On the other hand, the self-employed and employees in white-collar positions were more frequently burdened by higher repayment

Table 2.7 Structure of indebted households by source of income/maintenance (%)

Item	*Source of income/maintenance*					*Overall*	*Chi-squared statistic*	*p-value*	*Cramér's V coefficient*
	Own business/ self-employed	*Blue-collar employment*	*White-collar employment*	*Disability or retirement pension*	*Other*				
Debt type									
Credit or loan from a bank or credit union	73.49	60.93	71.87	71.25	67.86	68.20	13.98	0.007	0.112
Hire purchase at a retail outlet	31.33	38.80	34.26	31.25	33.93	34.87	4.41	0.354	0.063
Payday loan or loan from a loan company	3.61	4.64	1.95	4.38	7.14	3.70	6.07	0.194	0.074
Loans from private individuals	6.02	7.38	4.46	4.38	3.57	5.60	4.02	0.403	0.060
Workplace loans	5.42	9.84	18.94	4.38	1.79	10.93	41.16	0.000	0.193
Number of loans and credits									
1	57.23	63.11	55.71	68.13	62.50	60.52	27.52	0.281	0.079
2	29.52	24.32	27.86	25.00	28.57	26.56			
3	9.64	7.92	10.58	4.38	3.57	8.31			
4+	3.61	4.64	5.85	2.50	5.36	4.61			
Repayment amounts (PLN)									
Up to 200	15.66	24.73	12.92	33.54	25.93	20.86	118.69	0.000	0.164
(200–500]	22.29	35.16	22.47	31.01	25.93	28.05			
(500–1,000]	22.89	25.55	25.56	22.78	14.81	24.23			
(1,000–2,000]	27.71	12.91	28.37	8.86	22.22	20.04			
Above 2,000	11.45	1.65	10.67	3.80	11.11	6.83			
DSTI									
Up to 10%	38.78	45.82	36.88	31.51	42.55	39.72	35.60	0.003	0.090
(10–20%]	30.61	28.53	31.88	31.51	17.02	29.79			
(20–30%]	14.29	10.95	16.88	13.70	12.77	13.80			
Above 30%	16.33	14.70	14.38	23.29	27.66	16.68			
Repayment capacity									
From savings or current income	50.00	34.97	43.18	39.38	35.71	40.56	12.53	0.014	0.106
By selling a proportion of assets	87.35	78.69	85.24	76.88	80.36	81.93	6.29	0.179	0.098
By selling all assets	93.37	87.98	93.59	83.75	83.93	89.79	9.57	0.048	0.219

amounts: approximately 40% of respondents in each of these groups allocated more than PLN 1,000 every month to repayments. It is worth noting, however, that despite high repayments (compared to other groups), these groups had the greatest capacity to cover their debts both from current income or savings and from their assets.

Analysis of the DSTI ratio sheds a different light on households' objective debt burden. The high repayment amounts among self-employed households and employees in white-collar positions indicated earlier did not translate into a greater proportion of households with a DSTI ratio above 30%. For retirement pensioners, disability pensioners, and those supporting themselves from other sources of income, however, the DSTI ratio was above 30% for almost one in four respondents – despite the smaller number of loans and the lower nominal repayment amounts when compared with other socio-economic groups. Among households classified in these groups, just over one-third of those surveyed were able to repay their debts from current income or savings, while for just over 16% of households, even the sale of all of their assets would not have allowed them to fully satisfy their creditors.

The question of late, early, and punctual debt repayment represents an aspect of debt and its possible negative consequences that is different from those already considered. Of the surveyed group of indebted households, 80% settled their credit or loan liabilities on schedule, and 16% settled them ahead of schedule (Figure 2.2), which suggests that there exists a 'healthy' level of indebtedness that can be serviced without generating difficulties. The proportion of households in the surveyed sample for whom debt service was a problem and who settled their liabilities late was below 2%.

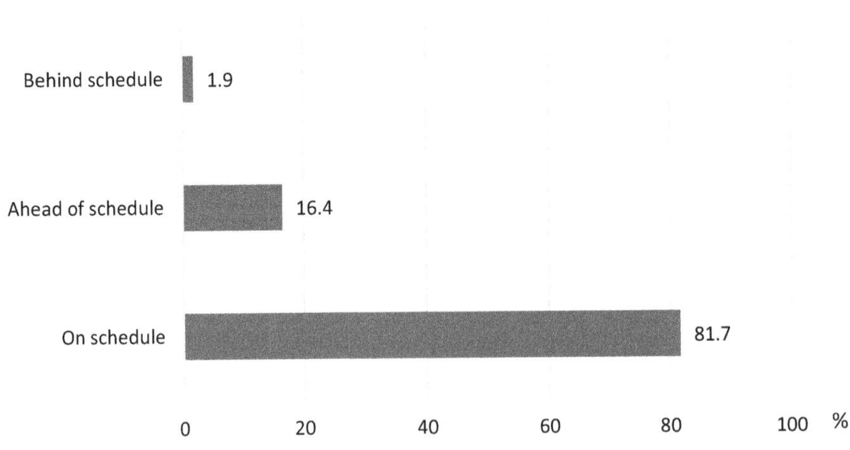

Figure 2.2 Late, early, and punctual repayment of credits and loans

2.3 Subjective assessment of indebtedness

No treatment of the indebtedness of households can be complete without supplementing the objective indicators, discussed earlier, with the subjective dimension. Numerous studies (Betti et al., 2007; D'Alessio & Iezzi, 2013) have confirmed that there is sometimes a disconnect between self-assessment of indebtedness and objective evaluations. What is more, the implications for their behaviour of the way households perceive indebtedness or, in broader terms, the way they perceive their financial situation, are not economic alone (Blomgren et al., 2016; Bridges & Disney, 2010; Richardson et al., 2013; Selenko & Batinic, 2011; Tay et al., 2017).

The subjective dimension was investigated by asking respondents how they felt about their indebtedness. Three gradations of respondents' assessments of indebtedness were adopted: (1) it is sometimes a source of stress and worry; (2) it is regarded as a severe psychological strain; and (3) it is identified as an unbearable psychological burden – the least favourable variant. In addition to assessing the psychological dimension of debt, respondents were asked whether they saw their physical health problems, such as high blood pressure or headaches, as resulting from their debt.

One further question that helped to shed light on respondents' subjective perceptions and to link them with objective indicators concerned the level of indebtedness households regarded as safe for them.

Studies suggest that debt can cause a variety of mental and physical health problems (Blomgren et al., 2016; Brown et al., 2005; Drentea & Lavrakas, 2000), including depression (Bridges & Disney, 2010). The responses associated with these problems – broken down by selected socio-demographic characteristics and aspects of indebtedness – are presented in Tables 2.8 and 2.9.

Table 2.8 Perceptions of indebtedness as a threat to health by selected socio-demographic characteristics (%)

Item	*Stress and worry*	*Severe psychological strain*	*Unbearable psychological burden*	*Difficulties with physical health*
Sex				
Women	28.54	9.29	2.21	9.73
Men	31.45	8.09	2.14	8.09
Age range				
18–34	35.98	4.57	0.00	3.96
35–54	29.18	8.45	1.21	7.65
55+	25.53	13.48	6.38	16.31
Education				
Basic vocational or lower	29.33	13.46	6.25	15.87
Secondary	32.18	7.99	1.51	8.86
Tertiary	28.67	6.88	0.91	5.28

(*Continued*)

Table 2.8 (Continued)

Item	*Stress and worry*	*Severe psychological strain*	*Unbearable psychological burden*	*Difficulties with physical health*
Number of people in household				
1	33.33	10.00	5.00	18.33
2	29.29	11.43	3.57	10.00
3	30.16	7.54	1.31	6.56
4	28.21	6.59	1.10	5.13
5+	34.11	7.75	0.78	10.08
Place of residence				
Rural	32.86	10.25	3.53	9.19
Small town[a]	31.71	8.54	1.83	9.55
Large town[b]	25.30	25.30	1.22	6.71

a – up to 100,000,
b – above 100,000.

Table 2.9 Perceptions of indebtedness as a threat to health by selected indebtedness characteristics (%)

Item	*Stress and worry*	*Severe psychological strain*	*Unbearable psychological burden*	*Difficulties with physical health*
Debt type				
Bank	28.44	8.81	4.08	8.07
Non-bank	22.44	5.68	8.12	6.53
Mixed bank and non-bank	48.10	12.86	3.33	14.29
Number of loans and credits				
1	22.39	5.82	1.49	6.27
2+	42.33	12.81	3.20	12.59
Repayment amounts (PLN)				
Up to 500	24.02	6.33	2.61	7.45
(500–1,000]	34.96	8.65	1.88	10.53
Above 1,000	37.63	12.88	1.69	9.83
DSTI				
Up to 0%	18.00	4.00	1.00	4.00
(10–20%]	30.33	6.67	1.33	6.33
(20–30%]	45.32	12.95	4.32	11.51
Above 30%	50.00	19.05	5.36	20.83
Repayment capacity				
From savings or current income	18.26	20.73	11.76	4.45
By selling a proportion of assets	25.25	22.71	21.15	6.17
By selling all assets	26.86	23.60	19.05	6.64

The general finding from the research is that the psychological aspect of the debt burden is more pronounced than that of physical health (cf. Dackehag et al., 2019; Drentea & Reynolds, 2012; Hojman et al., 2016; Keese & Schmitz, 2014; Richardson et al., 2017; Sweet et al., 2013, 2018). It is noteworthy that indebtedness was, at minimum, a source of stress and worry for one-third of those surveyed. It could be seen in respect of the weight of the mental burden associated with indebtedness that the proportion of people reporting both a severe and an unbearable psychological burden increased with age, while an inverse relationship was observed in the case of education and household size. No clear trend could be discerned with regard to place of residence.

Depending on the descriptor concerned, there were variations in respondents' feelings about the influence of indebtedness on health. As expected, there was an association between an increase in indebtedness levels expressed by any objective indicator (DSTI, repayment amounts, or the number of loans or credits) and an increase in the proportion of respondents finding indebtedness a severe or unbearable psychological burden. Interestingly, whereas the type of loan or credit had no significant influence on variations in subjective assessments of mental and physical health, simultaneous use of loans from banks and from non-bank lenders had a powerful impact – sufficient to produce a negative effect on three of the four components of the subjective dimension of indebtedness.

The respondents who most often perceived indebtedness as a source of serious health difficulties were women, those with a basic vocational education or lower, and people aged 55 and above. Respondents from one-person households, households with more than one credit or loan, and heavily indebted households (those with DSTI>30% and those able to repay their debts only by selling all of their assets) also indicated health problems connected with indebtedness. Indebtedness more often had a psychological dimension, however, among men, young people up to 34 years of age, and those with secondary education.

Subjective assessments of indebtedness relate to individuals' perceptions of the amount of debt considered safe – and not to health difficulties alone. They can be derived from personal attitudes, beliefs, or perspectives on risk and they can, in principle, be independent of the current objective level of indebtedness. An indebtedness ratio expressed as a multiple of monthly income was employed to produce a subjective assessment of the level of debt considered safe.

The research found that more than half of respondents (56.5%) considered indebtedness of up to 3 months' income as safe, while only approximately 10% considered indebtedness in excess of 1 year's income as safe. The level of debt considered safe did not depend on sex ($p = 0.507$): only a slightly higher percentage of men (10.78%) thought that debt above the equivalent of annual income was safe. The chi-square test of independence (at $p<0.01$) confirmed, though, that the amount of debt considered safe depended on age, educational level, debt type, number of loans and credits, repayment amounts, and the value of the DSTI ratio (Tables 2.10 and 2.11).

Table 2.10 Safe levels of indebtedness (expressed as a multiple of monthly incomes) in socio-demographic cross section (%)

Item	*Indebtedness level*					*Chi-squared statistic*	*p-value*	*Cramér's V coefficient*
	Up to 1 month	*Up to 3 months*	*Up to 6 months*	*Up to 12 months*	*Above 12 months*			
Sex								
Women	29.90	27.99	15.79	18.42	7.89	3.31	0.507	0.057
Men	30.88	24.67	15.69	17.97	10.78			
Age range								
18–34	30.50	29.25	16.04	14.15	10.06	24.77	0.002	0.110
35–54	25.97	24.68	16.74	20.82	11.80			
55+	39.02	24.39	13.41	18.29	4.88			
Education								
Basic vocational or lower	40.00	25.26	11.05	18.95	4.74	35.47	0.000	0.131
Secondary	31.34	28.11	17.51	16.13	6.91			
Tertiary	25.12	24.14	16.01	19.95	14.78			
Number of people in household								
1	32.08	27.36	12.26	13.21	15.09	19.78	0.230	0.069
2	34.77	24.61	17.58	16.41	6.64			
3	34.77	24.61	17.58	16.41	6.64			
4	28.35	26.82	15.71	18.39	10.73			
5+	23.73	33.90	14.41	21.19	6.78			
Place of residence								
Rural	31.18	25.86	13.69	19.01	10.27	13.99	0.301	0.067
Small town	31.10	28.29	17.49	14.90	8.21			
Large town	28.90	22.59	14.62	22.59	11.30			

Table 2.11 Safe levels of indebtedness (expressed as a multiple of monthly incomes) by selected characteristics of indebtedness (%)

Item	*Indebtedness level*					*Chi-squared statistic*	*p-value*	*Cramér's V coefficient*
	Up to 1 month	*Up to 3 months*	*Up to 6 months*	*Up to 12 months*	*Above 12 months*			
Debt type								
Bank	27.79	23.12	15.21	21.30	12.58	17.68	0.001	0.188
Non-bank	39.23	32.74	16.22	8.85	2.95			
Mixed bank and non-bank	22.22	21.72	16.16	26.26	13.64			
Number of credits and loans								
1	32.21	27.24	15.87	16.67	8.01	19.64	0.074	0.080
2+	27.83	24.14	15.52	20.44	12.07			
Repayment amounts (PLN)								
Up to 500	36.27	30.98	16.08	13.33	3.33	126.01	0.000	0.175
(500–1,000]	28.34	25.91	13.77	18.22	13.77			
Above 1,000	21.43	16.54	16.17	27.82	18.05			
DSTI								
Up to 10%	34.19	31.11	16.71	13.37	4.63	56.32	0.000	0.117
(10–20%]	27.46	24.30	17.96	19.37	10.92			
(20–30%]	25.00	26.56	9.38	18.75	20.31			
Above 30%	31.79	16.56	15.23	23.84	12.58			
Repayment capacity								
From savings or current income	32.87	27.74	17.95	15.15	6.29	16.58	0.002	0.127
By selling a proportion of assets	29.84	26.22	16.90	17.95	9.09	5.29	0.259	0.094
By selling all assets	29.69	26.05	16.51	17.90	9.86	6.73	0.151	0.198

The higher the educational level of respondents, the higher the proportion indicating a higher level of debt as safe. Respondents aged up to 34 and over 54 were more likely to report lower levels of debt as safe (up to the equivalent of 3 months' income). Regardless of size, households that considered indebtedness up to the amount of 1 month's income as safe were the most numerous. Households of five or more people, where almost 34% of respondents considered it safe to take on debt up to the amount of 3 months' income, were an exception. The highest proportion of those who regarded debt up to an amount above annual income as safe was found among one-person households (15.09%).

Respondents from towns with a population above 100,000 were more likely than others to indicate a higher level of indebtedness as safe (above the equivalent of 6 months' income). For respondents from small towns, however (approximately 77%), indebtedness up to the amount of 6 months' income was thought to be safe.

Households simultaneously holding a number of different types of debt (bank and non-bank) and those using only loans from banks were more likely to indicate a higher level of debt as safe (above 6 months' income). Meanwhile, those borrowing from non-bank lenders were more likely to indicate a level of indebtedness equivalent to 6 months' income as safe. It is possible that this difference in the perception of the level of safe debt is conditioned by the different customer profiles of these two credit-market segments (Jakubowska-Branicka, 2018; NBP, 2017a). On the other hand, it could result from the much higher public trust enjoyed by banks compared to loan companies (Idzik & Gieorgica, 2019).

Households holding a greater number of credits and loans regarded debt above 6 months' income as safe, while households with one loan most often regarded debt of up to 3 months' income as safe.

As monthly debt repayments increased, the proportion of households considering debt up to 3 months' income as safe decreased. By contrast, the proportion of respondents considering debt in excess of 6 months' income as safe increased as monthly debt repayments rose. These views appear to confirm that households took correct decisions (in the context, for example, of their attitude to risk) and, indirectly, to demonstrate that households did not feel overburdened by indebtedness.

An examination of the relationship between the value of the DSTI ratio and the level of indebtedness considered safe revealed a similar general pattern as in the case of repayment amounts. Respondents whose debt was low (DSTI<10%) indicated a relatively low debt of up to 3 months' income as safe. By contrast, respondents who were objectively more heavily indebted (DSTI>20%) displayed a greater subjective tolerance for debt. It can be indirectly confirmed on this basis that the level of indebtedness – expressed as a ratio of repayment amounts to income – is consistent with individual propensities to risk exposure.

2.4 Motives to borrow

The factors that motivate households to borrow can be random in nature or can, for example, be associated with long-term imbalances resulting from a natural lack of synchronisation of financial flows over the household life cycle

Table 2.15 Motives for indebtedness by household monthly income (%)

Item	*Income (PLN)*			*Overall*
	Up to 2,000	*2,000–6,000*	*Above 6,000*	
Current consumption expenditure (e.g. food, clothes, shoes)	23.87	10.39	7.14	11.74
House purchase or construction	12.90	26.95	55.04	31.98
Car purchase	6.45	13.96	18.49	13.46
Purchase of household and audio-visual appliances	30.97	30.03	25.21	29.00
Purchase of household furnishings (other durables)	8.39	11.36	6.30	9.12
House or flat refurbishment	20.00	21.27	12.18	18.70
Medical treatment and convalescence	3.87	1.30	0.42	1.54
Holidays and leisure	0.65	1.62	1.68	1.45
Training and education	0.65	0.97	0.84	0.81
Weddings and other celebrations	1.29	1.46	0.42	1.17
Other	10.32	6.33	8.40	7.86

Table 2.16 Motives for indebtedness by DSTI ratio (%)

Item	*DSTI*				*Overall*
	Up to 10%	*(10–20%)*	*(20–30%)*	*Above 30%*	
Current consumption expenditure (e.g. food, clothes, shoes)	10.25	9.67	11.51	18.45	11.74
House purchase or construction	10.25	39.00	52.52	51.19	31.98
Car purchase	10.25	16.33	20.86	12.50	13.46
Purchase of household and audio-visual appliances	41.25	20.00	22.30	21.43	29.00
Purchase of household furnishings (other durables)	10.00	10.67	6.47	10.12	9.12
House or flat refurbishment	14.25	23.00	18.71	22.62	18.70
Medical treatment and convalescence	1.00	1.00	2.16	2.98	1.54
Holidays and leisure	1.50	2.33	0.00	1.19	1.45
Training and education	1.25	0.67	1.44	0.00	0.81
Weddings and other celebrations	1.00	1.00	0.72	2.38	1.17
Other	9.00	4.67	6.47	9.52	7.86

often indicated by households in the middle age range. The wish to purchase household and audio-visual appliances was a common justification for taking on credits or loans in all age ranges. Almost one-quarter of households in the 55+ range indicated this way of spending borrowed funds, and buying household equipment was the primary motive for taking on debt for more than one-third of those in the 18–34 range. Organising weddings and other celebrations and financing medical treatment and convalescence (for the oldest age range) and paying for training and education (for the youngest age range) were indications belonging to the life cycle that stood out in comparison to other age groups but were mentioned far less frequently as reasons for taking on debt.

From the perspective of the respondents as a whole, the purchase of a house or flat proved to be the most important motive for taking on debt. This is unsurprising given the strong upward trend – reported in NBP statistics and mentioned earlier – in the mortgage liabilities of Polish households over the last 10 years or so, which is reflected, for example, in an increase in the frequency with which flats and houses are indicated in Social Diagnosis as reasons for indebtedness (Białowolski, 2014; Wałęga & Wałęga, 2016). In the sense that this type of debt is becoming more and more prevalent in Polish society and creating the conditions in which unfavourable macroeconomic trends could have very painful consequences for over-indebted households, this is a pertinent consideration.

From the perspective of educational attainment, it would appear that the variations in indications regarding the motives for indebtedness are to a significant extent determined by the greater wealth and higher incomes of households with higher levels of education (Ćwiek & Wałęga, 2016; Domański, 2018), which, in an obvious way, influences the wants that the various groups of households satisfy using credits or loans. Households with basic vocational education were much more likely to finance current consumer expenditure with credits and loans (Table 2.13) and were also more likely to look for external sources of financing to refurbish their flats or houses – as too were households with secondary education. There is one aspect – undoubtedly related to their higher incomes and resulting creditworthiness – in which the households of people with tertiary education differed significantly from the others: credit for the purchase or construction of real estate. While this motive was indicated with a frequency of 18–21% by households with at most secondary education, as many as 50% of households with tertiary education indicated a desire to own a flat or house as a reason for indebtedness.

The analysed sample of households was differentiated by other – though far less numerous – indications. An increase in educational level was, for example, accompanied by more frequent indications of taking out credits or loans for education and training, as well as for holidays and leisure, and less frequent indications of medical treatment and convalescence or weddings and other celebrations.

The purchase of household and audio-visual appliances proved to be a motive of great significance for all of the analysed groups. One in three households with a secondary educational level, and one in four in the other two groups, indicated this category of purchase as the reason for taking on a credit commitment. Moreover, it was the most frequent reason for households educated to a level other than tertiary and the second most frequent reason for households educated to tertiary level.

Regardless of place of residence, the three motives households most often indicated for taking on debt were to buy a flat – or possibly to build a house – to refurbish a flat or house, and to purchase household and audio-visual appliances (Table 2.14). They were not, however, of equal significance to rural and urban households. The most important motive for taking on debt among urban households – in both small and large towns – was the need to finance purchase of a flat or construction of a house. Yet the purchase of household and audio-visual appliances was the first priority in rural locations. What is more, the data revealed two distinct and interesting tendencies. As the size of the place of residence increased, so too did the frequency with which purchasing a flat (or building a house) was indicated as a motive for taking out credits or loans. This motive was selected by just over 25% of rural households, but by over 38% of households in large towns. The opposite tendency was detected in the case of expenditure on refurbishment, whereby the frequency of indications decreased as the size of the place of residence increased. As might be supposed, this pattern was determined by location-dependent differences in the specificities of the housing market, by differences in the income levels of rural and urban households, and by the strong, long-term trend of increasing rural housing standards by, for example, equipping houses with sanitary and technical installations (GUS, 2017).

Differences between rural and urban areas were also visible in borrowing for car purchases, which urban households did more often, and in respect of much less frequently indicated motives for indebtedness not directly related to material living conditions. Thus, rural households borrowed for weddings and other celebrations more often than those in other locations, households in small towns indicated medical treatment and convalescence as well as leisure more often than those in other locations, and households in large towns indicated education and training in a greater proportion than those in other locations.

The data set out in Table 2.15 would appear to confirm the unidirectional relationship between educational level and income mentioned earlier. Indeed, there was a striking overlap between the patterns of motives for indebtedness in the income cross section and those noted for respondents grouped by level of education (cf. NBP, 2017b). The poorest households – those with an income up to PLN 2,000 – took on loans and credits for current consumption expenditure (e.g. food, clothes, shoes) considerably more often than households in the remaining income bands. They took on credit obligations to finance refurbishment of a flat or house just as frequently as households in the PLN 2,000–6,000 income range, but much more frequently than those in the highest income range (above PLN 6,000).

The purchase of household and audio-visual appliances was a very common motive for indebtedness in the case of all income groups. Indeed, it was less frequent than borrowing to purchase a flat or build a house only in the case of households with an income above PLN 6,000, while in the remaining income groups it was the leading motive (over 30% of indications).

However, as income increased, the importance of two motives for indebtedness, purchasing a flat (or building a house) and purchasing a car, increased sharply. Households with average incomes (PLN 2,000–6,000) were twice as likely as the poorest households to indicate the first of these motives as the reason for taking out a loan, while the richest households (taking income as the measure of wealth) were more than four times as likely to do so, which means that the majority (55.04%) of households in this income group had a loan related to the purchase or construction of real estate. There was a similar, though slightly weaker, upward trend in the structure of responses to the second of the mentioned motives: car purchase. Households in the middle-income group were more than twice as likely as those in the income range up to PLN 2,000 to indicate car purchase as one of the sources of their credit commitments (13.96% as opposed to 6.45%), while the richest households were almost three times as likely to do so (18.49%).

Households with the highest incomes were less likely than other households to borrow money to finance medical treatment or family celebrations, while they were more likely than households with the lowest incomes to borrow to finance leisure activities such as holidays. It should be noted, however, that the number of indications for this group of reasons was low in all of the income ranges analysed.

The purchase of a flat or the construction of a house, which was indicated by more than half of the households whose DSTI exceeded 20% (Table 2.16), was the most frequent motive in the answers of households heavily burdened with debt, whereas the importance of buying a property faded, and that of purchasing household and audio-visual appliances rose (41%), in the indications of the households least burdened with debt (DSTI<10%). As a motive for taking on debt, the purchase of household and audio-visual appliances was also clearly present in the other groups of indebted households, and the frequency of its indications, although lower than for those with the lightest repayment burden, was relatively stable and slightly higher than, or equal to, 20%, depending on the group analysed. It was noticeable in relation to the other groups that the presence of motives such as refurbishing a flat or house (in the case of all groups with DSTI>10%) and car purchases (excluding the group of households with the heaviest repayment burden) was also much stronger.

It is interesting that – apart from the very high frequency of indications of flat purchase or house building as a motive for indebtedness mentioned earlier – the households most at risk of over-indebtedness had the highest percentage of indications of motives such as current consumption expenditure, medical treatment and convalescence, and organising weddings and other celebrations. In stating this, though, it should not be forgotten that the number of indications of the latter two motives was far lower than for current consumption expenditure. It can therefore be assumed that households with heavy repayment burdens possess other, very different characteristics. Some were comparatively wealthy households whose indebtedness derived from a wish to improve their housing situation, while others were poor households using credit to finance current consumption needs. The picture of the motives behind the heavy indebtedness of households would appear to be completed by certain obligations and imperatives linked to the organisation of important celebrations and to medical treatment.

2.5 Summary

Based on our original research, it can be concluded that household indebtedness in Poland is relatively low: the debt service-to-income (DSTI) ratio does not exceed 20% for the majority of respondents, while 60% of households have only one credit or loan. No serious difficulties in settling liabilities on time were detected in the sample studied.

The vast majority of respondents arranged their credits and loans with banks or credit unions. Workplace loans continued to be common for white-collar employees and those in older age groups. Overall, one in ten households held debt of this kind. Hire-purchase agreements with retail outlets and payday loans were more common, though, among young people and those living outside the large towns. This is almost certainly connected with their greater availability and convenience when compared with the instruments offered by conventional banks. Multi-person households and households supporting themselves from other sources of income (benefits, no regular income) used loan companies more often. Further in-depth research would therefore seem warranted to clarify the extent to which households' choices of types of instruments and sources of finance are due to reduced access to credit institutions (banks) and other credit constraints they might encounter.

Multi-person households and those at either end of the educational spectrum (lower secondary and below, and tertiary) were more likely to hold a number of loans or credits at the same time. It would appear that in spite of the different economic conditions they operate under, these households might face budget management difficulties that require constant monitoring.

It is worth noting that having multiple loans does not translate directly into a high relative repayment burden. The vulnerable groups with the highest repayment burden in relation to income were the households of retirement and disability pensioners, those supporting themselves from other sources of income, the poorly educated and one-person households. What is more, the highest proportion of households unable to cover their debts even by selling all of their assets was to be found among respondents with these characteristics.

The conducted analyses confirmed the negative impact of indebtedness on health. The strength of this impact is connected with the level of debt, but it is more pronounced in the psychological dimension than in relation to physical health. In general, the proportion of respondents with health problems increased with age, which may also be due to other factors than debt. However, to draw conclusions on this question requires caution and in-depth research, because without detailed data (a control group), indicating the extent and strength of the impact of debt on health could be imprecise.

The investigation of household indebtedness was complemented by a discussion of the motives for taking on credits and loans. According to the declarations concerning the different ways credits and loans were used, the most frequently indicated category of expenses they financed was house purchase or construction, while the refurbishment of flats and houses was a frequent category. Apart from the wish to satisfy housing needs, an important motive for indebtedness was the purchase of more expensive durables, such as cars, and household and audio-visual appliances. The purposes of indebtedness were generally consistent with changing needs over the family life cycle (van Raaij, 2016). The hierarchy of motives for indebtedness was modified by income and education: if credit supported current consumption expenditure more often for less well-off households – with the most common item on the list of motives being the purchase of household and audio-visual appliances – it supported more affluent and better-educated households most often in their purchases of flats or construction of houses.

The analysis of motives in relation to the DSTI ratio produced interesting conclusions in the context of the research problem. The households with a high DSTI ratio (>30%) were primarily those which drew on credit to satisfy housing needs (purchase, construction, refurbishment). However, households with a relatively heavy burden of loan repayments also had the highest percentages of indications for motives such as current consumption expenditure, medical treatment and convalescence, and arranging weddings and other celebrations. It would appear, therefore, that over-indebtedness can be experienced by households with very different characteristics – indeed, arguments for this inference will appear in later chapters of this book.

Note

1 If the null hypothesis – that the characteristics are not associated – is rejected in the chi-squared test of independence, the features under consideration are dependent. In this situation, the strength of the relationship can be measured using, for instance, Cramér's V coefficient, which produces a value in the range [0, 1]. See Brzezińska (2011) and Stanisz (2006) for an in-depth treatment of the chi-squared test of independence and measures of the relationships between qualitative characteristics.

References

Anderloni, L., & Vandone, D. (2008). *Households over-indebtedness in the economic literature* (Università degli Studi di Milano Working Paper No. 46). Milan: Università degli Studi di Milano.

Betti, G., Dourmashkin, N., Rossi, M., & Ping Yin, Y. (2007). Consumer over-indebtedness in the EU: Measurement and characteristics. *Journal of Economic Studies*, *34*(2), 136–156. https://doi.org/10.1108/01443580710745371

Białowolski, P. (2014). Patterns of debt possession among households in Poland – a multi-group latent class approach. *Bank i Kredyt*, *45*(2), 79–104.

Blomgren, J., Maunula, N., & Hiilamo, H. (2016). Over-indebtedness and chronic disease: A linked register-based study of Finnish men and women during 1995–2010. *International Journal of Public Health*, *61*(5), 535–544. https://doi.org/10.1007/s00038-015-0778-4

Bridges, S., & Disney, R. (2010). Debt and depression. *Journal of Health Economics*, *29*(3), 388–403. https://doi.org/10.1016/j.jhealeco.2010.02.003

Brown, S., Taylor, K., & Wheatley Price, S. (2005). Debt and distress: Evaluating the psychological cost of credit. *Journal of Economic Psychology*, *26*(5), 642–663. https://doi.org/10.1016/j.joep.2005.01.002

Brzezińska, J. (2011). Analiza korespondencji. In E. Gatnar & M. Walesiak (Eds.), *Analiza danych jakościowych i symbolicznych z wykorzystaniem programu R* (pp. 52–80). Warszawa: Wydawnictwo C.H. Beck.

Ćwiek, M., & Wałęga, A. (2016). Income of well-educated. Comparative analysis. In P. Lula & T. Rojek (Eds.), *Knowledge – Economy – Society. Contemporary aspects of economic transformations* (pp. 255–264). Cracow: Foundation of the Cracow University of Economics.

Dackehag, M., Ellegård, L.-M., Gerdtham, U.-G., & Nilsson, T. (2019). Debt and mental health: New insights about the relationship and the importance of the measure of mental health. *European Journal of Public Health*, *29*(3), 488–493. https://doi.org/10.1093/eurpub/ckz002

D'Alessio, G., & Iezzi, S. (2013). Household over-indebtedness: Definition and measurement with Italian data. *Bank of Italy Occasional Paper*, *149*. https://doi.org/10.2139/ssrn.2243578

Domański, H. (2018). Wpływ wykształcenia na rozkład zarobków w Polsce w latach 1988–2013. *Ekonomista*, *1*, 7–24.

Drentea, P., & Lavrakas, P. J. (2000). Over the limit: The association among health, race and debt. *Social Science & Medicine*, *50*(4), 517–529. https://doi.org/10.1016/S0277-9536(99)00298-1

Drentea, P., & Reynolds, J. R. (2012). Neither a borrower nor a lender be: The relative importance of debt and SES for mental health among older adults. *Journal of Aging and Health*, *24*(4), 673–695. https://doi.org/10.1177/0898264311431304

GUS. (2017). *Sytuacja społeczno-ekonomiczna gospodarstw domowych w latach 2000–2015. Zróżnicowanie miasto-wieś* (Informacje i Opracowania Statystyczne). Warszawa: Główny Urząd Statystyczny.

GUS. (2019). *Rocznik Statystyczny Rzeczypospolitej Polskiej 2019*. Warszawa: Główny Urząd Statystyczny. https://stat.gov.pl/obszary-tematyczne/roczniki-statystyczne/roczniki-statystyczne/rocznik-statystyczny-rzeczypospolitej-polskiej-2019,2,19.html

Hojman, D. A., Miranda, Á., & Ruiz-Tagle, J. (2016). Debt trajectories and mental health. *Social Science & Medicine*, *167*, 54–62. https://doi.org/10.1016/j.socscimed.2016.08.027

Idzik, M., & Gieorgica, J. (2019). Reputacja sektora bankowego w Polsce – wnioski z badania w 2019 roku. *Bezpieczny Bank*, *76*(3), 75–93. https://doi.org/10.26354/bb.4.3.76.2019

Jakubowska-Branicka, I. (2018). Profil klienta firm pożyczkowych. In I. Jakubowska-Branicka (Ed.), *Rynek firm pozyczkowych w Polsce. Teoria i praktyka* (pp. 205–239). Warszawa: Polskie Towarzystwo Ekonomiczne.

Keese, M., & Schmitz, H. (2014). Broke, ill, and obese: Is there an effect of household debt on health? *Review of Income and Wealth*, *60*(3), 525–541. https://doi.org/10.1111/roiw.12002

NBP. (2017a). *Rozwój systemu finansowego w Polsce w 2016 r.* Warszawa: Narodowy Bank Polski.

NBP. (2017b). *Zasobność gospodarstw domowych w Polsce. Raport z badania 2016 r.* Warszawa: Narodowy Bank Polski.

Richardson, T., Elliott, P., & Roberts, R. (2013). The relationship between personal unsecured debt and mental and physical health: A systematic review and meta-analysis. *Clinical Psychology Review*, *33*(8), 1148–1162. https://doi.org/10.1016/j.cpr.2013.08.009

Richardson, T., Elliott, P., Roberts, R., & Jansen, M. (2017). A longitudinal study of financial difficulties and mental health in a national sample of British undergraduate students. *Community Mental Health Journal, 53*(3), 344–352. https://doi.org/10.1007/s10597-016-0052-0

Selenko, E., & Batinic, B. (2011). Beyond debt. A moderator analysis of the relationship between perceived financial strain and mental health. *Social Science & Medicine, 73*(12), 1725–1732. https://doi.org/10.1016/j.socscimed.2011.09.022

Stanisz, A. (2006). *Przystępny kurs statystyki: Z zastosowaniem STATISTICA PL na przykładach z medycyny. Tom 1. Statystyki podstawowe*. Kraków: StatSoft.

Sweet, E., Kuzawa, C. W., & McDade, T. W. (2018). Short-term lending: Payday loans as risk factors for anxiety, inflammation and poor health. *SSM – Population Health, 5*, 114–121. https://doi.org/10.1016/j.ssmph.2018.05.009

Sweet, E., Nandi, A., Adam, E. K., & McDade, T. W. (2013). The high price of debt: Household financial debt and its impact on mental and physical health. *Social Science & Medicine, 91*, 94–100. https://doi.org/10.1016/j.socscimed.2013.05.009

Tay, L., Batz, C., Parrigon, S., & Kuykendall, L. (2017). Debt and subjective well-being: The other side of the income-happiness coin. *Journal of Happiness Studies, 18*(3), 903–937. https://doi.org/10.1007/s10902-016-9758-5

van Raaij, W. F. (2016). *Understanding consumer financial behavior: Money management in an age of financial illiteracy*. New York: Palgrave Macmillan.

Wałęga, A., & Wałęga, G. (2016). Bogaci i biedni na rynku kredytowym w Polsce. Analiza porównawcza dla lat 2000–2013. *Zeszyty Naukowe Uniwersytetu Ekonomicznego w Krakowie, 2*(950), 75–92. https://doi.org/10.15678/ZNUEK.2016.0950.0205

Zalega, T. (2016). *Segment osób w wieku 65+ w Polsce. Jakość życia – Konsumpcja – Zachowania konsumenckie*. Warszawa: Wydawnictwo Naukowe Wydziału Zarządzania Uniwersytetu Warszawskiego.

3 The nature of household over-indebtedness

Theory and measurement

3.1 The concept of over-indebtedness

The concept of over-indebtedness must be properly defined before the situation of households facing this problem can be studied. Various approaches to this issue are taken in the subject literature, and consequently there is no universally accepted definition (Bańkowska et al., 2015; D'Alessio & Iezzi, 2013; Disney et al., 2008; Ferretti & Vandone, 2019). This is due to the differences in legal systems at the international level as well as the disparate socio-economic, legal, and political contexts in which households operate (Anderloni & Vandone, 2008).

Usually, over-indebtedness is defined in terms of a household's capacity to service its obligations. It can be stated with reference to the theory of intertemporal choice that it arises where a household's assets are insufficient to offset the present value of future debts (Betti et al., 2007). Stefan Angel and Karin Heitzmann (2015) offer a succinct definition of over-indebtedness in stating that it is usually the result of a household losing liquidity. For Oliver Haas (2006), however, over-indebtedness describes a situation in which – despite reducing its standard of living – a household's income is insufficient to meet all of its payment obligations over the long term. Richard Disney and his colleagues (2008) argue that the most adequate definition is the one referring to late repayments. Yet in contending that overdue repayments are more symptomatic of over-indebtedness than they are synonymous with it, Andrea Falanga's diagnosis (2015) would appear more accurate.

Understood in a broad sense, over-indebtedness can be considered not only as a situation in which a household has difficulties in meeting its obligations but also as one in which it is at serious risk of such circumstances occurring. It is stressed in this connection, however, that the threat must be structural in character and stem from long-term factors (Oxera, 2004). It is for this reason that neither a temporary disparity between income and expenditure that leads to a considerable increase in indebtedness nor the accidental or intentional overlooking of a repayment instalment should be seen as indicating over-indebtedness.

The European Commission, which states in its assessment of the phenomenon that it is advisable to take account of all of a household's financial obligations – not only those connected with credits and loans – has also addressed the

DOI: 10.4324/9781003254706-4

task of formulating a definition of over-indebtedness (European Commission, 2008). Over-indebtedness is defined as a situation in which it is impossible to meet obligations and cover fixed expenditure without falling below a basic standard of living – even where a household draws upon its financial and tangible assets. Because sporadic difficulties with meeting obligations cannot in themselves be acknowledged as indicative of over-indebtedness, the European Commission's definition also points to the structural aspect of over-indebtedness.

In attempting a definition of over-indebtedness, four dimensions of it can be identified:

- economic – referring to a household's capacity to meet its obligations;
- temporal – it occurs in the medium or long term;
- social – it demands a substantial reduction in expenditure and therefore has a negative impact on living conditions;
- psychological – it is a source of stress and has an impact on mental health.

It should be emphasised that over-indebtedness cannot be reduced to questions of economics alone: it also involves emotional, psychological, and sociological states that usually extend over time and do not apply only to a particular moment in life.

Over-indebtedness can – but need not – result in consumer insolvency. This is a narrower concept than over-indebtedness and should not be equated with it. Consumer insolvency has an economic (financial) and legal dimension. In essence, it is above all a matter of loss of liquidity and the permanent loss of capacity to repay debt. A further concept connected with over-indebtedness needs to be mentioned here: bankruptcy. This represents the legal remedy for consumer insolvency and concerns the procedure for debt relief.

The above considerations allow for various conceptualisations of over-indebtedness. It can be understood in broad terms as a situation in which a household encounters difficulties in meeting its obligations, but manages to make ends meet by restricting even essential expenditure (economic over-indebtedness). In a different general understanding of over-indebtedness, the repayment burden has no significant effect on the satisfaction of essential needs but places a psychological burden on the household sufficient to reduce its quality of life (psychological over-indebtedness). When defined in these broad terms, it is of course also possible for over-indebtedness to occur simultaneously in the psychological and economic dimensions. Yet from a narrower perspective, over-indebtedness describes a situation in which – in addition to satisfying the conditions set out above – a household loses financial liquidity and is compelled to declare bankruptcy.

Given the difficulties in developing a universally accepted definition of over-indebtedness, and in an effort to comprehensively capture this complex phenomenon, a more pragmatic approach is proposed here. It relies on universal indicators of persistent debt strain (CPEC, 2013) or on a set of objective and subjective indicators (Chichaibelu & Waibel, 2018).

The subject literature uses a number of concepts, including financial difficulties, financial vulnerability, financial hardship, financial distress, and financial fragility, that are closely related to over-indebtedness. In this way, households that score highly on indicators of indebtedness are referred to by some scholars, such as Miguel Ampudia and his team (2016), and Marco Terraneo (2018), as financially vulnerable households. Luisa Anderloni and her associates (2012), who argue that the question for households of this kind is not only one of the difficulty in repaying credit obligations that can result from overborrowing but also one of a more broadly understood financial instability resulting, for example, from negative shocks (an increase in the interest rate applied to the debt) or an unbalanced budget (loss of source of income), interpret this definition differently. However, Marianna Brunetti and her colleagues (2016) employ the concept of fragile households and point out that the difficulty in their case is more a matter of non-optimal portfolio allocation than of the absolute level of debt. The notions of households in financial distress and households suffering financial hardship, which are defined as households with negative net wealth, also appear in the subject literature (Brown & Taylor, 2008; Giarda, 2013). Another means of assessing the extent of the financial difficulties faced by households is provided by indicators that link debt with income (Brown & Taylor, 2008; Faruqui, 2008; Jappelli et al., 2013; Keese, 2009). On the other hand, indicators of overdue repayment instalments are used to measure over-indebtedness in studies that equate the difficult situation of households with more serious financial problems (Georgarakos et al., 2010; Jappelli et al., 2013; Magri et al., 2011). For their part, Dimitrios Christelis and his colleagues (2009) and Yvonne McCarthy (2011) applied 'soft' indicators to evaluate the financial fragility of households, which they based on responses to questions asked of households about their ability to make ends meet, while Annamaria Lusardi and her associates (2011) investigated the same issue using a self-assessed measure of capacity to deal with financial shock.

Both the concept of over-indebtedness and that of financial difficulties (financial distress, financial hardship, financial vulnerability, financial fragility) refer to the question of households meeting their obligations (Bourova et al., 2019; Kempson, 2002). As is stressed by Luisa Anderloni and Daniela Vandone (2008), the difference between these definitions concerns the liabilities to which they refer. They can cover only indebtedness arising from loans and credits, but they can also include other debts (for example, arising from rents, fees, charges, taxes, and service provision agreements concluded by consumers). Another criterion for distinguishing over-indebtedness from financial difficulties is whether classification in a particular group is connected with actually being in arrears or only refers to households at risk of being in arrears.

Due to the nature of the data obtained in the research and the understanding of over-indebtedness that prevails in the literature, only debt related to loans and credits is considered for the purposes of this study.

3.2 Determinants of over-indebtedness: literature review

Though a survey of the literature on over-indebtedness indicates its complexity, most scholars share the view that – in the overwhelming majority of cases – it is a phenomenon that results from a variety of interrelated causes (Anderloni & Vandone, 2008). Moreover, they are not entirely separate from the causes that shape the process of becoming indebted itself, which under unfavourable conditions can likewise become the reason for over-indebtedness.

Two causes of over-indebtedness can be identified on the basis of economic theory (Betti et al., 2007). One is a result of the fact that households operate under conditions of uncertainty, which is a feature inherent to all economies. It must be assumed, therefore, that when faced with shocks, such as unforeseen events affecting employment, interest rates, the value of shares owned, health, or the family model or structure, rationally acting households will not be able to execute their optimal consumption plan and will thus be compelled to change it. This may have a negative impact on the prevailing, 'normal' standard of living they are accustomed to. This approach assumes that over-indebtedness is inevitable and does not depend on a household's consumption – or, more broadly, financial – plan, in which the extent of the indebtedness is determined by the life cycle (Baek & Hong, 2004; Betti et al., 2007; D'Alessio & Iezzi, 2013; Xiao & Yao, 2020; Yilmazer & DeVaney, 2005) and optimistic expectations of future income (Brown et al., 2005, 2008).

The social context in which a household operates, its attitude to risk, its temporal preferences, and its cognitive errors are also important for the occurrence of over-indebtedness. These factors lead to the second approach to explaining the causes of over-indebtedness. It assumes that household consumption plans, or household consumption decisions, are not intertemporally balanced due to individuals' bounded rationality (Anderloni & Vandone, 2011).

The imperfections of the credit market also influence the behaviour of households. Perhaps surprisingly, some scholars have argued that the causes of over-indebtedness include restricted access to credit (in particular restricted access to consumer credit) and financial exclusion (Crook, 2006; Grant, 2007). Households affected by these limitations are especially vulnerable to the negative consequences of fluctuations in current income (Jappelli, 1990). Demand for credit among this group of households that cannot be met by the banking system is satisfied by the non-bank market and alternative lenders, such as NGOs, where the conditions, including higher fees and inflexible repayment terms, are less favourable. In this way, even modest amounts of debt (used to plug a gap in the household budget) can lead to over-indebtedness (Desai & Elliehausen, 2017; Stegman & Faris, 2003).

The factors that foster over-indebtedness can be divided into five groups, relating them in turn to borrowers, lenders, the credit market, contingencies, and the environment.

Among the factors determining over-indebtedness, related to the characteristics of household members (borrowers), the following can be indicated:

- the household's income. Fundamentally, higher incomes are accompanied by higher levels of indebtedness, which entails greater repayment burdens and in turn increases the risk of over-indebtedness. This dependency can be explained by consumption aspirations and creditworthiness, which grow as income increases. There are nevertheless a number of studies (Anderloni & Vandone, 2008; Bridges & Disney, 2004) that indicate low income as a reason for over-indebtedness, which arises in this case from the need to resort to more expensive forms of credit (e.g. loans from loan companies) and less resilience in the face of the consequences of unexpected events. People who are poor, whose cognitive capacity is undermined by poverty and the pressures they are under, making it difficult for them to take sound intertemporal decisions, are particularly vulnerable (Carvalho et al., 2016; Mullainathan & Shafir, 2013; Ong et al., 2019);

- employment status. This influences the capacity to generate income and its amount, while also determining the stability of income streams over time. On the one hand, stable employment makes it possible to access a greater number of credit instruments at lower rates of interest. On the other hand, the above factors can provide an incentive for borrowing that, in absolute terms, is too high (Anderloni & Vandone, 2008). People who are unemployed and have no regular and reliable source of income are more likely to experience difficulty in servicing their debt (del Río & Young, 2008; Du Caju et al., 2016; Keese, 2009) and to feel over-indebted much more often (Keese, 2012);
- household size and structure. One-person households (Haas, 2006) and multi-person households (Worthington, 2006) are over-indebted to the greatest degree. Research suggests that the number of children may be a factor that increases the risk of over-indebtedness, due to the greater rigidity of some expenditure and the lower number of hours parents can on average devote to paid work (Keese, 2009). Other dependents who do not earn income may also constitute a risk factor. Family breakdown and divorce also fall into the household size and structure category of reasons for over-indebtedness (Disney et al., 2008);
- housing tenure. Andrea Falanga (2015) identifies two particularly vulnerable groups of households: those with mortgages (high repayment burden) and renters (higher living expenses). The high proportion of households in arrears among renters is noted by Elaine Kempson and her colleagues (2004) and by Sarah Bridges and Richard Disney (2004). Similar conclusions are drawn by Orla May and her associates (2004): though on average renters are less indebted, they are at greater risk of repayment difficulties because they can only access unsecured credit products at higher rates of interest;
- psychological and socio-cultural factors, lifestyles, and, especially, borrowers' attitudes to risk, consumption and indebtedness (Białowolski et al., 2020; Kamleitner et al., 2012; Kamleitner & Kirchler, 2007; Meyll & Pauls, 2019; Pattarin & Cosma, 2012; Webley & Nyhus, 2001). For the reason that their societies are less approving of the extensive use of credit (more stigma is attached to it), the risk of over-indebtedness is lower in countries whose credit markets are less developed. By contrast, the subjective debt burden is lower in countries with well-developed mortgage markets (Georgarakos et al., 2010);

- cognitive limitations due to psychological and behavioural determinants of borrowing (Ferretti & Vandone, 2019). Research suggests that an excessive propensity for risk (Brown et al., 2013), difficulty in self-control, and a tendency to make impulsive purchases could all be sources of problems with indebtedness (McCarthy, 2011; Ottaviani & Vandone, 2018). According to Jason Kilborn (2005), an important role in the emergence of over-indebtedness can be assigned to anomalies – identified within the disciplines of behavioural and experimental economics – in the decisions taken by individuals, which include the following: (1) forming opinions based on their own experiences of over-indebtedness rather than on an assessment of real probabilities (the availability heuristic), which leads them to underestimate the risk of debt problems, and (2) relying on stereotypes (the representativeness heuristic). Over-optimism (in respect of resources held and negative phenomena such as sickness and loss of employment) causes the debt-to-income ratio to increase (Hyytinen & Putkuri, 2018). Present-biased preferences, which result from hyperbolic discounting (as manifested in the slogan 'buy now, pay later'), represent a further factor conducive to over-indebtedness (Anderloni & Vandone, 2011; Meier & Sprenger, 2010);
- age. According to the life-cycle theory, age determines not only the amount of expenditure but also the capacity to obtain income. On the basis of data from developed countries, Luisa Anderloni and Daniela Vandone (2008) show that people aged between 30 and 40 are at the greatest risk of over-indebtedness. Generally, indebtedness declines with age (Cavalletti et al., 2020; D'Alessio & Iezzi, 2013), so it can be expected that over-indebtedness will be less prevalent among households in the older age groups. Empirical research shows that the vulnerable groups are those from the youngest cohorts (Betti et al., 2007; del Río & Young, 2008; Majamaa et al., 2019);
- health. The appearance of ill health is associated with increased expenditure and, at the same time, the possibility of a fall in income – or even of loss of employment. That falling ill often happens unexpectedly has an additional, negative impact on a household's capacity to manage its liquidity. With the reservation that the issue has not yet been widely addressed in economic research, it can be ventured that addictions – for example, to alcohol, drugs, and gambling – constitute a separate factor in this category and one that would appear to increase the probability of over-indebtedness (D'Alessio & Iezzi, 2013; Meltzer et al., 2013; Valins, 2004);
- education. Education determines individuals' ability to get good jobs, and the quality of the positions secured is reflected in income levels and the stability of employment. Furthermore, when they possess economic knowledge, individuals can manage household budgets better and understand complicated financial instruments (Anderloni & Vandone, 2011; French & McKillop, 2016; Lusardi & Tufano, 2015). It is for this reason that households with less educated individuals are more often at risk of over-indebtedness (Anderloni et al., 2012; Schicks, 2014);

- belonging to an ethnic minority. As it is hypothesised that less educated people, who are more likely to be renters and derive low incomes from less stable forms of employment, will be over represented in the group of households composed of ethnic minorities, being a member of one increases the risk of over-indebtedness (Anderloni & Vandone, 2008). Yet a note of caution should be sounded. This group is particularly heterogeneous and – at least where Europe is concerned – under-researched. No studies of this group of households have yet been conducted in Poland.

Factors associated with the supply side of the credit market form a further set of elements likely to give rise to over-indebtedness. The following actions taken by lenders stimulate this negative phenomenon:

- changes to banks' lending policies whereby borrowers are offered advantageous loan conditions and criteria (Wałęga, 2015). Easing the minimum standards for assessing creditworthiness can lead to excessive increases in indebtedness – especially among vulnerable groups of households. These observations are supported by the simulations run by Matthew Chambers and his colleagues (2009), who found that, particularly for young people and people on low incomes, a small deposit is a very significant factor when taking out mortgage loans;
- the fact that borrowers are often guided by what is quickly, or instantly, available, and do not have sufficient knowledge to select a suitable financial instrument, is exploited by financial intermediaries to offer households unsuitable credit products (Autio et al., 2009). That debt rollover is facilitated (Li et al., 2009; Samolyk, 2007) and customers are given the option to pay only the minimum amount when debt repayments are due (Elliehausen & Lawrence, 2001) also constitute factors that increase the risk of entering a debt spiral;
- making remuneration at financial institutions directly dependent on sales plans, which encourages employees to use aggressive sales tactics so that the highest possible number of agreements can be signed. These tactics are often supported by similar marketing techniques. They include the automatic renewal or raising of credit limits on current accounts and credit cards, lowering minimum repayment requirements, and offering reduced interest rates in the event of debt consolidation. As Elaine Kempson has demonstrated (2002), the households most susceptible to these activities are those from the high-risk group, which means people who are predisposed to over-indebtedness;
- unethical debt-recovery practices that involve imposing excessive penalties on borrowers and charging them additional fees for late payment.

The risk to households of over-indebtedness can be driven by factors resulting from the structure of the credit market in a given country. At the level of both products and institutions, the degree of competitiveness of the particular credit market is important when analysing this phenomenon. This is confirmed in relation to European countries by Dimitrios Christelis and his colleagues (2009) and Catarina Frade and Claudia Lopes (2009), who show that levels of debt and difficulties in servicing it correlate positively with the degree of credit market development. The presence of a greater number of financial institutions (commercial banks, mortgage banks, credit unions) affects price levels (interest rates) and makes it easier for households to access a wider range of suitable credit instruments. This, however, increases the risk of financial difficulties (Melzer, 2011). For their part, other lending institutions (loan companies) often operate on the fringes of the regulated financial system, offering payday loans at high rates of interest. Such loans can be seen as factors that lead to over-indebtedness (del Río & Young, 2008). Meanwhile, Anu Raijas and her colleagues (2010) cite the widespread uptake of credit cards in the 1990s and, later, the spread of instant loans via the Internet and SMS, as causes of over-indebtedness. Indeed, it is argued that technological progress, reflected in simplified procedures and shorter waiting times for borrowed funds, can be regarded as a determinant of over-indebtedness – especially among the youngest age groups (Autio et al., 2009; Majamaa et al., 2019).

In the context of market determinants of over-indebtedness, attention is also drawn to changes in the institutional environment (e.g. credit reference agencies) and in the legal environment (e.g. insolvency regulations) (Coletta et al., 2019; Fay et al., 2002; Jappelli et al., 2013).

Random factors, which are immanent in all economic activity, constitute a separate group of causes of household over-indebtedness. They are seen as a reason for the occurrence of passive over-indebtedness (Ferretti & Vandone, 2019). Among the most notable random events are loss of income (such as in a pandemic) or assets (theft, fraud), unexpected costs (e.g. connected with flood damage), changes in the overall economic situation and in basic economic indicators (interest rates, exchange rates), and changes in household structure (e.g. the death of a family's main breadwinner, divorce). It is worth noting that some scholars (Anderloni & Vandone, 2008; Gutiérrez-Nieto et al., 2017) do not define a separate category for random events, which they instead treat as one of a number of circumstances pertaining to borrowers.

The environments in which households function – economic, political, cultural, and social – also play a role in the processes associated with the appearance of indebtedness. Christopher Whelan and his colleagues (2017) take the view that one of the reasons for difficulties with over-indebtedness is the occurrence of macroeconomic shocks, which are triggered, for example, by changes in the prices of food, fuel, incomes, property, and rents. This is confirmed for the euro area by the work of Katarzyna Bańkowska and her associates (2015) and Miguel Ampudia and his colleagues (2016), and for the Republic of South Africa by the work of Shaun de Wet and his team (2015).

Over-indebtedness is determined by the socio-economic system adopted and by the economic policies applied. Massimo Coletta and his co-researchers

(2019) found that higher levels of indebtedness are likely to arise in countries with social-democratic and liberal welfare models. The main factors that triggered the rise in indebtedness in the global economy include the enlargement of the European Union and the consequent fall in interest rates; liberalisation and cross-border cooperation, which enabled credit-sector growth; and the integration of countries in economic transition into the global financial system (CPEC, 2013).

Catarina Frade and Claudia Lopes (2009) point out that income inequalities or, more broadly, economic inequalities are factors that give rise to financial difficulties and over-indebtedness. The widespread use of credit instruments is a means by which the less well-off can attain a standard of living closer to that of people in higher income brackets. Such attempts to secure a higher position on the socio-economic ladder require, therefore, a conscious financial strategy. Nevertheless, they carry a considerable, and inevitable, burden of risk. It is worth remembering that in many highly developed countries the path to social advancement is taken by paying for courses of higher education, which means, given the steady increases in fees at the best universities, taking on debt. What is more, for the middle and lower classes, there is a concomitant reduction in the number of stable career paths, which results in an increased risk of over-indebtedness – especially if they are young adults at the start of their working lives (Hodson et al., 2014). In addition, in some countries, such as Poland or Spain, the underdeveloped rental market and the under-supply of social housing have led to a situation in which the majority of households can satisfy their housing needs only by purchasing property on credit. This, in turn – whether inadvertently or not – has produced a sort of cult of home ownership (Martínez, 2008; Nettleton & Burrows, 1998; Sánchez-Martínez et al., 2016).

The factors that limit tensions in the credit market include the scope and quality of regulation and the efficiency of the judicial system (Duygan-Bump & Grant, 2009). Indeed, the strictness of the debt-recovery process (the severity of the sanctions) and the accessibility and straightforwardness of the debt-relief procedure (as an element of insolvency arrangements) are related to the number of insolvency proceedings. Increased difficulties with loan repayment are also linked to the efficiency of systems for sharing credit information (Jappelli et al., 2013). To this Dimitris Georgarakos and Sven Fürth (2015) add corruption, which they identify as a factor differentiating the percentages of households in arrears found in different countries.

Numerous studies confirm that social and cultural elements determine levels of indebtedness (Kamleitner & Kirchler, 2007; Marron, 2012). For instance, Elizabeth Sweet has shown how neoliberalism shapes a specific perception of debt, which in turn has further implications in terms of its impact on health (Sweet, 2018; Sweet et al., 2018). In some cultures, the use of credit is entirely natural and has positive connotations, while in others it is freighted with stigma (Frade & Lopes, 2009). What is more, perceptions of both consumption and borrowing have altered over recent decades. Indeed, in some cultures credit has become a way of life. Freedom is manifested through consumption and continuously rising indebtedness, which inevitably generates an increased number of over-indebted households. This is confirmed by the research of, among others, John J. Watson (2003) and Ragna B. Garðarsdóttir and Helga Dittmar (2012), which suggests that there is a direct correlation between materialism, a propensity for making impulsive, uncontrolled purchases, and the degree of indebtedness.

The cultural determination of over-indebtedness is also connected with taking responsibility for debts and being committed to repaying them on time (Anderloni & Vandone, 2008). Thus, the problem of over-indebtedness is diminished in countries where institutions are trusted more, where there are deeper reserves of social capital, and where people observe and feel bound by generally agreed norms. It would appear that the stigma (social sanction) attached to non-payment of debts guarantees a high rate of repayment (Fay et al., 2002; Georgarakos & Fürth, 2015). These dependencies are, however, strongly connected with individual experiences and the environment in which households operate (French & Vigne, 2019).

Followers of different religions have different attitudes to debt (Chunping et al., 2016; Sipon et al., 2014). For example, indebtedness is powerfully associated with feelings of guilt and sinfulness for Catholics, so that they view debt negatively, while the history of Protestantism suggests a positive attitude towards debt (Kiesel & Noth, 2016). It is for this reason that the proportion of over-indebted individuals is lower among Catholics than it is among Protestants (Hasan et al., 2019). What is more, some scholars (Beck et al., 2014; Georgarakos & Fürth, 2015) have found that religious belief is a factor that limits the proportion of households that default. Religious belief therefore plays a role in fostering financial responsibility and shaping attitudes to risk and saving (Renneboog & Spaenjers, 2012).

3.3 Indicators of over-indebtedness

Just as there is no consensus in the subject literature on the definition of over-indebtedness, likewise there is no unanimity on its measurement (Frade & Lopes, 2009). The indicators employed to analyse over-indebtedness are dependent on the available sources of data (see subsection 1.2).

Some of these indicators refer to over-indebtedness at the macroeconomic level and are based on data aggregated from financial market institutions, including banks and credit reference agencies. Such indicators have the advantage of being relatively highly internationally comparable and easy to calculate, due to the widespread availability of public datasets.

A separate group of indicators is based on data from the judicial system and from debtor-support institutions of various kinds, such as restructuring advisors, debt-relief offices, and bailiffs. The limited scope of application of indicators based on these types of data sources results mainly from the fragmentary nature of the data and the non-uniform methods used to collect them.

For their part, studies of over-indebtedness at the microeconomic (household) level employ numerous subjective and objective indicators based on data from multi-topic surveys of indebtedness. Here, one must agree with Pru Cox and her colleagues (2002): aggregated data do not permit detailed analysis of over-indebtedness – especially given the varying socio-economic situations of the different groups of households.

It may be concluded from even a cursory review of the relevant subject literature (see Betti et al., 2007) that a wide range of indicators, often constructed ad hoc, is used to measure over-indebtedness, and that selecting appropriate indicators is itself objectively difficult (Falanga & Financité, 2015). Table 3.1 gives an overview of these measures of over-indebtedness.

The core indicators of over-indebtedness are those based on quantitative data. One of the most popular of these, debt to income (DTI), is calculated as the level of indebtedness in relation to income (usually 12-month income). It is predominantly applied to aggregated data (at the macroeconomic level). However, it can also be calculated on the basis of individual data.

Another core measure of over-indebtedness is debt to wealth (DTW). To calculate it, a number of categories of wealth are employed – for example, debt to savings (DTS), which can be calculated with the exclusion of the property the

Table 3.1 Indicators of over-indebtedness

Name	*Description (construction)*	*Threshold value for over-indebtedness*
Objective indicators		
DTI	Ratio of debt to income	100–300%
DTW	Ratio of debt to wealth	50–100%
DTA	Ratio of debt to financial assets	
DTS	Ratio of debt to savings	
DSTI	Ratio of debt service (monthly debt repayments) to income	30–40%
FM	Financial Margin: income after deducting debt repayments and essential expenditure	Less than zero
BPL	Below the Poverty Line: income after deducting debt repayments	Value of income is below the designated poverty line
NL	Number of credit and loan agreements	Four or more
A	Arrears: late repayment of credit obligations	Debt repayment arrears of 3 months or more
D	Defaults: insolvency proceedings	Declaration of insolvency
Subjective indicators		
SB (Subjective Burden of Debt)	Subjective perception of debt burden	Feeling of being over-indebted
MEM (Make Ends Meet)/MME (Meet a Major Expense)	Ability to make ends meet/ Ability to meet major expenses	Inability to make ends meet/Inability to meet major expenses

Source: authors' original work.

household uses as its dwelling place, or with the inclusion of all the properties it owns. Some studies and reports use a different version of the debt-to-savings indicator, which is known as debt to assets (DTA).

An undoubted advantage of these indicators is that they are intuitive, based on hard data, and can be easily compared. Yet they also have serious weaknesses. First of all, they are not constructed to account for changes in levels of income, wealth, and indebtedness over the life cycle, which means that identical values of the indicators cannot be interpreted in the same way for all of the various categories of households. What is more, they cannot specify real capacity to service debt: a high level of debt does not necessarily mean a heavy repayment burden on a household's budget. For this reason, it is difficult to define a threshold value for these indicators. For DTA, an assumption of 50–100% is usually made in the literature (Baek & DeVaney, 2004; Garrett & James III, 2013), while for DTI, it is usually 100–300% (Falanga & Financité, 2015; Ferretti & Vandone, 2019; Terraneo, 2018). Second, in the case of DTI, there is a serious methodological objection to comparing streams (income) with resources (debt). One of the limitations of indicators based on wealth (financial assets) is the availability and quality of data (imprecision in respondents' valuations and estimations) (see Bucks & Pence, 2015).

The next in this group of indicators, debt service to income (DSTI), is calculated as the ratio of monthly debt repayments to monthly incomes. It is also possible to employ data relating to a longer time horizon, such as annual data. DSTI can be calculated in two different ways (Faruqui, 2008). The first considers only interest, but it is rarely applied because information as detailed as this is usually unavailable. The second adds principal repayments – at their minimum value or at the value arising from the adopted repayment schedule – to the debt-servicing costs.

Debt service to income is regarded as the most useful of the objective indicators because it shows the ability to service debt on an ongoing basis without resorting to asset sales (Brown & Taylor, 2008). What is more, DSTI incorporates interest rate changes, which enables better evaluation of a household's ability to service its debt compared to the DTI (CPEC, 2013).

In the case of DTSI, the majority of studies take the threshold value for over-indebtedness to be 30% or 40% (D'Alessio & Iezzi, 2013, 2016; Michelangeli & Pietrunti, 2014; Sánchez-Martínez et al., 2016; Tiongson et al., 2009). Federico Ferretti and Daniela Vandone (2019), meanwhile, postulate a DSTI threshold of 25% for consumer credit. There are other scholars who rely on a higher value of 50% for this indicator (Chichaibelu & Waibel, 2018; Oxera, 2004), which would appear justified for countries in which households are served by highly developed credit markets.

As with the indicators discussed earlier, in order to properly assess over-indebtedness, it is necessary to establish a DSTI threshold value beyond which a household will be considered over-indebted (Ampudia et al., 2016). Moreover, despite the fact that it is a relative measure, many scholars argue that its value should be assessed in the context of income (D'Alessio & Iezzi, 2016;

Falanga & Financité, 2015). It is possible, they argue, that where the amount of nominal disposable income is high, even a relatively high level of DSTI may not place a heavy burden on the household's budget or carry a high risk of over-indebtedness.

When calculating debt indicators, some researchers contend that it is necessary to distinguish between indebtedness that is unsecured by assets or wealth – in simple terms: consumer debt – and indebtedness that is secured against property (del Río & Young, 2008). This follows from the observation that unsecured debt is characterised, among other things, by comparatively high rates of interest, and therefore represents a greater burden for borrowers. Indeed, it is usually the most expensive method of borrowing money. Thus, a higher risk of over-indebtedness can be expected with this type of liability (Brown & Taylor, 2008; May et al., 2004). In practice, however, the range of liability categories considered is broad and largely dictated by the availability of data.

Using the concept of financial margin represents an opportunity to overcome the objective limitation set out previously: the need to fix threshold values for indicators of over-indebtedness a priori. This measure is calculated as income remaining after subtracting debt repayments and covering essential expenditure (Ampudia et al., 2016). Where the financial margin is negative, a household has difficulty in settling its liabilities. The result is either a lower standard of living (through a reduction in expenditure) or falling into arrears. If the latter, the household can be regarded as being over-indebted. It is worth emphasising, however, that a negative financial margin can be financed temporarily from other sources: from savings or by selling a portion of assets or wealth, for example.

Debt repayment expenditure is always included when calculating the financial margin (FM); the selection of all other categories is, however, arbitrary. Giovanni D'Alessio and Stefano Iezzi (2016) choose essential consumption expenditure, for example, while Marianna Brunetti (2016) and Alessandra Bettocchi (2018) and their teams employ the category of expected expenses, which they define as total expenditure on non-durable goods, rents, alimony, and insurance premiums. For their part, Sławomir Zajączkowski and Dawid Żochowski (2007) take account of a category defined as fixed consumption expenditure, which, if unmet, can have grave consequences, such as threatening the biological existence of household members, their health, and their capacity to generate income. Bjørn Vatne (2006) points out that a variety of margin types can be calculated (e.g. after deducting interest only or including the household's bank deposits). The widespread use of financial margins is most often constrained by the unavailability of such detailed expenditure categories.

The solution proposed to the objective difficulties encountered when attempting to study over-indebtedness from the perspective of consumption expenditure is the use of an indicator based on the poverty line: below the poverty line (BPL). In its intuitiveness and its reference to universally accepted thresholds (benchmarks), which make it a straightforward platform for international comparison, it has definite advantages. It is assumed that the conditions for an over-indebted household are met if, after deducting credit and loan repayments from income, it falls below a poverty line (for income per equivalent unit or per capita income) set at 60% of the median reference income. Despite the fact that this indicator embraces two dimensions of over-indebtedness (economic and social) and possesses considerable power to inform, it is seldom employed. This can be explained by the need for an adequate data source that not only covers questions of indebtedness but also provides detailed information on the number of people in a household. The weakness of the BPL indicator lies in its sensitivity to large, one-off loan repayments. Giovanni D'Alessio and Stefano Iezzi used it in studies of over-indebtedness in Italian households (2013), Lungile Ntsalaze and Sylvanus Ikhide did likewise for households in the Republic of South Africa (2017), and it was first employed to investigate indebted Polish households by Grzegorz Wałęga and Agnieszka Wałęga (2021).

In addition to relative measures, assessments of over-indebtedness also make use of households' debt repayment arrears (A). Falling behind with repayments is a sign of serious financial difficulties – especially if it is structural in nature. Debt repayment arrears is one of the primary indicators used by authorities at the macroeconomic level (European Commission, 2008). The scale of over-indebtedness is usually analysed through the number of overdue payments and their duration. Yet the value of overdue payments must be taken into account if this indicator is to produce a reliable assessment, so as to exclude cases in which minor arrears would be grounds for classifying a household as over-indebted. This indicator faces an additional limitation in the form of the frequent lack of reliable data: households often do not divulge the full extent of their overdue liabilities, which is probably due to the sensitive nature of the subject (Falanga & Financité, 2015). It is necessary furthermore to separate loan repayment arrears determined by long-term and structural factors from one-off or unintentional occurrences of arrears. The level of this indicator is, moreover, largely determined by the cultural and legal context in which households operate (Aller & González Chapela, 2013; Duygan-Bump & Grant, 2009), which further complicates its application and interpretation in the international context.

The number of credit and loan agreements held (NL) is another indicator employed to measure over-indebtedness. The research conducted by Elaine Kempson (2002) has revealed a link between being in arrears and the number of loans held. In accordance with the findings of behavioural economics, a large number of loans can indicate problems with self-control and budget management. For Giovanni D'Alessio and Stefano Iezzi (2013), holding four or more credit agreements is indicative of over-indebtedness. Because it does not include the amounts (values) of debt and can therefore produce a misleading picture of a household's situation, the deficiencies of the NL indicator are similar to those of the arrears indicator (A). The threshold adopted for the number of loan agreements indicative of over-indebtedness is, too, largely notional as it cannot be analysed in isolation from the developmental level of the credit market in the relevant country.

The use of subjective indicators of indebtedness, which measure the probability of financial difficulties based on households' own appraisals of their situation and declarations of their debt repayment capacity, represents another approach to the assessment of over-indebtedness (Betti et al., 2007; D'Alessio & Iezzi, 2016; Oxera, 2004). The rationale for employing this indicator is the assumption that the household is the best judge of its own financial situation. An over-indebted household is therefore one that sees itself as such. What is measured in this approach is not only the subjective – or psychological – burden of the debt held but also the perception of its repayment. This burden is manifested in the anxiety, stress, or pressure that household members are subjected to (Tay et al., 2017). Subjective evaluation of over-indebtedness based on household members' preferences and opinions can refer both to a household's present situation and to a factor that objective indicators do not take account of, namely predictions of its future financial situation (Białowolski & Węziak-Białowolska, 2014).

In practice, diverse questions are employed to elicit households' own assessments of their financial situation and indebtedness. Elaine Kempson (2002), for example, asked her respondents how they perceived their indebtedness and whether they felt over-committed, while Dimitrios Christelis and his team (2009) and Yvonne McCarthy (2011) enquired about households' ability to make ends meet. For their part, Annamaria Lusardi and her associates (2011) analysed the risk of over-indebtedness based on household members' beliefs about their capacity to cope with unplanned (unexpected) expenses. The issue of the subjective evaluation of financial difficulties is also present in research undertaken by EU-SILC, in which respondents were asked, among other things, about the subjective burden of mortgage repayments, hire purchase, and the repayment of other debts, as well as about their capacity to cover substantial, unexpected expenses, and their ability to make ends meet (CPEC, 2013).

The chief flaw in subjective indicators of indebtedness stems from the fact that being classified as over-indebted largely depends on how the question is posed (on how over-indebtedness is defined). To employ definitions that are too general (too broad) can result in an overestimation of the number of households classified on their basis, or it can result in the opposite if respondents systematically underestimate the risk of external shocks. Moreover, Marianna Brunetti and her colleagues (2016) are correct in stating that self-assessments can be too arbitrary, since households may indicate that indebtedness is a serious burden on them even where the objective (nominal) value of the loans is low. Sarah Bridges and Richard Disney (2010) also point to the weak relationship between objective indicators of indebtedness and psychological well-being, as well as to a possible reverse causality. Matthias Keese (2012) lists a number of factors that explain the differences between objective levels of indebtedness and subjective perceptions of it. These include a household's current financial situation (higher earners generally perceive their indebtedness as less of a burden), individual attitudes towards indebtedness (young people find it more natural to be indebted), and expectations of future incomes.

The objective evaluation of over-indebtedness is augmented by indicators based on data from judicial (administrative) systems. They include the number of court cases concerning unpaid loans (Majamaa et al., 2019), the number of proceedings that have resulted in debt restructuring (Raijas et al., 2010), and the number of insolvencies (DeVaney & Lytton, 1995; Skiba & Tobacman, 2019). It should not be forgotten, however, that these indicators identify over-indebtedness only narrowly (as indebtedness that leads to illiquidity), while entirely overlooking cases in which the consequences of over-commitment have a detrimental impact on household consumption plans and constitute a psychological burden for household members. In countries where there is a developed system of institutions offering debt management support for households in financial difficulty, the number of cases handled can serve as an indirect indicator of over-indebtedness and function as a sort of early-warning signal (Raijas et al., 2010; Valins, 2004). In practice, however, there are limitations on the use of this indicator: case numbers can fluctuate due to external factors, such as the launch of an advertising campaign for debt advice services or increased funding for them. What is more, the severity of the financial difficulties can vary greatly from case to case. In some countries, the extent of over-indebtedness can also be inferred from the number of people in receipt of loans designed for the poorest in society or the number benefiting from support (shelter) programmes for those who have problems repaying debts.

To summarise this review of indicators of over-indebtedness at the microeconomic level, it should be stated that each of the discussed indicators illustrates only a selected aspect of indebtedness. As Elena Giarda emphasises (2013), indicators of over-indebtedness complement each other quantitatively and qualitatively, and to better comprehend the phenomenon in question, it would therefore appear justified to use a combination of indicators. This is especially so as over-indebtedness has a psychological and social dimension as well as an economic one. Such an approach builds a more complete picture of the debt burden at the level of individual households (Ampudia et al., 2016; Brunetti et al., 2016). The implementation of a set of indicators also facilitates longitudinal and cross-sectional comparisons at the international level. For example, to identify over-indebtedness and households at risk of it, the CPEC (2013) report uses statistics on late repayments, the number of insolvency cases that go to court or that are handled by debt restructuring advisers, households' own assessments of their debt burdens, and two further indicators: DTI and DSTI.

An in-depth analysis of over-indebtedness should be conducted using composite indicators, but these have not been widely used in the subject literature to date. So, for example, Marianna Brunetti and her colleagues (2016) employed only objective categories to construct an index of the risk of financial fragility, while Luisa Anderloni and her associates (2012) relied on a range of subjective indicators of over-indebtedness. To overcome the constraints of selecting only one of these types of indicators, it is necessary to take into account both objective and subjective varieties. This approach is taken by Piotr Białowolski and Dorota Węziak-Białowolska (2014) when assessing the financial situation of Italian households, by Sri Noerhidajati and team (2021) when evaluating the financial situation of Indonesian households, and by Declan French and Dolan McKillop (2017) when examining the relationship between over-indebtedness and health.

3.4 Summary

To offer a precise definition of over-indebtedness poses many difficulties. For as we have seen, it is not just an economic phenomenon but a psychological and sociological one too. Two features of over-indebtedness are clear: it is structural in nature and adversely affects the ability to satisfy needs and wants. A variety of approaches to over-indebtedness can be found in the subject literature. In a narrow sense, it is equated with debt-servicing problems and loss of liquidity, which in extreme cases will push households into bankruptcy. In a broader sense, it is pointed out that over-indebtedness is inherent in the very threat of being unable to meet credit obligations, which in turn modifies consumer behaviour and the functions households perform. It can thus be defined both through the lens of objective difficulties in managing household budgets and wealth and within the context of subjective feelings associated with the holding of financial obligations. Although over-indebtedness usually refers to debts arising from credits and loans, it is also possible to assess it in connection with other forms of liability.

The emergence of problems with indebtedness is determined by a number of factors. In economic theory, the occurrence of over-indebtedness results from the uncertainty of the environment in which households operate, the insufficient application of bounded rationality in decision-making, and the imperfections of the market mechanism. A group of factors conducive to the emergence of the phenomenon of over-commitment can be identified on the basis of this thorough review of the existing research into over-indebtedness. First, over-indebtedness can be induced by certain socio-demographic features of households and their economic situation. Second, the structure of credit markets at the institutional and product level, their institutional development, and technological change determine the availability of loans to households, which can in turn lead to the emergence of over-indebtedness. This phenomenon can also be detected in the economic, political, cultural, and social environments in which households operate. The causes of over-indebtedness also include changes in the labour and property markets, changes in legal regulations, macroeconomic shocks, the globalisation of consumer behaviour, and the increasing economic stratification of societies.

The over-indebtedness of households can be measured at various levels of aggregation. Owing to the nature of this study, the focus is on over-indebtedness indicators applied in microeconomic research, that is, research related to households. In practice, there are two approaches to assessing the difficulties associated with indebtedness.

The first is based on objective categories relating to the economic situation of households (expressed in monetary units of income, consumption, and indebtedness) and selected data on the debt itself (number of credits and loans, number of overdue liabilities, and number of recovery proceedings and bankruptcies). In this understanding of the phenomenon, the primary indicators used to analyse over-indebtedness are debt to income (DTI), debt service to income (DSTI), and debt to assets (DTA). The main limitation in the use of these indicators, and the key issue for the reliability of the results, is the adoption of an arbitrary level (value) for each indicator, above which a case is treated as over-indebtedness. Other indicators – including financial margin (FM) and below the poverty line (BPL) – that at least partially mitigate these limitations have been proposed. The remaining objective indicators are usually treated as supplementary, since either they do not permit direct determination of debt-servicing difficulties – instead enabling only the identification of people with the potential to experience such problems (e.g. the number of credit obligations) – or they only register cases of narrowly defined over-indebtedness, in which loss of liquidity has already occurred (e.g. cessation of debt repayments or bankruptcy).

If it is accepted that over-indebtedness also applies to situations in which the credits and loans they possess influence households' consumer behaviour and well-being (by forcing them, for example, to limit some of their expenditure, or by generating stress and worry), it is necessary to include subjective assessments of indebtedness in the research. Such indicators are constructed on the basis of households' diverse declarations of their perceived debt burden, their difficulties in managing a household budget encumbered by debt repayments, and their capacity to cope with unexpected expenses and debt repayments. The subjectivity of this approach, however, is thought to be at once its main advantage and main disadvantage.

References

Aller, C., & González Chapela, J. (2013). Misclassification of the dependent variable in a debt – repayment behavior context. *Journal of Empirical Finance*, *23*, 162–172. https://doi.org/10.1016/j.jempfin.2013.06.001

Ampudia, M., van Vlokhoven, H., & Żochowski, D. (2016). Financial fragility of euro area households. *Journal of Financial Stability*, *27*, 250–262. https://doi.org/10.1016/j.jfs.2016.02.003

Anderloni, L., Bacchiocchi, E., & Vandone, D. (2012). Household financial vulnerability: An empirical analysis. *Research in Economics*, *66*(3), 284–296. https://doi.org/10.1016/j.rie.2012.03.001

Anderloni, L., & Vandone, D. (2008). *Households over-indebtedness in the economic literature* (Università degli Studi di Milano Working Paper No. 46). Milan: Università degli Studi di Milano.

Anderloni, L., & Vandone, D. (2011). Risk of over-indebtedness and behavioural factors. In C. Lucarelli & G. Brighetti (Eds.), *Risk tolerance in financial decision making* (pp. 113–132). London: Palgrave Macmillan.

Angel, S., & Heitzmann, K. (2015). Over-indebtedness in Europe: The relevance of country-level variables for the over-indebtedness of private households. *Journal of European Social Policy*, *25*(3), 331–351. https://doi.org/10.1177/0958928715588711

Autio, M., Wilska, T.-A., Kaartinen, R., & Lähteenmaa, J. (2009). The use of small instant loans among young adults – A gateway to a consumer insolvency? *International Journal of Consumer Studies, 33*(4), 407–415. https://doi.org/10.1111/j.1470-6431.2009.00789.x

Baek, E., & DeVaney, S. A. (2004). Assessing the baby boomers' financial wellness using financial ratios and a subjective measure. *Family and Consumer Sciences Research Journal, 32*(4), 321–348. https://doi.org/10.1177/1077727X04263826

Baek, E., & Hong, G.-S. (2004). Effects of family life-cycle stages on consumer debts. *Journal of Family and Economic Issues, 25*(3), 359–385. https://doi.org/10.1023/B:JEEI.0000039946.59422.5f

Bańkowska, K., Lamarche, P., Osier, G., & Pérez-Duarte, S. (2015). Measuring household debt vulnerability in the euro area. In Bank for International Settlements (Ed.), *Indicators to support monetary and financial stability analysis: Data sources and statistical methodologies proceedings of the seventh IFC conference, 4–5 September 2014 (IFC Bulletin No 39)*. Basel: Bank for International Settlements.

Beck, J. H., Hackney, D. D., Hackney, J., & McPherson, M. Q. (2014). Regional differences in chapter 13 filings: Southern legal culture or religion? *Review of Social Economy, 72*(2), 186–208. https://doi.org/10.1080/00346764.2013.861644

Betti, G., Dourmashkin, N., Rossi, M., & Ping Yin, Y. (2007). Consumer over-indebtedness in the EU: Measurement and characteristics. *Journal of Economic Studies, 34*(2), 136–156. https://doi.org/10.1108/01443580710745371

Bettocchi, A., Giarda, E., Moriconi, C., Orsini, F., & Romeo, R. (2018). Assessing and predicting financial vulnerability of Italian households: A micro-macro approach. *Empirica, 45*(3), 587–605. https://doi.org/10.1007/s10663-017-9378-2

Białowolski, P., Cwynar, A., Cwynar, W., & Węziak-Białowolska, D. (2020). Consumer debt attitudes: The role of gender, debt knowledge and skills. *International Journal of Consumer Studies, 44*(3), 191–205. https://doi.org/10.1111/ijcs.12558

Białowolski, P., & Węziak-Białowolska, D. (2014). The index of household financial condition, combining subjective and objective indicators: An appraisal of Italian households. *Social Indicators Research, 118*(1), 365–385. https://doi.org/10.1007/s11205-013-0401-0

Bourova, E., Ramsay, I., & Ali, P. (2019). The Experience of financial hardship in Australia: Causes, impacts and coping strategies. *Journal of Consumer Policy, 42*(2), 189–221. https://doi.org/10.1007/s10603-018-9392-1

Bridges, S., & Disney, R. (2004). Use of credit and arrears on debt among low-income families in the United Kingdom. *Fiscal Studies, 25*(1), 1–25. https://doi.org/10.1111/j.1475-5890.2004.tb00094.x

Bridges, S., & Disney, R. (2010). Debt and depression. *Journal of Health Economics, 29*(3), 388–403. https://doi.org/10.1016/j.jhealeco.2010.02.003

Brown, S., Garino, G., & Taylor, K. (2008). Mortgages and financial expectations: A household-level analysis. *Southern Economic Journal, 74*(3), 857–878. https://doi.org/10.2307/20112000

Brown, S., Garino, G., & Taylor, K. (2013). Household debt and attitudes toward risk. *Review of Income and Wealth, 59*(2), 283–304. https://doi.org/10.1111/j.1475-4991.2012.00506.x

Brown, S., Garino, G., Taylor, K., & Price, S. W. (2005). Debt and financial expectations: An individual- and household-level analysis. *Economic Inquiry, 43*(1), 100–120. https://doi.org/10.1093/ei/cbi008

Brown, S., & Taylor, K. (2008). Household debt and financial assets: Evidence from Germany, Great Britain and the USA. *Journal of the Royal Statistical Society: Series A (Statistics in Society), 171*(3), 615–643. https://doi.org/10.1111/j.1467-985X.2007.00531.x

Brunetti, M., Giarda, E., & Torricelli, C. (2016). Is financial fragility a matter of illiquidity? An appraisal for Italian households. *Review of Income and Wealth*, *62*(4), 628–649. https://doi.org/10.1111/roiw.12189

Bucks, B., & Pence, K. (2015). Wealth, pensions, debt, and savings: Considerations for a panel survey. *Journal of Economic and Social Measurement*, *40*(1–4), 151–175. https://doi.org/10.3233/JEM-150396

Carvalho, L. S., Meier, S., & Wang, S. W. (2016). Poverty and economic decision-making: Evidence from changes in financial resources at payday. *American Economic Review*, *106*(2), 260–284. https://doi.org/10.1257/aer.20140481

Cavalletti, B., Lagazio, C., Lagomarsino, E., & Vandone, D. (2020). Consumer debt and financial fragility: Evidence from Italy. *Journal of Consumer Policy*, *43*(4), 747–765. https://doi.org/10.1007/s10603-020-09458-w

Chambers, M. S., Garriga, C., & Schlagenhauf, D. (2009). The loan structure and housing tenure decisions in an equilibrium model of mortgage choice. *Review of Economic Dynamics*, *12*(3), 444–468. https://doi.org/10.1016/j.red.2009.01.003

Chichaibelu, B. B., & Waibel, H. (2018). Over-indebtedness and its persistence in rural households in Thailand and Vietnam. *Journal of Asian Economics*, *56*, 1–23. https://doi.org/10.1016/j.asieco.2018.04.002

Christelis, D., Jappelli, T., Paccagnella, O., & Weber, G. (2009). Income, wealth and financial fragility in Europe. *Journal of European Social Policy*, *19*(4), 359–376. https://doi.org/10.1177/1350506809341516

Chunping, Z., Li, P., & Lingwei, S. (2016). Do religious beliefs affect borrowing behavior? Evidence from Chinese households. *Review of Economics of the Household*, *14*(4), 989–1005. https://doi.org/10.1007/s11150-016-9324-2

Coletta, M., De Bonis, R., & Piermattei, S. (2019). Household debt in OECD countries: The role of supply-side and demand-side factors. *Social Indicators Research*, *143*(3), 1185–1217. https://doi.org/10.1007/s11205-018-2024-y

Cox, P., Whitley, J., & Brierley, P. (2002). Financial pressures in the UK household sector: Evidence from the British household panel survey. *Bank of England Quarterly Bulletin*, *Q4*, 410–419.

CPEC. (2013). *The over-indebtedness of European households: Updated mapping of the situation, nature and causes, effects and initiatives for alleviating its impact*. Berlin: Civic Consulting of the Consumer Policy Evaluation Consortium.

Crook, J. N. (2006). Household debt demand and supply: A cross-country comparison. In G. Bertola, C. Grant, & R. Disney (Eds.), *The economics of consumer credit* (pp. 63–92). Cambridge, MA: MIT Press.

D'Alessio, G., & Iezzi, S. (2013). Household over-indebtedness: Definition and measurement with Italian data. *Bank of Italy Occasional Paper*, *149*. https://doi.org/10.2139/ssrn.2243578

D'Alessio, G., & Iezzi, S. (2016). Over-indebtedness in Italy: How widespread and persistent is it? *Bank of Italy Occasional Paper*, *349*. https://doi.org/10.2139/ssrn.2772485

del Río, A., & Young, G. (2008). The impact of unsecured debt on financial pressure among British households. *Applied Financial Economics*, *18*(15), 1209–1220. https://doi.org/10.1080/09603100701604233

Desai, C. A., & Elliehausen, G. (2017). The effect of state bans of payday lending on consumer credit delinquencies. *The Quarterly Review of Economics and Finance*, *64*, 94–107. https://doi.org/10.1016/j.qref.2016.07.004

DeVaney, S. A., & Lytton, R. H. (1995). Household insolvency: A review of household debt repayment, delinquency, and bankruptcy. *Financial Services Review*, *4*(2), 137–156. https://doi.org/10.1016/1057-0810(95)90008-X

de Wet, S., Botha, I., & Booyens, M. (2015). Measuring the effect of the national credit act on indebtedness in South Africa. *Journal of Economic and Financial Sciences, 8*(1), 83–104. https://doi.org/10.4102/jef.v8i1.85

Disney, R., Bridges, S., & Gathergood, J. (2008). *Drivers of over-indebtedness.* Nottingham: Centre for Policy Evaluation, The University of Nottingham.

Du Caju, P., Rycx, F., & Tojerow, I. (2016). *Unemployment risk and over-indebtedness: A micro-econometric perspective* (ECB Working Paper No. 1908). Frankfurt am Main: European Central Bank.

Duygan-Bump, B., & Grant, C. (2009). Household debt repayment behaviour: What role do institutions play? *Economic Policy, 24*(57), 108–140. https://doi.org/10.1111/j.1468-0327.2009.00215.x

Elliehausen, G., & Lawrence, E. C. (2001). *Payday advance credit in America: An analysis of customer demand* (Monograph No. 35). Washington, DC: Georgetown University, McDonough School of Business, Credit Research Center.

European Commission. (2008). *Towards a common operational European definition of over-indebtedness.* Brussels: European Commission.

Falanga, A., & Financité, R. (2015). *Over-indebtedness in the EU: From figures to expert opinions.* Brussels: Réseau Financité & European Financial Inclusion Network.

Faruqui, U. (2008). *Indebtedness and the household financial health: An examination of the Canadian debt service ratio distribution* (Bank of Canada Working Paper No. 46). Ottawa: Bank of Canada.

Fay, S., Hurst, E., & White, M. J. (2002). The household bankruptcy decision. *American Economic Review, 92*(3), 706–718. https://doi.org/10.1257/00028280260136327

Ferretti, F., & Vandone, D. (2019). *Personal debt in Europe: The EU financial market and consumer insolvency.* Cambridge: Cambridge University Press.

Frade, C., & Lopes, C. A. (2009). Overindebtedness and financial stress: A comparative study in Europe. In J. Niemi, I. Ramsay, & W. C. Whitford (Eds.), *Consumer credit, debt and bankruptcy: Comparative and international perspectives* (pp. 249–272). Oxford: Hart Publishing.

French, D., & McKillop, D. (2016). Financial literacy and over-indebtedness in low-income households. *International Review of Financial Analysis, 48*, 1–11. https://doi.org/10.1016/j.irfa.2016.08.004

French, D., & McKillop, D. (2017). The impact of debt and financial stress on health in Northern Irish households. *Journal of European Social Policy, 27*(5), 458–473. https://doi.org/10.1177/0958928717717657

French, D., & Vigne, S. (2019). The causes and consequences of household financial strain: A systematic review. *International Review of Financial Analysis, 62*, 150–156. https://doi.org/10.1016/j.irfa.2018.09.008

Garðarsdóttir, R. B., & Dittmar, H. (2012). The relationship of materialism to debt and financial well-being: The case of Iceland's perceived prosperity. *Journal of Economic Psychology, 33*(3), 471–481. https://doi.org/10.1016/j.joep.2011.12.008

Garrett, S., & James III, R. N. (2013). Financial ratios and perceived household financial satisfaction. *Journal of Financial Therapy, 4*(1), 4. https://doi.org/10.4148/jft.v4i1.1839

Georgarakos, D., & Fürth, S. (2015). Household repayment behavior: The role of social capital and institutional, political, and religious beliefs. *European Journal of Political Economy, 37*, 249–265. https://doi.org/10.1016/j.ejpoleco.2014.10.001

Georgarakos, D., Lojschova, A., & Ward-Warmedinger, M. E. (2010). *Mortgage indebtedness and household financial distress* (ECB Working Paper No. 1156). Frankfurt am Main: European Central Bank. http://doi.org/10.2139/ssrn.1456593

Giarda, E. (2013). Persistency of financial distress amongst Italian households: Evidence from dynamic models for binary panel data. *Journal of Banking & Finance, 37*(9), 3425–3434. https://doi.org/10.1016/j.jbankfin.2013.05.005

Grant, C. (2007). Estimating credit constraints among US households. *Oxford Economic Papers, 59*(4), 583–605. https://doi.org/10.1093/oep/gpm024

Gutiérrez-Nieto, B., Serrano-Cinca, C., & de la Cuesta-González, M. (2017). A multivariate study of over-indebtedness' causes and consequences. *International Journal of Consumer Studies, 41*(2), 188–198. https://doi.org/10.1111/ijcs.12324

Haas, O. J. (2006). *Overindebtedness in Germany* (Working Paper No. 44). Geneva: International Labour Organization.

Hasan, I., Kiesel, K., & Noth, F. (2019). *'And forgive US our debts': Do Christian moralities influence over-indebtedness of individuals?* (IWH Discussion Papers No. 8). Halle: Halle Institute for Economic Research.

Hodson, R., Dwyer, R. E., & Neilson, L. A. (2014). Credit card blues: The middle class and the hidden costs of easy credit. *The Sociological Quarterly, 55*(2), 315–340. https://doi.org/10.1111/tsq.12059

Hyytinen, A., & Putkuri, H. (2018). Household optimism and overborrowing. *Journal of Money, Credit and Banking, 50*(1), 55–76. https://doi.org/10.1111/jmcb.12453

Jappelli, T. (1990). Who is credit constrained in the U.S. economy? *The Quarterly Journal of Economics, 105*(1), 219–234. https://doi.org/10.2307/2937826

Jappelli, T., Pagano, M., & Di Maggio, M. (2013). Households' indebtedness and financial fragility. *Journal of Financial Management, Markets and Institutions, 1*(1), 23–46. https://doi.org/10.12831/73631

Kamleitner, B., Hoelzl, E., & Kirchler, E. (2012). Credit use: Psychological perspectives on a multifaceted phenomenon. *International Journal of Psychology, 47*(1), 1–27. https://doi.org/10.1080/00207594.2011.628674

Kamleitner, B., & Kirchler, E. (2007). Consumer credit use: A process model and literature review. *European Review of Applied Psychology, 57*(4), 267–283. https://doi.org/10.1016/j.erap.2006.09.003

Keese, M. (2009). *Triggers and determinants of severe household indebtedness in Germany* (Ruhr Economic Paper No. 150). RWI – Leibniz-Institut für Wirtschaftsforschung, Ruhr-University Bochum, TU Dortmund University, University of Duisburg-Essen.

Keese, M. (2012). Who feels constrained by high debt burdens? Subjective vs. objective measures of household debt. *Journal of Economic Psychology, 33*(1), 125–141. https://doi.org/10.1016/j.joep.2011.08.002

Kempson, E. (2002). *Over-indebtedness in Britain* [Report]. Bristol: Personal Finance Research Centre, University of Bristol.

Kempson, E., McKay, S., Willitts, M., Great Britain, Department for Work and Pensions, University of Bristol, & Personal Finance Research Centre. (2004). *Characteristics of families in debt and the nature of indebtedness* (Research Report No. 211). Bristol: Personal Finance Research Centre, University of Bristol.

Kiesel, K., & Noth, F. (2016). When debt spells sin: Does religiosity guard against over-indebtedness? *Annual conference 2016 (Augsburg): Demographic change*. Verein für Socialpolitik/German Economic Association.

Kilborn, J. J. (2005). Behavioral economics, overindebtedness & comparative consumer bankruptcy: Searching for causes and evaluating solutions. *Emory Bankruptcy Developments Journal, 22*(1), 13–45.

Li, W., Parrish, L., Ernst, K., & Davis, D. (2009). *Predatory profiling: The role of race and ethnicity in the location of payday lenders in California*. Durham: Center for Responsible Lending.

Lusardi, A., Schneider, D. J., & Tufano, P. (2011). *Financially fragile households: Evidence and implications* (NBER Working Paper No. 17072). Cambridge, MA: National Bureau of Economic Research. https://doi.org/10.3386/w17072

Lusardi, A., & Tufano, P. (2015). Debt literacy, financial experiences, and overindebtedness. *Journal of Pension Economics and Finance*, *14*(4), 332–368. https://doi.org/10.1017/S1474747215000232

Magri, S., Pico, R., & Rampazzi, C. (2011). Which households use consumer credit in Europe? *Bank of Italy Occasional Paper*, *100*. https://doi.org/10.2139/ssrn.1998749

Majamaa, K., Lehtinen, A.-R., & Rantala, K. (2019). Debt judgments as a reflection of consumption-related debt problems. *Journal of Consumer Policy*, *42*(2), 223–244. https://doi.org/10.1007/s10603-018-9402-3

Marron, D. (2012). Producing over-indebtedness. *Journal of Cultural Economy*, *5*(4), 407–421. https://doi.org/10.1080/17530350.2012.703144

Martínez, M.-T. S. (2008). The Spanish financial system: Facing up to the real estate crisis and credit crunch. *European Journal of Housing Policy*, *8*(2), 181–196. https://doi.org/10.1080/14616710802037425

May, O., Tudela, M., & Young, G. (2004). British household indebtedness and financial stress: A household-level picture. *Bank of England Quarterly Bulletin*, *Q4*, 414–428.

McCarthy, Y. (2011). *Behavioural characteristics and financial distress* (ECB Working Paper No. 1303). Frankfurt am Main: European Central Bank. https://econpapers.repec.org/paper/ecbecbwps/20111303.htm

Meier, S., & Sprenger, C. (2010). Present-biased preferences and credit card borrowing. *American Economic Journal: Applied Economics*, *2*(1), 193–210. https://doi.org/10.1257/app.2.1.193

Meltzer, H., Bebbington, P., Brugha, T., Farrell, M., & Jenkins, R. (2013). The relationship between personal debt and specific common mental disorders. *The European Journal of Public Health*, *23*(1), 108–113. https://doi.org/10.1093/eurpub/cks021

Melzer, B. T. (2011). The real costs of credit access: Evidence from the payday lending market. *The Quarterly Journal of Economics*, *126*(1), 517–555. https://doi.org/10.1093/qje/qjq009

Meyll, T., & Pauls, T. (2019). The gender gap in over-indebtedness. *Finance Research Letters*, *31*. https://doi.org/10.1016/j.frl.2018.12.007

Michelangeli, V., & Pietrunti, M. (2014). A microsimulation model to evaluate Italian households' financial vulnerability. *International Journal of Microsimulation*, 7(3), 53–79. https://doi.org/10.34196/ijm.00107

Mullainathan, S., & Shafir, E. (2013). *Scarcity: Why having too little means so much*. London: Allen Lane.

Nettleton, S., & Burrows, R. (1998). Mortgage debt, insecure home ownership and health: An exploratory analysis. *Sociology of Health & Illness*, *20*(5), 731–753.

Noerhidajati, S., Purwoko, A. B., Werdaningtyas, H., Kamil, A. I., & Dartanto, T. (2021). Household financial vulnerability in Indonesia: Measurement and determinants. *Economic Modelling*, *96*, 433–444. https://doi.org/10.1016/j.econmod.2020.03.028

Ntsalaze, L., & Ikhide, S. (2017). The threshold effects of household indebtedness on multidimensional poverty. *International Journal of Social Economics*, *44*(11), 1471–1488. https://doi.org/10.1108/IJSE-03-2016-0086

Ong, Q., Theseira, W., & Ng, I. Y. H. (2019). Reducing debt improves psychological functioning and changes decision-making in the poor. *Proceedings of the National Academy of Sciences*, *116*(15), 7244–7249. https://doi.org/10.1073/pnas.1810901116

Ottaviani, C., & Vandone, D. (2018). Financial literacy, debt burden and impulsivity: A mediation analysis. *Economic Notes*, *47*(2–3), 439–454. https://doi.org/10.1111/ecno.12115

Oxera. (2004). *Are UK households over-indebted?* Oxford: Oxera. www.oxera.com/Oxera/media/Oxera/downloads/reports/Are-UK-householdsoverindebted. pdf?ext=.pdf

Pattarin, F., & Cosma, S. (2012). Psychological determinants of consumer credit: The role of attitudes. *Review of Behavioural Finance*, *4*(2), 113–129. https://doi.org/10.1108/19405971211284899

Raijas, A., Lehtinen, A.-R., & Leskinen, J. (2010). Over-indebtedness in the Finnish consumer society. *Journal of Consumer Policy*, *33*(3), 209–223. https://doi.org/10.1007/s10603-010-9131-8

Renneboog, L., & Spaenjers, C. (2012). Religion, economic attitudes, and household finance. *Oxford Economic Papers*, *64*(1), 103–127. https://doi.org/10.1093/oep/gpr025

Samolyk, K. A. (2007). Payday lending: Evolution, issues, and evidence. In S. Agarwal & B. W. Ambrose (Eds.), *Household credit usage: Personal debt and mortgages* (pp. 175–200). New York: Palgrave Macmillan. https://doi.org/10.1057/9780230608917_11

Sánchez-Martínez, M. T., Sanchez-Campillo, J., & Moreno-Herrero, D. (2016). Mortgage debt and household vulnerability: Evidence from Spain before and during the global financial crisis. *International Journal of Housing Markets and Analysis*, *9*(3), 400–420. https://doi.org/10.1108/IJHMA-07-2015-0038

Schicks, J. (2014). Over-indebtedness in microfinance – an empirical analysis of related factors on the borrower level. *World Development*, *54*, 301–324. https://doi.org/10.1016/j.worlddev.2013.08.009

Sipon, S., Othman, K., Ghani, Z. A., & Radzi, H. M. (2014). The impact of religiosity on financial debt and debt stress. *Procedia – Social and Behavioral Sciences*, *140*, 300–306. https://doi.org/10.1016/j.sbspro.2014.04.424

Skiba, P. M., & Tobacman, J. (2019). Do payday loans cause bankruptcy? *The Journal of Law and Economics*, *62*(3), 485–519. https://doi.org/10.1086/706201

Stegman, M. A., & Faris, R. (2003). Payday lending: A business model that encourages chronic borrowing. *Economic Development Quarterly*, *17*(1), 8–32. https://doi.org/10.1177/0891242402239196

Sweet, E. (2018). "Like you failed at life": Debt, health and neoliberal subjectivity. *Social Science & Medicine*, *212*, 86–93. https://doi.org/10.1016/j.socscimed.2018.07.017

Sweet, E., DuBois, L. Z., & Stanley, F. (2018). Embodied neoliberalism: Epidemiology and the lived experience of consumer debt. *International Journal of Health Services*, *48*(3), 495–511. https://doi.org/10.1177/0020731418776580

Tay, L., Batz, C., Parrigon, S., & Kuykendall, L. (2017). Debt and subjective well-being: The other side of the income-happiness coin. *Journal of Happiness Studies*, *18*(3), 903–937. https://doi.org/10.1007/s10902-016-9758-5

Terraneo, M. (2018). Households' financial vulnerability in Southern Europe. *Journal of Economic Studies*, *45*(3), 521–542. https://doi.org/10.1108/JES-08-2016-0162

Tiongson, E. R., Sugawara, N., Sulla, V., Taylor, A., Gueorguieva, A. I., Levin, V., & Subbarao, K. (2009). *The crisis hits home: Stress-testing households in Europe and Central Asia* [Raport]. Washington, DC: The World Bank. https://doi.org/10.1596/978-0-8213-8222-6

Valins, O. (2004). *When debt becomes a problem: A literature study*. Wellington: Ministry of Social Development.

Vatne, B. H. (2006). How large are the financial margins of Norwegian households? An analysis of micro data for the period 1987–2004. *Economic Bulletin*, 77(4), Norges Bank, 173–180.

Wałęga, G. (2015). Zmiany w polityce kredytowej banków a zadłużenie polskich gospodarstw domowych. *Konsumpcja i Rozwój*, *1*(10), 44–55.

Wałęga, G., & Wałęga, A. (2021). Over-indebted households in Poland: Classification tree analysis. *Social Indicators Research, 153*(2), 561–584. https://doi.org/10.1007/s11205-020-02505-6

Watson, J. J. (2003). The relationship of materialism to spending tendencies, saving, and debt. *Journal of Economic Psychology, 24*(6), 723–739. https://doi.org/10.1016/j.joep.2003.06.001

Webley, P., & Nyhus, E. K. (2001). Life-cycle and dispositional routes into problem debt. *British Journal of Psychology, 92*(3), 423–446. https://doi.org/10.1348/000712601162275

Whelan, C. T., Nolan, B., & Maitre, B. (2017). Polarization or "squeezed middle" in the Great Recession?: A comparative European analysis of the distribution of economic stress. *Social Indicators Research, 133*(1), 163–184. https://doi.org/10.1007/s11205-016-1350-1

Worthington, A. C. (2006). Debt as a source of financial stress in Australian households. *International Journal of Consumer Studies, 30*(1), 2–15. https://doi.org/10.1111/j.1470-6431.2005.00420.x

Xiao, J. J., & Yao, R. (2020). Debt types and burdens by family structures. *International Journal of Bank Marketing, 38*(4), 867–888. https://doi.org/10.1108/IJBM-07-2019-0262

Yilmazer, T., & DeVaney, S. A. (2005). Household debt over the life cycle. *Financial Services Review, 14*, 285–304.

Zajączkowski, S., & Żochowski, D. (2007). *Obciążenia gospodarstw domowych spłatami długu: Rozkłady i stress testy – na podstawie badań budżetów gospodarstw domowych GUS* (Materiały i Studia No. 221). Warszawa: Narodowy Bank Polski.

4 Characteristics of over-indebted households

Empirical analysis

4.1 The level of over-indebtedness

The indicators discussed in subsection 3.3 were employed to extract households regarded as over-indebted from the sample of indebted households investigated. Consideration was given to:[1]

- debt service to income in excess of 30% (DSTI30);
- an indicator based on the poverty line – income per capita after deducting credit and loan repayments is below a poverty line set at 60% of the median per capita income (BPL);
- repayment arrears of more than 3 months (A3);
- the number of credits or loans is greater than or equal to 4 (NL4);
- subjective debt burden[2] – the respondent declared that they felt over-indebted (SB).

Each of the indicators used corresponds to a different aspect of over-indebtedness, which represents a response to the view widespread in the literature that the nature of the phenomenon under investigation is complex (D'Alessio & Iezzi, 2013; Disney et al., 2008). Overall, 47.67% of the surveyed households can be considered over-indebted according to at least one of the five indicators considered, 17.78% according to at least two indicators, 7.05% according to at least three indicators, and only 1.09% according to four or five indicators.

The DSTI indicator exceeds 30% in 16.73% of over-indebted households (Table 4.1), while one-third of the households studied were classified as over-indebted based on the BPL indicator. The proportion of households indebted according to DSTI30 and BPL is similar to that determined by Giovanni D'Alessio and Stefano Iezzi (2013). Only 1.90% of households do not repay their debts for a period exceeding 3 months.[3] Because the frequency of arrears usually concerns a comparatively small proportion of households (Georgarakos et al., 2010), this is a typical value for this indicator. Households with more than three credit agreements constituted 4.61% of the sample. Households feel subjectively over-indebted more frequently than is indicated by objective

DOI: 10.4324/9781003254706-5

Table 4.1 Matrix of over-indebtedness indicators (%)

Item	*DSTI30*	*BPL*	*A3*	*NL4*	*SB*
DSTI30	16.73	10.86	0.50	1.59	6.87
BPL	10.86	33.07	1.00	2.19	8.17
A3	0.50	1.00	1.90	0.63	1.36
NL4	1.59	2.19	0.63	4.61	2.26
SB	6.87	8.17	1.36	2.26	17.07

measures. Of the households surveyed, 17.07% considered themselves over-indebted, which roughly corresponds to the proportion of households whose debt service-to-income ratio exceeds 30% of monthly income.

Over-indebtedness can, and should, therefore be assessed using an array of measurements and not by reference to a single symptom (Anderloni & Vandone, 2011; Betti et al., 2007). For example, when analysing the proportion of over-indebted households for the combined DSTI30 and BPL indicators in relation to the values calculated for the individual indicators, it is noticeable, first, that the majority of people for whom debt-servicing (DSTI30) accounts for a significant share of their budgets are below the poverty line. Second, there is among the indebted a large group of households facing financial difficulties and poverty even though their debt repayment burden is not excessive in relation to their income.

The data displayed in Table 4.1 also make it possible to assess the scale of indebtedness of households simultaneously classified as over-indebted on the basis of two different types of indicator: objective and subjective. If this frame of reference is taken as appropriate for the estimation of over-indebtedness, the proportion of over-indebted households does not exceed 8.17% (SB and BPL) and 6.87% (SB and DSTI30). The proportion of over-indebted households in the sample studied does not exceed 2.3% in the remaining cases in which two indicators are applied.

On the one hand, these values suggest that over-indebtedness, when measured in this way, is limited in scope in Poland, and on the other hand, they signal a need to consider whether the choice of indicators is correct. To satisfy the conditions for over-indebtedness according to two indicators at the same time is a criterion that limits the sample size of over-indebted households considerably. It is for this reason that subsequent stages of the research employed two objective indicators – DSTI30 and BPL – as well as a subjective, supplementary indicator (SB) to identify people describing themselves as over-indebted. In this way, the analysis is carried out both in relation to respondents defined as over-indebted according to only one of these criteria and in relation to those defined as over-indebted according to an objective and a subjective indicator simultaneously. In that the subjective approach possesses a dimension that is indeed highly complementary – given that the over-indebted groups are largely disjointed when captured in objective and subjective terms – this is all the more justified (Figure 4.1). The choice of these three fundamental indicators

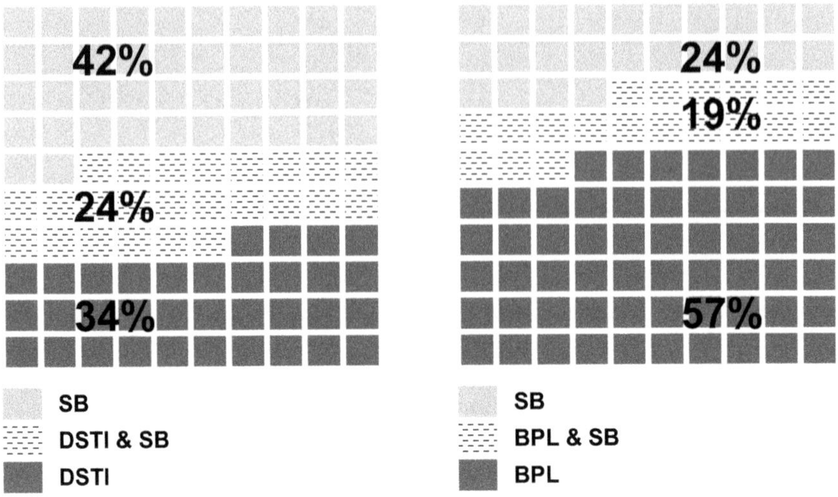

Figure 4.1 Over-indebted households – relationships between objective and subjective over-indebtedness

of over-indebtedness makes it possible, then, both to capture the dual (objective and subjective) nature of the phenomenon under analysis and to identify similarities and differences in the characteristics of over-indebted households according to DSTI30 and BPL. The use of the BPL indicator also makes it possible to reflect the social dimension of this phenomenon.

In the group of households identified on the basis of DSTI30 and SB, only 24% are indebted to objective and subjective measures at the same time. Moreover, only slightly more than 41% of households selected according to DSTI30 describe themselves as over-indebted (SB) or, looking at it another way, only 36% of households who feel themselves to be over-indebted really are so in objective terms (according to DSTI30).[4]

Similar observations can be made in respect of the second of the objective indicators to be analysed: BPL. Households that meet the criterion for over-indebtedness according to both indicators at the same time (BPL and SB) constitute 19% of those analysed (that is, households whose indebtedness, when these indicators are employed, permits them to be classified as over-indebted objectively or subjectively). In the group of households whose per capita income after deducting loan repayment instalments falls below the adopted poverty line, only 25% feel themselves to be over-indebted. The proportion of households objectively indebted according to the BPL indicator in the group of households self-reporting as over-indebted was much greater – just over 44% (although it is worth noting that this is still below 50% of the group studied).

4.2 Cross-sectional analysis of over-indebted households

Table 4.2 presents the proportion of over-indebted households broken down according to selected socio-demographic features, economic features, and debt characteristics, which are identified on the basis of the three indicators discussed earlier.

The feeling of being over-indebted is greater among women than men: it affects every fifth woman but only every seventh man. In large measure, the

Table 4.2 Proportion of over-indebted households broken down according to socio-demographic features, economic features, and debt characteristics (%)

Item	*DSTI30*	*BPL*	*SB*
Sex			
Woman	17.37	31.76	20.35
Man	16.30	33.94	14.81
Age range			
Up to 34	11.88	35.31	12.80
35–54	18.14	33.19	18.11
55+	20.08	30.12	20.21
Education			
Basic vocational or lower	20.10	50.52	22.60
Secondary	15.33	38.92	16.20
Tertiary	16.58	17.88	15.37
Number of people in household			
1	30.36	23.21	21.67
2	14.96	22.05	15.00
3	18.28	29.75	19.67
4	13.47	37.14	15.38
5+	10.53	66.67	14.73
Place of residence			
Rural	20.00	45.77	18.37
Small town	13.78	30.22	15.85
Large town	18.43	26.28	17.68
Income (PLN)			
Up to 2,000	36.60	84.31	24.52
(2,000–6,000]	15.17	32.46	16.23
Above 6,000	7.98	1.68	15.55
Source of income/maintenance			
Own firm/self-employed	16.33	28.57	13.86
Blue-collar work	14.74	43.64	18.31
White-collar work	14.42	15.99	13.09
Retirement pension or disability pension	23.29	38.36	23.75
Other	28.26	69.57	25.00

(*Continued*)

Table 4.2 (Continued)

Item	*DSTI30*	*BPL*	*SB*
Debt type			
Bank	20.70	30.85	16.88
Non-bank	4.60	36.20	8.24
Mixed	27.18	33.33	32.38
Number of credits and loans			
1	11.15	31.95	11.34
2+	25.06	34.74	25.86

differences between the sexes can be attributed to different perceptions of the future, personality traits, and different levels of caution where financial matters are concerned. The results obtained are consistent with the findings of Matthias Keese (2012), Jenni Blomgren and her team (2016), and Julia Callegari and her colleagues (2020). On the other hand, looking at the proportion of objectively over-indebted households broken down by sex, we see that it is basically identical (a difference of 1–2 percentage points), though women are slightly ahead of men for DSTI30 and men slightly ahead of women for BPL.

A distinct tendency is noticeable when attention is turned to age: the proportion of over-indebted households identified on the basis of the DSTI30 and SB indicators rises through the successive age ranges. These results are the opposite of what theoretical predictions would suggest, which is that the proportion of over-indebted households should fall in the higher age ranges (D'Alessio & Iezzi, 2013; Ntsalaze & Ikhide, 2016; Yilmazer & DeVaney, 2005). The greater burden of debt repayment among older households could suggest material deprivation associated with low current income and the lack of a sufficient stock of accumulated wealth with which to finance consumption needs. For their part, it is most likely that younger households encounter restrictions in accessing credit due to the lack of a reliable credit history. Turning to the BPL indicator, however, the proportion of over-indebted households in the 34 and younger age range is approximately 5 percentage points higher than among those in the oldest age range. Where subjective over-indebtedness is concerned, it may be supposed that the detected pattern is most likely associated with the greater experience that comes with age, lower tolerance of (or propensity for) risk, and, perhaps, also partially with the phases of the family life cycle characteristic of particular age groups. Another explanation for this pattern could be the change in the perception of debt that has occurred over the last few decades (Drentea & Reynolds, 2012).

Irrespective of the indicator, it is a general rule that the proportion of over-indebted households is lower among better-educated people. These findings are consistent with expectations and with earlier research results (see Chichaibelu & Waibel, 2018; Lusardi et al., 2011). Not only does education allow for better long-term consumption planning (which translates into a lower proportion of households with debt repayment burdens that exceed 30% of income among those with tertiary education when compared to those educated to the lowest level), but it also – thanks to greater awareness of the mechanisms of the real world, including its economic mechanisms – makes it possible to reduce (or to rationalise) the psychological burden of debt. Interestingly, the results obtained for the best educated households in Poland differ from those describing the situation of households in Spain (Sánchez-Martínez et al., 2016).

The problem of over-indebtedness primarily affects single-person households. The proportion of such households on the DSTI30 indicator is almost 20 percentage points higher than among households with five or more people. The difference between the same two household sizes for the SB indicator is not quite 7 percentage points. It is possible that these differences are explained by the generally lower capacity among the least numerous households to build up a financial buffer or to spread some of the individual risk factors (job loss, illness). For this reason, the fact that single-person households struggle alone with debt repayments may be associated with a greater feeling of over-indebtedness (CPEC, 2013). Matthias Keese (2012) obtained similar results for objective and subjective indicators. When applying the BPL indicator, the greatest proportion of over-indebted households was identified among the most numerous households. In this group, as many as two out of three households with five or more members are over-indebted. Given that poverty in Poland is, in the main, experienced by households with multiple children, these results are unsurprising. Even if the debt repayments are not objectively high, the strain they place on the budgets of these families exacerbates the problem of pauperisation in this group.

While the variation in the proportion of over-indebted households broken down according to place of residence is not great, the level of income has a powerful influence on the occurrence of this phenomenon. Although higher-income households are understandably less often affected by over-indebtedness (as measured by the DSTI30 indicator) than others, these differences are not so large when it comes to subjective over-indebtedness. Over 36% of households with incomes of up to PLN 2,000 can be considered objectively over-indebted, while this is true of just under 8% of households on the best incomes in excess of PLN 6,000. Similar relationships between income and the proportion of over-indebted households have been established by Federico Ferretti and Daniela Vandone (2019) and by Luisa Anderloni and the latter (2008). This disproportion is considerably smaller where subjective over-indebtedness is concerned. The proportion of households in the lowest income group classified as over-indebted based on the BPL indicator is very high: over 84% are faced with this problem, which also affects nearly one-third of households whose incomes do not exceed PLN 6,000. These results shed new light on the social dimension of over-indebtedness: for households that are not particularly well-off, servicing debt must place consumption plans under serious strain – and hence determine their quality of life.

When broken down according to source of income/maintenance, the greatest proportion of over-indebted households is to be found among those supporting themselves from 'other' sources of income/maintenance (benefits, no regular income) and among disability pensioners and retirement pensioners. Blue-collar households are also heavily burdened with debt repayments: once these repayments are taken into account, almost 44% of them can be classified as below the poverty line. The smallest proportion of subjectively over-indebted households can be identified among those supporting themselves from self-employment and from white-collar work. Where the latter are concerned, the proportion of over-indebted households is the lowest no matter which indicator of over-indebtedness is applied. In the case of difficulties with over-indebtedness, the situation of the self-employed in Poland is better than in other European countries. This may be explained by the relatively low level of overall debt (including mortgage debt), which reduces the risk of financial difficulties occurring when there are extreme income fluctuations, to which this group of households is particularly exposed (Bartiloro et al., 2015).

The next two breakdowns that shape the profile of over-indebtedness are connected with debt type and with the number of credits and loans. The results reveal that the proportion of objectively over-indebted households (DSTI30) is greater among those who borrow from banks and credit unions than it is among those who borrow exclusively from non-bank sources. In the case of the BPL indicator, the proportion of over-indebted households is greater among those who borrow from loan companies and other non-bank lenders than it is among those who borrow from within the mainstream banking system. This would appear to suggest a feedback loop between poverty and the use of loan companies, which is consistent with the findings of research into the loan-company sector carried out by Iwona Jakubowska-Branicka (2018) and studies conducted at the international level (Carvalho et al., 2016; Melzer, 2011). Significantly. the highest values for both the DSTI30 and SB indicators apply to households with mixed debts (from bank and non-bank institutions simultaneously). This provides the grounds for asserting that combining different sources of borrowing can constitute a significant predictor of over-indebtedness.

In the case of the number of loans, the research results confirmed expectations: where they hold two or more loans, the proportion of households both objectively and subjectively over-indebted is more than twice as great when compared to households that possess only one credit or loan commitment.

What is important from the point of view of the aim of this study is to define the characteristics of people (households) classified as over-indebted. The results displayed in Table 4.3 were employed to create a profile (portrait) of over-indebted households. As before, the analysis was performed on the basis of the three fundamental indicators of over-indebtedness: DSTI30, BPL, and SB. Furthermore, to obtain a more complete picture of over-indebted households, a combination of two indicators was also taken into account (DSTI30 and SB, and BPL and SB), thus fusing the objective and subjective dimensions of the phenomenon under investigation.

Table 4.3 Structure of over-indebted households by selected socio-demographic features, economic features, and debt characteristics (%)

Item	*DSTI30*	*BPL*	*SB*	*DSTI30 and SB★*	*BPL and SB★*
Sex					
Woman	41.67	38.55	48.68	44.93	46.34
Man	58.33	61.45	51.32	55.07	53.66
Age range					
Up to 34	21.43	32.23	22.22	11.59	18.29
35–54	48.81	45.18	47.62	55.07	51.22
55+	29.76	22.59	30.16	33.33	30.49
Education					
Basic vocational or lower	23.21	29.52	24.87	28.99	36.59
Secondary	38.69	49.7	39.68	37.68	41.46
Tertiary	38.10	20.78	35.45	33.33	21.95
Number of people in household					
1	20.24	7.83	13.76	21.74	15.85
2	22.62	16.87	22.22	20.29	15.85
3	30.36	25.00	31.75	31.88	31.71
4	19.64	27.41	22.22	20.29	23.17
5+	7.14	22.89	10.05	5.80	13.41
Place of residence					
Rural	30.95	35.84	27.66	33.33	35.37
Small town	36.90	40.96	41.49	37.68	41.46
Large town	32.14	23.19	30.85	28.99	23.17
Income (PLN)					
Up to 2,000	33.33	38.86	21.71	36.23	41.46
(2,000–6,000]	55.36	59.94	57.14	50.72	57.32
Above 6,000	11.31	1.20	21.14	13.04	1.22
Source of income/maintenance					
Own firm/self-employed	14.29	12.65	12.17	15.94	10.98
Blue-collar work	30.36	45.48	35.45	33.33	41.46
White-collar work	27.38	15.36	24.87	21.74	14.63
Retirement pension or disability pension	20.24	16.87	20.11	23.19	20.73
Other	7.74	9.64	7.41	5.80	12.20
Debt type					
Bank	59.52	44.88	48.68	49.28	50.00
Non-bank	8.93	35.54	15.34	5.80	12.20
Mixed	31.55	19.58	35.98	44.93	37.80
Number of credits and loans					
1	39.88	57.83	40.21	28.99	39.02
2+	60.12	42.17	59.79	71.01	60.98

★ Households classified as over-indebted in subjective and objective terms at the same time.

Broken down by sex, men predominate among over-indebted households irrespective of the indicator used. The majority of over-indebted people are middle aged (35–54 years), which is consistent with the results from other countries (Michelangeli & Pietrunti, 2014; Ntsalaze & Ikhide, 2016). Indeed, approximately one-third of over-indebted households are those of respondents aged over 55. This proportion is generally higher for older people than for people from the youngest age group. In this respect, the structure under analysis differs from that in other European countries, where the proportion of over-indebted households (DSTI>30%) declines with age (Ferretti & Vandone, 2019). These results may demonstrate that, due to either high consumption aspirations or a relatively low level of wealth, consumption plans in Polish households in the older age ranges cannot be implemented without indebtedness, which increases the risk of the occurrence of over-indebtedness. It was only for the BPL indicator that a slightly different age profile was identified: here almost 33% of over-indebted households were constituted by people aged 34 and below, while for the oldest age range the proportion was not quite 23%. This proves that there is a significant group among young people whose debt repayment burden is high enough to lead to poverty.

Interestingly, the proportion of the youngest households (up to 34 years of age; and *only* those households) in the group of households that are subjectively and objectively over-indebted at the same time (as identified by DSTI30 and SB) falls significantly compared to when over-indebted households are identified only by DSTI30 or only by SB. This points to the conclusion that, to a greater extent than among other households, there exists a more distinct division among young people into two groups: one heavily burdened with debt that does not, however, represent a psychological burden, and one feeling over-indebted though their repayment amounts are not great in relation to their income. Overall, the results broken down by age confirm the observations made by Rachel Dwyer and her colleagues (2011), namely, that the psychological burden (stress) of debt grows with age.

People who have completed either secondary or tertiary education, that is, the groups of households that make most frequent use of the credit market, predominate among the over-indebted (Ferretti & Vandone, 2019). Only when applying the BPL indicator does the structure of over-indebtedness show a slightly different distribution of households in the breakdown of this characteristic. Applying BPL to education, it can be seen that the proportion of the poorest educated is greater than that of the best educated among over-indebted households. This is consistent with previous research, which established that, especially among vulnerable social groups, educational level (and the associated numeracy and ability to manage a budget) is correlated with over-indebtedness (French & McKillop, 2016).

Turning to household size, two-, three-, and four-person units predominate among over-indebted households, which is connected with the fact that these are the most numerous groups in the sample studied. As with the breakdowns discussed earlier, a slight difference in structure between the DSTI30 and BPL indicators is noticeable. The structure of over-indebtedness by place of residence is, in turn, relatively stable irrespective of the indicator applied.

Over half of the over-indebted households fall within the PLN 2,000–6,000 income range. The conducted analyses demonstrate that the nature of over-indebtedness is linked to income. The proportion of over-indebted households with the highest income is highest among the subjectively over-indebted (21.14%), while low-income households are most common among the over-indebted classified by the BPL indicator (38.86%) and the combined BPL and SB indicators (41.46%). This confirms Stefan Angel's (2017) finding that over-indebtedness is associated with low income and poverty.

Irrespective of the indicator adopted, those who derive their living from blue-collar or white-collar employment form the greatest proportion of the over-indebted (approximately 55–60% of the total). If retirement and disability pensioners are also included, these three groups make up the vast majority of over-indebted households in Poland. Considering the structure of households by source of income/maintenance, this is an unsurprising result. It is worth noting the increased disproportion in the structure of over-indebtedness in respect of the BPL indicator between households deriving a living from white-collar employment and those whose livelihood depends on blue-collar employment (when compared with the other indicators). This may reflect the different income positions of these two groups of households.

The structure of over-indebtedness by debt type reveals that more than 91% of those indebted according to DSTI30, and almost 85% of those indebted according to SB, use bank credit, which is either their only source of debt or represents one of the debt types they hold. Since it is basically the banks that are the major source of indebtedness for households, this structure is no surprise. Of the households that are impoverished once debt repayments are accounted for, one-third use non-bank sources of finance. If it is remembered that the clients of loan companies and other non-bank lenders are often less wealthy individuals who face restrictions in accessing the mainstream credit market, this is unsurprising (Kowalski & Wałęga, 2022). By turning to the non-bank market, they are often forced to accept worse credit terms, which has an impact on their subjective debt burden.

The final analytical breakdown is by the number of loans and credits a household possesses. As a rule, among over-indebted households the proportion of households with two or more credit obligations is higher than among those with only one. The difference is approximately 20 percentage points for DSTI30 and SB, while for the combined DSTI30 and SB indicator of over-indebtedness it is above 40 percentage points. The structure of over-indebtedness by the number of credits and loans appears somewhat different when it is determined using BPL: the majority of the households (57.83%) possess a single credit or loan, which can be explained by the income levels and creditworthiness of this group, which are on average lower.

In conclusion, it can be stated that the simultaneous application of two criteria (objective and subjective) for distinguishing over-indebted households in

Poland does not significantly change their profile and the conclusions drawn when compared to those distinguished on the basis of single indicators.

Respondents classified as over-indebted (according to at least one of the three indicators – DSTI30, BPL, or SB) are predominantly male, aged 35–54, and with higher education (Figure 4.2). The monthly income of the overwhelming proportion of over-indebted households is above PLN 2,000, but not higher than PLN 6,000. The majority of households possess a single loan, which in most cases is taken out to purchase a house or flat. The source of loan funds is exclusively a bank in the case of nearly half of over-indebted households.

There is no significant variation in the major motives for taking on debt among the households distinguished on the basis of the various indicators of over-indebtedness (Table 4.4). Regardless of whether the focus is on objective indebtedness according to the DSTI indicator, on subjective indebtedness, or on the set of households that meet both of the criteria applied, the most common and by far the most prominent reason for borrowing is to purchase a flat or to build a house. The order of the remaining, significant reasons for borrowing is also the same for the three indicators adopted: house or flat refurbishment, purchase of household and audio-visual appliances, and current consumption expenditure.

It is possible by analysing the frequency with which different reasons for borrowing are indicated to capture one of the significant differences between households over-indebted according to DSTI30 and those over-indebted according to the subjective indicator (SB). The latter indicate the purchase of a

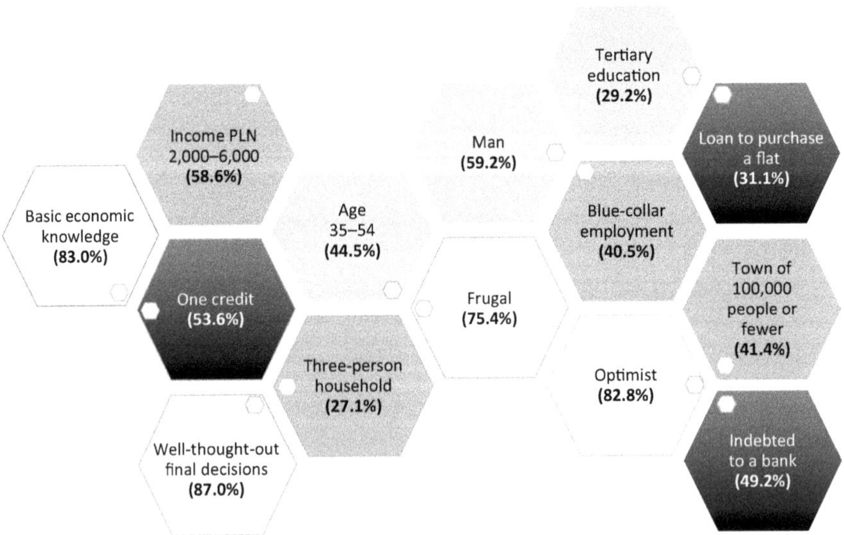

Figure 4.2 Representation of over-indebted households

Note: the bracketed data represent the greatest frequencies for households that satisfy the criteria for over-indebtedness on at least one of the indicators adopted (DSTI30, BPL, and SB).

Table 4.4 Over-indebted households' reasons for borrowing (%)

Item	*DSTI30*	*SB*	*BPL*	*DSTI30 and SB*	*BPL and SB*
Current consumption expenditure (e.g. food, clothes, shoes)	18.45	19.58	15.06	23.19	23.17
House/flat purchase, house construction	51.19	37.57	22.59	49.28	30.49
Car purchase	12.50	12.17	11.75	7.25	8.54
Purchase of household and audio-visual appliances	21.43	22.22	34.04	24.64	29.27
Purchase of household furnishings (other durables)	10.12	11.11	11.45	14.49	15.85
House or flat refurbishment	22.62	26.46	21.69	31.88	28.05
Medical treatment and convalescence	2.98	3.70	2.71	4.35	4.88
Holidays and leisure	1.19	0.53	1.20	0.00	0.00
Training and education	0.00	1.59	0.90	0.00	1.22
Weddings and other celebrations	2.38	2.12	1.51	4.35	2.44
Other	9.52	13.76	8.73	13.04	15.85

flat or house (construction of a house) far more rarely as a reason for borrowing than households that are objectively indebted (a difference in indications of almost 14 percentage points). Leaving aside unimportant and rarely indicated motives, this is the only very striking disproportion in the reasons for borrowing between households identified as over-indebted based on DSTI30 and SB. It may suggest that the nature of the motive and the decision associated with it – conscious, well-thought-out, and long-term – attenuates households' tendency to feel over-indebted.

Interestingly, although the four fundamental reasons for becoming indebted are repeated in the case of over-indebtedness according to the BPL indicator, the purchase of household and audio-visual appliances comes distinctly to the fore as the most prominent reason for borrowing in this group of households, while – when compared with other indicators – the frequency with which the purchase of a house or flat is indicated decreases considerably. This shift in emphasis is not surprising given the nature of the indicator analysed, which determines the characteristics of the households identified by means of it.

4.3 The spatial differentiation of over-indebtedness

The greatest proportion of households financing their expenditure from more than one source is to be found in the Lubelskie and Opolskie Voivodships (Figure 4.3), while the inhabitants of the Warmińsko-Mazurskie and Pomorskie Voivodships most often have only one loan. The great majority of households use bank loans, but there are some who borrow exclusively from non-banks – especially in the Podlaskie and Warmińsko-Mazurskie Voivodships. It would appear that this could be connected with the fact that there are fewer bank

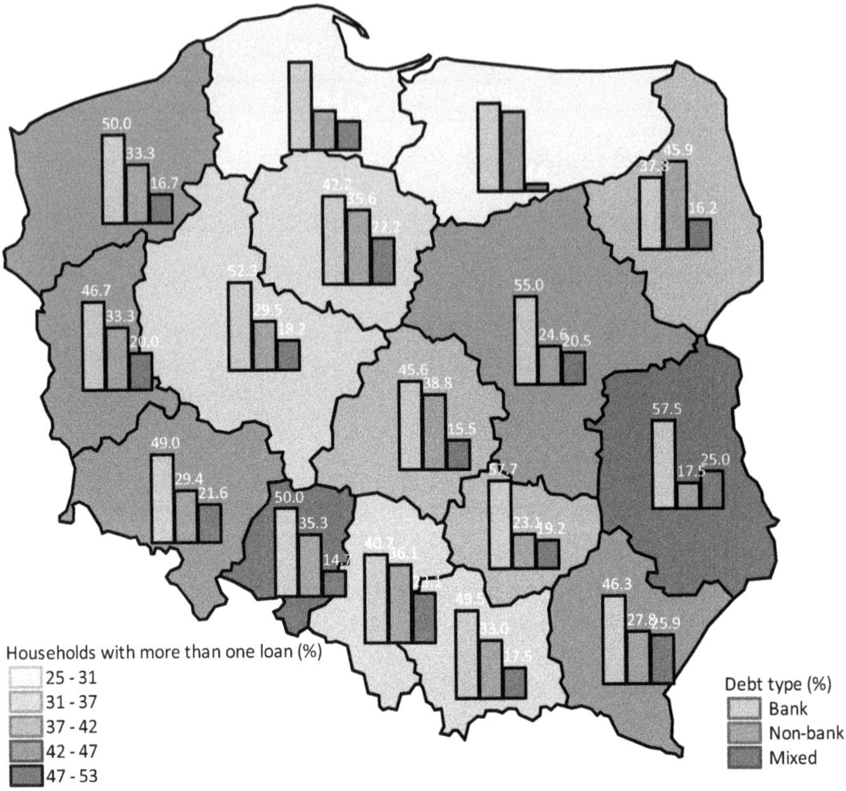

Figure 4.3 Selected characteristics of household debt by voivodship (%)

branches in the north-eastern voivodships, such that the greater use of non-bank loans, which are often available in the borrowers' immediate vicinity, can almost be said to be enforced. Mixed forms of debt are more often used by the inhabitants of the Podkarpackie and Lubelskie Voivodships compared to households in other voivodships.

Irrespective of the criteria used to distinguish the voivodships, there is considerable variation between them (coefficient of variation *Vs*>20%) with respect to the proportion of households classified as over-indebted (Table 4.5). The application of the Kruskal–Wallis test[5] confirms this observation for the DSTI30 indicator (H = 32.27; p = 0.0059) and the BPL indicator (H = 23.01; p = 0.0840). The result of the test, which is statistically significant, indicates that there are differences between the voivodships. However, the result of the test in respect of the SB indicator (H = 15.02; p = 0.4503) does not permit rejection of the hypothesis that variation among the voivodships in respect of this indicator is absent. The concordance produced when the voivodships are ranked by proportion of over-indebted households is also small. The greatest

Table 4.5 Proportion of over-indebted households by voivodship (%)

Voivodship	*DSTI30*	*SB*	*BPL*
Dolnośląskie	14.43	24.51	30.93
Kujawsko-Pomorskie	9.76	15.56	29.27
Lubelskie	22.22	12.50	36.11
Lubuskie	10.26	11.11	41.03
Łódzkie	13.27	15.53	38.78
Małopolskie	13.79	16.49	25.29
Mazowieckie	25.66	20.47	31.58
Opolskie	17.65	20.59	38.24
Podkarpackie	28.89	20.37	40.00
Podlaskie	2.86	8.11	45.71
Pomorskie	24.07	15.25	31.48
Śląskie	9.09	15.74	23.23
Świętokrzyskie	15.00	19.23	50.00
Warmińsko-Mazurskie	16.07	14.52	44.64
Wielkopolskie	21.52	18.18	31.65
Zachodniopomorskie	9.38	8.33	18.75

similarity is revealed when they are ranked according to the SB and DSTI30 indicators (Spearman's rank correlation coefficient = 0.49).

What are the similarities between the voivodships in respect of the proportion of over-indebted households according to objective and subjective indicators? If we search for those voivodships in which over-indebted households constitute a comparatively low proportion of indebted households – irrespective of the over-indebtedness indicator consulted – it is the Zachodniopomorskie Voivodship that comes to the fore. It registers below 20% on the DSTI, SB, and BPL indicators. From this perspective, a relatively small proportion of over-indebted households can also be found in the Śląskie, Kujawsko-Pomorskie, and Małopolskie Voivodships, while the Podkarpackie, Opolskie, Wielkopolskie, and Mazowieckie Voivodships are in the worst position in this respect. However, to formulate far-reaching conclusions about the similarities between voivodships in terms of the values of the indicators identifying over-indebted households requires more than a simple analysis of the data set out in Table 4.5. To that end, the voivodships were grouped by Ward's method (with Euclidean distance), and the *k*-means method was then applied. At this stage of the analysis, the unit of investigation is the voivodship. The proportion of households over-indebted according to the SB (X_1) indicator and the proportion of households over-indebted according to one of the objective indicators, DSTI30 or BPL (X_2), were taken as the diagnostic features characterising individual voivodships. The values of these variables were calculated on the basis of unit data and therefore denote the average values of the variables for the various voivodships. The adopted diagnostic features show sufficient variation (determined by a coefficient of variation of 24–44%) across the set of voivodships, which in the light of the adopted features demonstrates the diversity of these territorial divisions in terms of over-indebtedness. The variables are not, furthermore, strongly correlated with each other, because the values of the Pearson linear coefficients of correlation do not exceed r = 0.7. It can therefore be assumed that the absence of excessive correlation of features was satisfied as a criterion of variable selection. As the proposed variables are expressed as percentages, it was not necessary to normalise them.

The number of subsets of voivodships was defined on the basis of dendrograms following demarcation of a critical cut-off line (Figures 4.4 and 4.5).

By grouping voivodships using the DSTI30 and SB indicators, it was possible to distinguish the following groups of voivodships (Figure 4.4):

- Group 1: objective and subjective indicators at the 14–18% level with a predominance of households indebted in subjective terms,
- Group 2: the lowest levels of the indicators – the lowest proportion of over-indebted households,
- Group 3: the highest levels of the indicators (the largest number of over-indebted households) with a predominance of households over-indebted in objective terms.

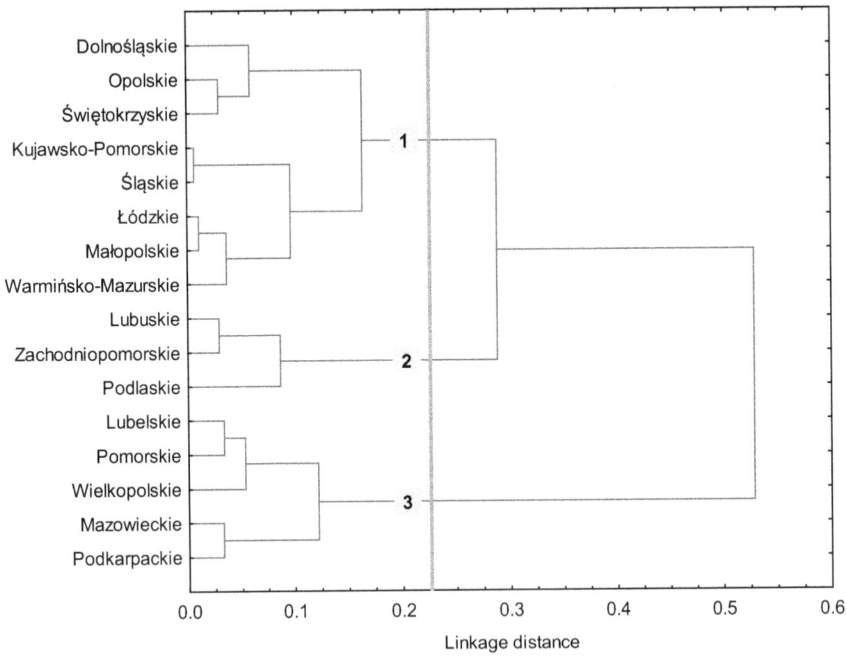

Figure 4.4 Results of voivodship grouping by Ward's method according to DSTI30 and SB

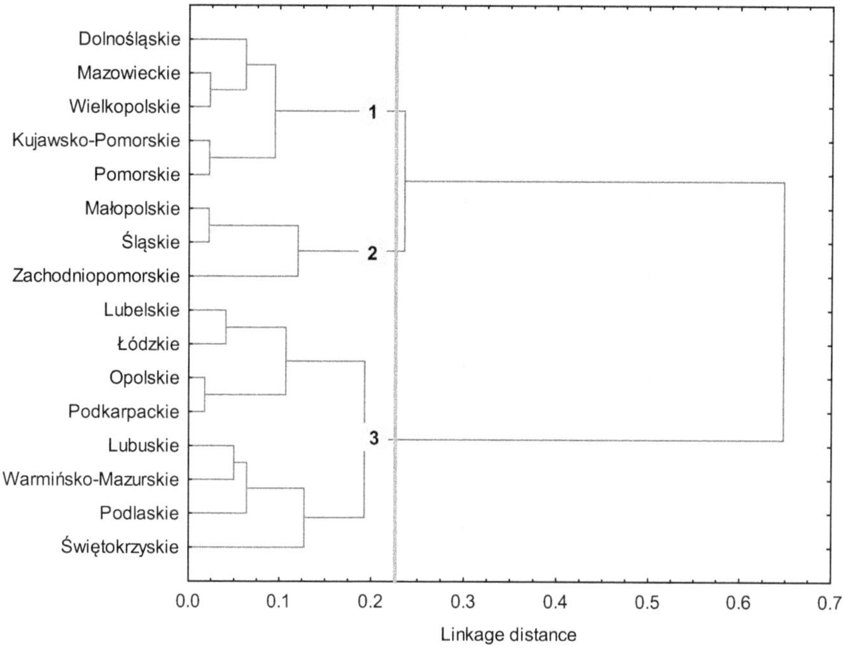

Figure 4.5 Results of voivodship grouping by Ward's method according to BPL and SB

The groups of voivodships distinguished using the BPL and SB indicators (Figure 4.5) differ in respect of the level of both of the indicators considered, with the proportion of over-indebted households according to the BPL indicator greater than the proportion of households over-indebted in subjective terms in each group. The second group (Małopolskie, Śląskie, Zachodniopomorskie) represents the voivodships with the lowest proportion of over-indebted households. The most numerous group (Group 3) is made up of the voivodships in the worst situation in respect of over-indebtedness: it is here that the largest percentage of over-indebted households is to be found.

It is noticeable when the similarity of the voivodship groupings is investigated using the method proposed by Marcin Salamaga (2010) that the subgroups produced show no significant similarity. An indicator at a level of 0.328 means that the results obtained from the grouping differ from each other.

To identify the voivodships similar in respect of over-indebtedness and its characteristics, the following features were considered during grouping: proportion of over-indebted households according to the SB indicator (X_1), proportion of over-indebted households according to the DSTI30 indicator (X_2), proportion of over-indebted households according to the BPL indicator (X_3), proportion of households with more than one credit or loan (X_4), proportion of households with non-bank loans (X_5), and the proportion of households with mixed loans (X_6).

By applying Ward's method, it is possible to distinguish three groups of voivodships that are similar in respect of over-indebtedness and its characteristics (Figure 4.6). Consequently, using the *k*-means method, an identical number of clusters were adopted. Both methods produced the same classification results in respect of group composition:[6]

- Group 1: Dolnośląskie (0.0442), Lubelskie (0.0548), Mazowieckie (0.0341), Opolskie (0.0654), Podkarpackie (0.0424), Pomorskie (0.0595), Świętokrzyskie (0.0646), and Wielkopolskie (0.04269);
- Group 2: Kujawsko-Pomorskie (0.0264), Małopolskie (0.0223), Śląskie (0.0195), and Zachodniopomorskie (0.0437);
- Group 3: Lubuskie (0.0483), Łódzkie (0.0265), Podlaskie (0.0460), and Warmińsko-Mazurskie (0.0688).

The distances between the centroids of the groups were determined in order to evaluate the distance between the groups obtained.[7] According to the calculations, clusters 1 and 3 (0.0869) are the farthest apart, and therefore the most dissimilar, while the voivodships in clusters 1 and 2 are the closest together (0.0774). Based on the calculations in Table 4.6, it can be observed that, when compared to the two other clusters, the greatest proportion of over-indebted households

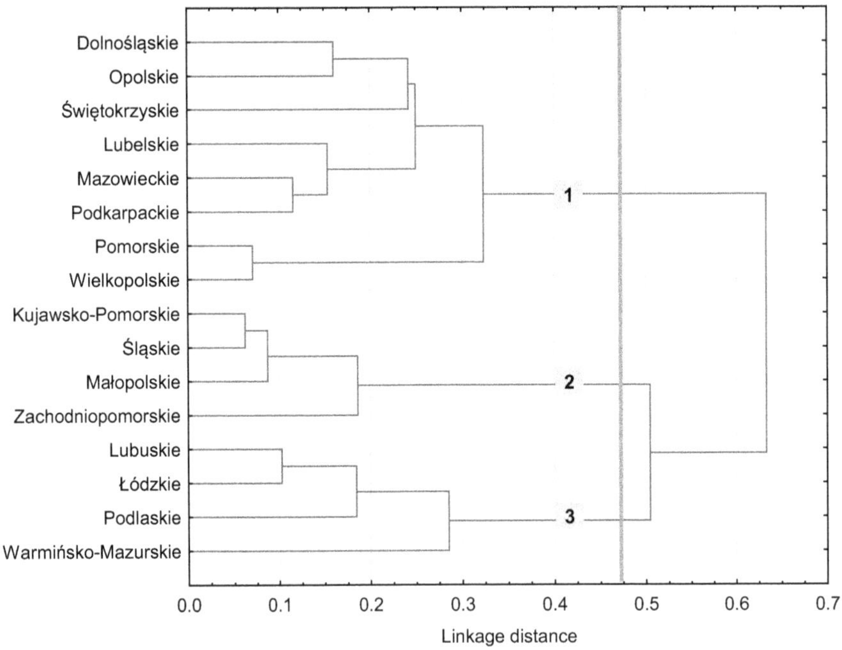

Figure 4.6 Results of voivodship grouping by Ward's method according to over-indebtedness and its characteristics

Table 4.6 Average values of variables in each cluster obtained by the *k*-means method

Item	*Cluster averages*		
	Group 1	*Group 2*	*Group 3*
SB (X_1)	0.1889	0.1403	0.1232
DSTI30 (X_2)	0.2118	0.1050	0.1061
BPL (X_3)	0.3625	0.2413	0.4254
More than one loan (X_4)	0.4158	0.3805	0.3763
Non-bank debt (X_5)	0.2657	0.3450	0.4082
Mixed debt (X_6)	0.2047	0.1989	0.1415

according to a subjective (SB) and an objective criterion (DSTI30) is to be found in the voivodships that form cluster 1. The greatest percentage of households that possess more than one loan, and the greatest percentage of those that have mixed forms of debt, is also to be found in this cluster. In turn, the voivodships that constitute cluster 3 have the greatest proportion of over-indebted households according to the BPL indicator and the greatest percentage of households in possession of non-bank debt. In this group, the remaining variables either reach the lowest average values or are very close to the minimum value (as in the case of DSTI30). The proportion of households over-indebted according to BPL and DSTI30 is smallest in the voivodships belonging to cluster 2.

Despite similarities in respect of over-indebtedness and its characteristics, the groups that emerged do not constitute spatially coherent regions formed of adjacent voivodships. Voivodships in south-east Poland, as well as in the western and northern parts of the country, are both to be found in the first group. Meanwhile, the third group is composed of voivodships from the north-eastern, central, and western areas of Poland. Group 2, for its part, is the most territorially diffuse in respect of the voivodships that make it up.

The question of the reasons for the spatial variation in the characteristics of household indebtedness is undoubtedly complicated. A deeper interpretation of the results would require the use of data on the supply side of the credit market in Poland, including aggregated data at the voivodship level, which is beyond the scope of the book.

4.4 Determinants of over-indebtedness: regression analysis

The factors that determine the risk of inclusion in the group of over-indebted households were identified with the aid of a logit model.[8] A dummy variable (dependent variable), whereby an over-indebted household is assigned a value of one, was constructed for this purpose. Two objective criteria (DSTI30 and BPL), and a subjective criterion (SB), for the identification of over-indebted households were considered, and a separate model was estimated for each. The proposed explanatory variables are set out in Table 4.7.

Table 4.7 Explanatory variables in the logit model for over-indebted households: economic, social, and behavioural factors

Name	*Designation of variable*	*Description*
Characteristics of households		
Income (PLN) (INC)	INC_1	Up to 2,000 (reference variable)
	INC_2	(2,000–4,000]
	INC_3	(4,000–6,000]
	INC_4	(6,000–8,000]
	INC_5	Above 8,000
Subjective assessment of financial situation (SAFS)	SAFS_1	We lack money for even basic, everyday expenditure (reference variable)
	SAFS_2	We have enough money for our basic needs and nothing more
	SAFS_3	We live frugally in order to meet at least our basic needs, and sometimes we succeed in putting some money aside for larger purchases
	SAFS_4	We have enough to satisfy all of our needs
	SAFS_5	We live very well and we can satisfy all of our needs – however sophisticated
Source of income/ maintenance (SI)	SI_1	Own firm/self-employed (reference variable)
	SI_2	Blue-collar work
	SI_3	White-collar work
	SI_4	Retirement pension or disability pension
	SI_5	Other
Number of loans (NL)	NL_1	1–4+
	NL_2	
	NL_3	
	NL_4	
Debt type (DT)	DT_1	Bank (reference variable)
	DT_2	Non-bank
	DT_3	Mixed
Number of people in household (NUM)	NUM_1	1–5+
	NUM_2	
	NUM_3	
	NUM_4	
	NUM_5	
Place of residence (RESID)	RESID_1	Rural (reference variable)
	RESID_2	Town with population of 100,000 or fewer
	RESID_3	Town with population of 100,000–500,000
	RESID_4	Town with population above 500,000
Socio-demographic characteristics of respondent		
Sex (SEX)	0	Woman
	1	Man

Name	*Designation of variable*	*Description*
Education (EDU)	EDU_1	Lower secondary at most (reference variable)
	EDU_2	Basic vocational
	EDU_3	Secondary vocational
	EDU_4	General secondary
	EDU_5	Tertiary
Age range (AGE)	AGE_1	Up to 34 (reference variable)
	AGE_2	35–54
	AGE_3	55+
Behavioural traits of respondent (BEH) – dummy variables		
Impulsive	BEH_1	I sometimes purchase on the spur of the moment (advertising, tastings, promotions)
Imitator	BEH_2	I sometimes purchase so as to have the same things as my friends
Original	BEH_3	I sometimes purchase so as to stand out from the crowd
Stylish	BEH_4	I sometimes purchase to follow fashion
Optimist	BEH_5	I am an optimist
Frugal	BEH_6	I am frugal
Knowledgeable	BEH_7	I have a basic knowledge of economics
Strategist	BEH_8	My financial decisions are usually very well thought out

The results of the parameter estimations for the logit models are displayed in Table 4.8. The results of the likelihood-ratio test indicate rejection of the hypothesis that the model's explanatory variables, when taken together, have no significant influence on the probability of inclusion in the group of over-indebted households. Although the values of the *pseudo-*R^2 coefficient, which in the case of the estimated models are 0.28, 0.26, and 0.26, respectively, are not high, they are acceptable in the case of these types of models when applied to individual data (Gruszczyński, 2012). The lack of significance returned by the Hosmer–Lemeshow test (in each of the models) allows us to conclude that the observed and predicted values are sufficiently close.[9] It may therefore be assumed that the models represent a good fit with the actual data.

As has been established, some of the proposed explanatory variables do not significantly influence the probability of inclusion in the group of over-indebted households. The use of stepwise backward regression made it possible to estimate model parameters in which all of the estimates are statistically significantly different from zero (the majority at the level of $p<0.05$). When their values are positive, the risk of over-indebtedness is greater.

Table 4.8 Results of parameter estimation of the logit model for the dependent variables identifying over-indebted households: economic, social, and behavioural factors (models 1–3)

Item	*Model 1 (DSTI30)*				*Model 2 (BPL)*				*Model 3 (SB)*			
	Coef.	*Std err*	*Wald*	*p-value*	*Coef.*	*Std err*	*Wald*	*p-value*	*Coef.*	*Std err*	*Wald*	*p-value*
Intercept	−1.219	0.495	6.067	0.014	2.685	0.619	18.817	0.000	2.436	0.532	20.926	0.000
INC	−0.775	0.102	57.348	0.000	–	–	–	–	–	–	–	–
SAFS	–	–	–	–	−0.532	0.090	34.690	0.000	−0.856	0.101	71.951	0.000
NL	0.855	0.134	40.579	0.000	–	–	–	–	0.586	0.097	36.694	0.000
DT_2	−2.212	0.313	50.089	0.000	–	–	–	–	−1.054	0.236	19.956	0.000
DT_3	−0.632	0.275	5.277	0.022	–	–	–	–	–	–	–	–
NUM	–	–	–	–	0.532	0.070	57.832	0.000	–	–	–	–
RESID	–	–	–	–	−0.145	0.084	2.986	0.084	–	–	–	–
SEX	–	–	–	–	–	–	–	–	−0.393	0.180	4.746	0.029
EDU	0.139	0.082	2.868	0.090	−0.456	0.066	48.325	0.000	–	–	–	–
AGE	–	–	–	–	−0.378	0.116	10.665	0.001	–	–	–	–
BEH_5	–	–	–	–	−0.403	0.219	3.390	0.066	−0.604	0.241	6.275	0.012
BEH_6	0.680	0.263	6.659	0.010	0.609	0.181	11.314	0.001	–	–	–	–
BEH_7	0.606	0.315	3.687	0.055	−0.466	0.215	4.704	0.030	−0.461	0.257	3.220	0.073
BEH_8	−0.978	0.324	9.125	0.003	–	–	–	–	−0.538	0.266	4.108	0.043
Statistics for the model												
Likelihood ratio	184.24; $p<0.001$				201.60; $p<0.001$				188.62; $p<0.001$			
Hosmer-Lemeshow test	2.36; $p = 0.968$				6.69; $p = 0.570$				3.53; $p = 0.831$			
AIC	734.12				1079.34				832.75			
Nagelkerke's R^2	0.2839				0.2551				0.2632			
Log (likelihood)	−358.06				−530.67				−408.37			

Note: designation of variables as in Table 4.7. Categorical variables are employed in the models, and dummy variables have been used in cases where a digit appears in the designation of a variable.

The risk of over-indebtedness rises with the number of loans (models 1 and 3), with the number of people in a household (model 2), and with educational level (model 1). The direction of the effect of these variables is consistent with expectations and with the findings of other authors (Chichaibelu & Waibel, 2017; Kempson, 2002).

The probability of becoming over-indebted declines, however, with an increase in income (model 1) and with an improvement in households' subjective assessments of their financial situation (SAFS – models 2 and 3), which also, indirectly, could be linked with the level of income obtained.[10] Where identification of over-indebted households based on the BPL indicator is concerned (model 2), the chance of inclusion in the group of over-indebted households also declines along with the size of the place of residence, the educational level, and the age of the respondent. An identical direction of effect in connection with a respondent's age and educational level can be found in the work of Lungile Ntsalaze and Sylvanus Ikhide (2016). When the subjective indicator is considered (model 3), the probability of over-indebtedness decreases if the respondent is male. Matthias Keese (2012) detected a greater subjective debt burden among women than among men.

The risk of inclusion in the group of over-indebted households is also dependent on debt type. Households with non-bank debt (DT_2) are less likely to be in the over-indebted group according to SB (model 3), while in the case of the DSTI30 indicator (model 1) those with mixed forms of debt (DT_3) are also less likely than households with bank debt to be in the over-indebted group of households.

Where respondents' behavioural traits are concerned, the probability of inclusion in the group of over-indebted households decreases when they declare that their financial decisions are well thought out – BEH_8 (models 1 and 3). As expected, prudent behaviour is a factor that reduces the risk of over-indebtedness. The BEH_5 variable (I am an optimist), which reduces the likelihood of being classified as subjectively over-indebted (model 3) and of being over-indebted according to the BPL indicator, has the same effect. The impact of the BEH_7 variable (I have a basic knowledge of economics) is, however, ambiguous. In the case of the DSTI index (model 1), it increases the likelihood of being classified as an over-indebted household, while in the case of BPL and SB it decreases this likelihood (models 2 and 3). The influence of the BEH_6 variable (I am frugal) on the likelihood of inclusion in the group of over-indebted households was a surprise, as declaring frugality (models 1 and 2) increases the risk of over-indebtedness.

In most cases, the categorical variables introduced in models 1–3, such as education, place of residence, and age, proved to have no significant influence on the risk of over-indebtedness. This could be linked to the nature of the variables, which capture the impact of these features on the dependent variable too comprehensively. To this end, all of the categorical variables were recoded as dummy variables and the parameters of three additional models (models 4–6) were estimated. Their parameter estimation results are presented in Table 4.9.

Table 4.9 Results of parameter estimation of the logit model for the dependent variables identifying over-indebted households: economic, social, and behavioural factors (models 4–6)

Item	*Model 4 (DSTI30)*				*Model 5 (BPL)*				*Model 6 (SB)*			
	Coef.	*Std err*	*Wald*	*p-value*	*Coef.*	*Std err*	*Wald*	*p-value*	*Coef.*	*Std err*	*Wald*	*p-value*
Intercept	−0.169	0.444	0.146	0.703	1.228	0.530	5.376	0.020	1.312	0.434	9.136	0.003
INC_2	−1.484	0.270	30.207	0.000	–	–	–	–	–	–	–	–
INC_3	−1.861	0.292	40.603	0.000	–	–	–	–	–	–	–	–
INC_4	−2.758	0.441	39.059	0.000	–	–	–	–	–	–	–	–
INC_5	−2.812	0.421	44.677	0.000	–	–	–	–	–	–	–	–
SAFS_2	–	–	–	–	0.832	0.380	4.789	0.029	–	–	–	–
SAFS_3	–	–	–	–	–	–	–	–	−1.360	0.339	16.146	0.000
SAFS_4	−0.462	0.208	4.921	0.027	−0.679	0.196	12.022	0.001	−2.333	0.345	45.809	0.000
SAFS_5	–	–	–	–	−1.002	0.221	20.479	0.000	−2.964	0.381	60.426	0.000
SI_3	–	–	–	–	−0.602	0.214	7.904	0.005	−0.455	0.213	4.560	0.033
SI_4	–	–	–	–	0.648	0.305	4.512	0.034	–	–	–	–
SI_5	–	–	–	–	1.325	0.383	11.961	0.001	0.639	0.361	3.136	0.077
NL_2	0.965	0.255	14.333	0.000	–	–	–	–	0.610	0.209	8.540	0.003
NL_3	2.146	0.366	34.441	0.000	–	–	–	–	1.211	0.288	17.664	0.000
NL_4+	2.236	0.446	25.121	0.000	0.646	0.365	3.131	0.077	1.967	0.356	30.479	0.000
DT_2	−2.303	0.325	50.099	0.000	–	–	–	–	−1.037	0.238	19.032	0.000
DT_3	−0.722	0.290	6.205	0.013	–	–	–	–	–	–	–	–
NUM_3	–	–	–	–	0.623	0.220	8.042	0.005	0.409	0.198	4.245	0.039
NUM_4	–	–	–	–	1.011	0.231	19.187	0.000	–	–	–	–
NUM_5+	–	–	–	–	2.112	0.283	55.785	0.000	–	–	–	–
RESID_2	−0.434	0.199	4.752	0.029	−0.292	0.167	3.076	0.079	–	–	–	–
RESID_4	–	–	–	–	−0.498	0.285	3.051	0.081	0.602	0.256	5.518	0.019
SEX	–	–	–	–	–	–	–	–	−0.378	0.183	4.281	0.039

EDU_2	–	–	–	–	−1.123	0.458	6.002	0.014	–	–	–	–
EDU_3	–	–	–	–	−1.407	0.448	9.842	0.002	–	–	–	–
EDU_4	–	–	–	–	−1.212	0.460	6.924	0.009	–	–	–	–
EDU_5	–	–	–	–	−2.112	0.460	21.076	0.000	–	–	–	–
AGE_2	0.352	0.202	3.030	0.082	−0.405	0.195	4.343	0.037	–	–	–	–
AGE_3	–	–	–	–	−1.094	0.296	13.657	0.000	–	–	–	–
BEH_3	–	–	–	–	−0.414	0.250	2.737	0.098	–	–	–	–
BEH_5	–	–	–	–	–	–	–	–	−0.562	0.250	5.065	0.024
BEH_6	0.607	0.263	5.338	0.021	0.541	0.192	7.950	0.005	–	–	–	–
BEH_7	0.802	0.326	6.034	0.014	−0.452	0.226	4.022	0.045	–	–	–	–
BEH_8	−1.068	0.324	10.867	0.001	–	–	–	–	−0.627	0.264	5.650	0.017
Statistics for the model												
Likelihood ratio	208.57; $p<0.01$				271.92; $p<0.01$				208.26; $p<0.01$			
Hosmer-Lemeshow test	10.86; $p = 0.210$				8.51; $p = 0.385$				10.08; $p = 0.259$			
AIC	723.79				1035.01				831.76			
Nagelkerke's R^2	0.3176				0.3326				0.2869			
Log (likelihood)	−345.89				−495.5				−400.88			

Note: designation of variables as in Table 4.7. Dummy variables are used in the models.

The likelihood-ratio test indicates that the model's explanatory variables, when taken together, have a significant influence on the risk of over-indebtedness. The values of the *pseudo*-R^2 coefficient are 0.32, 0.33, and 0.29, respectively, while the application of the Hosmer–Lemeshow test permits the conclusion that the observed and predicted values are sufficiently close. It may therefore be assumed that, as in the case of models 1–3, the models in Table 4.9 represent a good fit to the actual data.

As the number of people in a household increases, the risk of over-indebtedness also increases (model 5), although in this case the parameter values adjacent to the NUM variable (number of people in household) are only significant for households of three people and above. It would appear to follow logically that the pressure exerted on budgets by debt repayments is heavier among households with a greater number of household members (Keese, 2012). Three-person households are also more at risk (than the remaining household sizes) of inclusion in the group of over-indebted households based on the subjective indicator of over-indebtedness (model 6).

The greater the income, the smaller the risk of over-indebtedness (model 4) and, as a rule, the better a household views its financial situation, the less likely is over-indebtedness (SAFS_4 and SAFS_5 – models 5 and 6). If a household deems its needs are met, it can be expected that it will be less willing to increase its indebtedness, which in itself limits the risk of over-commitment. Yet for households that see their financial position as bad (we have enough money for our basic needs and nothing more – SAFS_2), the probability of inclusion in the group of objectively over-indebted households grows in comparison to those who lack the money for even basic expenditure (model 5). When compared to other households, those with sufficient money to satisfy all of their needs (SAFS_4 – model 4) have a smaller chance of being considered over-indebted.

Where households' sources of income/maintenance are concerned, the overall risk of over-indebtedness (models 5 and 6) is greater for households supporting themselves from other sources (benefits and other income not derived from employment) – especially compared to households that are self-employed or run their own firms. Households made up of retirement pensioners and disability pensioners are also at greater risk of over-indebtedness (model 5). Yet when compared to those supporting themselves by self-employment, households supporting themselves from white-collar employment (models 5 and 6) are less likely to be included in the group of over-indebted households.

As with models 1 and 3, the relationship whereby a rise in the number of credits increases the probability that a household will be classified as over-indebted was confirmed. In model 5, only households holding four or more credit obligations were at a greater risk of over-indebtedness. As with models 1 and 3, the influence of debt type on the risk of over-indebtedness was also confirmed.

The use of a set of dummy variables for categorical variables permits the statement that, in addition to the regularities identified in respect of income, subjective assessment of financial situation, number and type of loans, and number of people in a household, the influence of place of residence, educational level, and age on the risk of an excessive burden of debt is noticeable.

Households in towns of 100,000 people or fewer (models 4 and 5) and those in towns above 500,000 people (model 5) are less exposed to the risk of inclusion in the group of over-indebted households when compared to those in rural areas. It can be seen when over-indebtedness is identified with the aid of the SB indicator, however, that households in large towns above 500,000 people are more exposed to over-indebtedness than those in towns of other sizes.

In general, compared to those with at most a lower secondary education, the higher the educational level of the respondent, the lower the risk of over-indebtedness in a household (model 5). Elena Giarda detected a similar relationship (2013), although, for example, in the research done by Bezawit Beyene Chichaibelu and Hermann Waibel (2018), a lower level of education corresponded with less likelihood of over-indebtedness (this could, however, have been dictated by the characteristics of the credit markets in the countries studied, which meant that credit products were less available to less educated individuals). The effect of the influence of education on over-indebtedness may in reality, then, be uncertain. On the one hand, households with low levels of education more often encounter restrictions in accessing the credit market, and therefore are less likely to become over-committed. On the other hand, this is the group of households that is most often compelled by negative circumstances (e.g. unexpected expenditure) to go into debt and that possesses less knowledge of credit instruments (Schicks, 2014). This variable also has a multi-directional impact on over-indebtedness in the case of the best educated households. As a rule, better education tends to be accompanied by higher income levels, which in turn is a factor – in the light of the considerations in subsection 3.2 – that increases the level of indebtedness and thus the risk of over-indebtedness (Haq et al., 2018; Yilmazer & DeVaney, 2005). At the same time, a better overall level of education translates into a higher level of financial literacy (Cwynar et al., 2019), which, in the light of international studies, is a factor that limits the risk of over-indebtedness (Bridges & Disney, 2004; French & McKillop, 2016). What is more, the households of people with tertiary education display little susceptibility, at least in Poland, to indebtedness arising from limited rationality (Kośny, 2020).

Where the age profile of respondents is concerned, it may be noted that the probability of inclusion in the group of over-indebted households declines with age when over-indebtedness is identified with the aid of the BPL indicator (model 5). Tansel Yilmazer and Sharon A. DeVaney (2005), among others, confirmed the negative effect of age on over-indebtedness, but this was in respect of the DTA indicator. However, the households of those in the 35–54 age range are at greater risk of inclusion in the group of over-indebted households when the DSTI30 indicator is employed to identify over-indebtedness.

The impact of behavioural traits on the likelihood of classification as an over-indebted household is similar to that in models 1–3. Finally, it was noted that the BEH_3 variable had a negative effect (at a significance threshold of $p<0.1$) on the risk of over-indebtedness according to the BPL indicator (model 5).

4.5 Summary

Bearing in mind the limitations of the ways in which over-indebtedness can be measured, which are addressed in Chapter 3, both objective indicators (an indicator of the burden that debt repayment places on income with a threshold value of 30% – DSTI30, an indicator that refers to the poverty line – BPL, and debt repayment arrears stretching beyond 3 months – A3) and a subjective indicator (subjective debt burden – SB) were employed to assess the scale of over-indebtedness among households. This combination made it possible to exploit the strengths of each approach and thus, the authors believe, to better identify the problem of over-indebtedness in Poland.

The general observation to be made on the level of over-indebtedness in Poland is that it is not high: the proportion of households classified as over-indebted according to at least two indicators at the same time does not exceed 18%. Fewer than 2% of respondents declare that they face the most acute category of arrears in settling credit obligations: that of being over 3 months late with repayments. Indeed, these results are similar to those in other countries. Irrespective of whether DSTI greater than 30%, or households' feelings with regard to being overloaded with debt, is taken as the measure of over-indebtedness, households deemed to be over-committed constitute approximately 17% of the overall total. For one in three respondents, the consequence of debt repayment is to fall below the poverty line. This proportion appears quite high for the BPL indicator, but the result may have been encumbered by the limitations ascribed to income-based measures of poverty. In-depth analyses show that the objective and subjective groups of over-indebted households are largely disjointed.

The results of investigations into over-indebtedness lead to the conclusion that it is a phenomenon more often observed among households with particular socio-demographic and economic characteristics. One of the basic determinants of over-indebtedness is income. The greatest proportion of households classified both objectively and subjectively as over-indebted is to be found among people with the lowest incomes. Interestingly, subjective perceptions of over-indebtedness are mitigated only to a limited extent by a higher income.

Using the BPL indicator, it can be observed that over 84% of the poorest households are confronted with the problem of over-indebtedness. They are also individuals with low levels of education who live in households made up of four or more people. For these people, who are already in a difficult financial situation, over-indebtedness represents an additional burden.

Those in the 55+ age range – especially disability and retirement pensioners – make up a group that is particularly vulnerable to the difficulties entailed by an excessive debt burden (DSTI>30%). A significant proportion of one-person households (20–30%) was, moreover, classified as over-indebted (no matter the indicator adopted). There is no doubt that these households are less able to build up a surplus fund (understood as the difference between income and expenditure) compared to multi-person households, which leads to a significant burden of debt repayments on the household budget. Moreover, because they are left to face their debt alone (more so than other households), they are more likely to feel overwhelmed by its size.

The research made it possible to identify the most poorly educated households as those which, irrespective of the indicator employed, are at greatest risk of over-indebtedness. Here, the Polish case deviates from tendencies observed elsewhere in the world. This may indicate the special role of this debt as a means of balancing the household budget[11] and as a tool for satisfying consumption aspirations. These results illuminate the role played by financial knowledge and the ability to manage a household budget in countering over-indebtedness. This is also particularly important in the context of the remaining results: a higher proportion of over-indebted households according to BPL among those who use non-bank loans and those who hold two or more credit obligations.

The most common reasons for borrowing declared by households classified as over-indebted according to DSTI30 and SB are those associated with housing needs (construction, purchase, refurbishment). The second most frequent group of reasons is the purchase of durables (household and audio-visual appliances, cars). Both in relation to households over-indebted according to the other indicators and in relation to the overall number of indebted households (see subsection 2.4), the purchase of household and audio-visual appliances is a reason for borrowing that distinguishes households over-indebted according to the BPL indicator. This distribution of responses among the economically disadvantaged may suggest a substitution of debt-financed housing expenditure with purchases of durables, which are relatively more accessible due to their lower market value.

There is noticeable spatial variation in indicators of over-indebtedness and the features that characterise indebtedness, such as the number of loans and the type of debt. The attempt made to distinguish similar voivodships using cluster analysis made it possible to divide them into three groups that are internally coherent in respect of the features investigated. The resulting clusters do not, however, constitute any larger, spatially cohesive territorial units (regions). It would therefore be desirable to extend the analysis to include additional characteristics of the units (voivodships) under examination, such as the availability of lending institutions in terms of their spatial distribution.

The use of the logit model to assess the probability of households being classified as over-indebted confirmed the influence of income, number of loans, number of people in a household, age, education, place of residence, and subjective assessment of financial situation on the probability of classification as over-indebted. The direction of impact of the variables in the models is consistent with expectations and with the results of previous studies. With respect to behavioural traits, only some proved statistically significant, and the influence of some of these on over-indebtedness turned out to be contrary to theoretical assumptions. The caveat is that the results obtained for the behavioural variables, which were constructed on the basis of the respondents' direct declarations, are probably not fully reliable, as the question itself may have elicited answers that, rather than being true, spring from a desire to be viewed favourably by others and maintain self-esteem (social desirability bias). It would seem, therefore, that to properly capture the role of the psychological determinants of financial behaviour requires a specialised and more elaborate research methodology.

Notes

1 Cases in which lack of data made it impossible to calculate indicators of over-indebtedness were excluded from the analyses (for example, where a respondent did not state their income).

2 Subjective burden of debt is defined based on respondents' declarations of whether or not they feel over-indebted (1–Yes; 0–No). There are examples in the literature where over-indebtedness is assessed with the aid of categorical variables indicating the strength/intensity of over-indebtedness (CPEC, 2013; Keese, 2012; Lusardi et al., 2011).

3 Given the small percentage of respondents who are in arrears with debt repayments, it is not possible to conduct an in-depth analysis of this problem (including broken down into socio-economic categories). Respondents were most often in arrears in respect of rent payments, service charges, and utilities (38.5%). This is followed in declining order of frequency by arrears connected with other payments, such as goods deliveries, and repayment of credit and loan instalments. Even fewer respondents were in arrears in respect of TV, telephone, and Internet bills, while the fewest were in arrears in the payment of tax and social insurance contributions. The most frequent reasons given for late payment were unemployment or loss of employment (38%), followed by unforeseen events (29%) and reduced income (24%). Other researchers who have investigated this phenomenon as a cause of over-indebtedness have also found that unemployment and low income are among the primary causes of arrears (Anderloni & Vandone, 2008; CPEC, 2013; Haas, 2006). Similar conclusions as to types of repayment arrears emerge from *Diagnoza Społeczna* (Panek & Czapiński, 2015), which found that households were most often in arrears in respect of rent, gas, and electricity, and, to a lesser extent, mortgage repayments. It should be added, however, that the proportion of indebted households in mortgage arrears is comparatively small: in 2015, it was 1.4%.

4 Owing to the difference in the number of households from which it was possible to identify households over indebted in objective terms (DSTI, BPL) and subjective terms (SB), it is not possible to calculate the proportion of objectively indebted households among the subjectively over indebted households based on the data displayed in Table 4.1.

5 The Kruskal–Wallis test, which represents an alternative to analysis of variance and does not demand that a series of assumptions be satisfied, was employed because application of the Levene test for each of the variables analysed resulted in rejection of the null hypothesis of the equality of variances.

6 Distance from the centre of the cluster is given in brackets.

7 These distances were calculated according to the Euclidean metric.

8 Discussion of the model's assumptions, methods of parameter estimation, and testing can be found in, for instance, Gruszczyński (2012) and Maddala (2001).

9 In the original version of model 2, there were no grounds for rejecting the null hypothesis in the Hosmer–Lemeshow test. A decision was therefore taken to exclude the INC explanatory variable from this model, which supports the conclusion that it represents a good fit with the actual data.

10 Interpretations of model parameters are given on the *ceteris paribus* assumption.

11 The problem of low incomes and poverty among the most poorly educated is well known and has been confirmed in numerous studies.

References

Anderloni, L., & Vandone, D. (2008). *Households over-indebtedness in the economic literature* (Università degli Studi di Milano Working Paper No. 46). Milan: Università degli Studi di Milano.

Anderloni, L., & Vandone, D. (2011). Risk of over-indebtedness and behavioural factors. In C. Lucarelli & G. Brighetti (Eds.), *Risk tolerance in financial decision making* (pp. 113–132). London: Palgrave Macmillan.

Angel, S. (2017). *Persistent household over-indebtedness and exits from over-indebtedness. Evidence from EU-SILC.* mimeo.

Bartiloro, L., Michelangeli, V., & Rampazzi, C. (2015). *The vulnerability of indebted households during the crisis: Some evidence from the euro area.* Banca d'Italia, mimeo.

Betti, G., Dourmashkin, N., Rossi, M., & Ping Yin, Y. (2007). Consumer over-indebtedness in the EU: Measurement and characteristics. *Journal of Economic Studies, 34*(2), 136–156. https://doi.org/10.1108/01443580710745371

Blomgren, J., Maunula, N., & Hiilamo, H. (2016). Over-indebtedness and chronic disease: A linked register-based study of Finnish men and women during 1995–2010. *International Journal of Public Health, 61*(5), 535–544. https://doi.org/10.1007/s00038-015-0778-4

Bridges, S., & Disney, R. (2004). Use of credit and arrears on debt among low-income families in the United Kingdom. *Fiscal Studies, 25*(1), 1–25. https://doi.org/10.1111/j.1475-5890.2004.tb00094.x

Callegari, J., Liedgren, P., & Kullberg, C. (2020). Gendered debt – a scoping study review of research on debt acquisition and management in single and couple households. *European Journal of Social Work, 23*(5), 742–754. https://doi.org/10.1080/13691457.2019.1567467

Carvalho, L. S., Meier, S., & Wang, S. W. (2016). Poverty and economic decision-making: Evidence from changes in financial resources at payday. *American Economic Review, 106*(2), 260–284. https://doi.org/10.1257/aer.20140481

Chichaibelu, B. B., & Waibel, H. (2017). Borrowing from "Pui" to pay "Pom": Multiple borrowing and over-indebtedness in rural Thailand. *World Development, 98*, 338–350. https://doi.org/10.1016/j.worlddev.2017.04.032

Chichaibelu, B. B., & Waibel, H. (2018). Over-indebtedness and its persistence in rural households in Thailand and Vietnam. *Journal of Asian Economics, 56*, 1–23. https://doi.org/10.1016/j.asieco.2018.04.002

CPEC. (2013). *The over-indebtedness of European households: Updated mapping of the situation, nature and causes, effects and initiatives for alleviating its impact.* Berlin: Civic Consulting of the Consumer Policy Evaluation Consortium.

Cwynar, A., Cwynar, W., & Wais, K. (2019). Debt literacy and debt literacy self-assessment: The case of Poland. *Journal of Consumer Affairs, 53*(1), 24–57. https://doi.org/10.1111/joca.12190

D'Alessio, G., & Iezzi, S. (2013). Household over-indebtedness: Definition and measurement with Italian data. *Bank of Italy Occasional Paper, 149.* https://doi.org/10.2139/ssrn.2243578

Disney, R., Bridges, S., & Gathergood, J. (2008). *Drivers of over-indebtedness.* Nottingham: Centre for Policy Evaluation, The University of Nottingham.

Drentea, P., & Reynolds, J. R. (2012). Neither a borrower nor a lender be: The relative importance of debt and SES for mental health among older adults. *Journal of Aging and Health, 24*(4), 673–695. https://doi.org/10.1177/0898264311431304

Dwyer, R. E., McCloud, L., & Hodson, R. (2011). Youth debt, mastery, and self-esteem: Class-stratified effects of indebtedness on self-concept. *Social Science Research, 40*(3), 727–741. https://doi.org/10.1016/j.ssresearch.2011.02.001

Ferretti, F., & Vandone, D. (2019). *Personal debt in Europe: The EU financial market and consumer insolvency*. Cambridge: Cambridge University Press.

French, D., & McKillop, D. (2016). Financial literacy and over-indebtedness in low-income households. *International Review of Financial Analysis, 48*, 1–11. https://doi.org/10.1016/j.irfa.2016.08.004

Georgarakos, D., Lojschova, A., & Ward-Warmedinger, M. E. (2010). *Mortgage indebtedness and household financial distress* (ECB Working Paper No. 1156). Frankfurt am Main: European Central Bank. http://doi.org/10.2139/ssrn.1456593

Giarda, E. (2013). Persistency of financial distress amongst Italian households: Evidence from dynamic models for binary panel data. *Journal of Banking & Finance, 37*(9), 3425–3434. https://doi.org/10.1016/j.jbankfin.2013.05.005

Gruszczyński, M. (2012). *Empiryczne finanse przedsiębiorstw. Mikroekonometria finansowa*. Warszawa: Difin.

Haas, O. J. (2006). *Overindebtedness in Germany* (Working Paper No. 44). Geneva: International Labour Organization.

Haq, W., Ismail, N. A., & Satar, N. M. (2018). Investigation of household debt through multilevel multivariate analysis: Case of a developing country. *Journal of Reviews on Global Economics*, 7, 297–316. https://doi.org/10.6000/1929-7092.2018.07.26

Jakubowska-Branicka, I. (Ed.). (2018). *Rynek firm pożyczkowych w Polsce. Teoria i praktyka*. Warszawa: Polskie Towarzystwo Ekonomiczne.

Keese, M. (2012). Who feels constrained by high debt burdens? Subjective vs. objective measures of household debt. *Journal of Economic Psychology, 33*(1), 125–141. https://doi.org/10.1016/j.joep.2011.08.002

Kempson, E. (2002). *Over-indebtedness in Britain* [Report]. Bristol: Personal Finance Research Centre, University of Bristol.

Kośny, M. (2020). Economic resourcefulness as a determinant of saving and borrowing in Poland. *Post-Communist Economies, 32*(6), 793–812. https://doi.org/10.1080/14631377.2020.1727264

Kowalski, R., & Wałęga, G. (2022). Regulation of usury: Justification, consequences, and some lessons from Polish experiences. *Gospodarka Narodowa*, forthcoming.

Lusardi, A., Schneider, D. J., & Tufano, P. (2011). *Financially fragile households: Evidence and implications* (NBER Working Paper No. 17072). Cambridge, MA: National Bureau of Economic Research. https://doi.org/10.3386/w17072

Maddala, G. S. (2001). *Introduction to econometrics* (3rd ed.). Chichester: Wiley.

Melzer, B. T. (2011). The real costs of credit access: Evidence from the payday lending market. *The Quarterly Journal of Economics, 126*(1), 517–555. https://doi.org/10.1093/qje/qjq009

Michelangeli, V., & Pietrunti, M. (2014). A microsimulation model to evaluate Italian households' financial vulnerability. *International Journal of Microsimulation*, 7(3), 53–79. https://doi.org/10.34196/ijm.00107

Ntsalaze, L., & Ikhide, S. (2016). Household over-indebtedness: Understanding its extent and characteristics of those affected. *Journal of Social Sciences, 48*(1–2), 79–93. https://doi.org/10.1080/09718923.2016.11893573

Panek, T., & Czapiński, J. (2015). Warunki życia gospodarstw domowych. Warunki mieszkaniowe. Diagnoza Społeczna 2015. Warunki i jakość życia Polaków – Raport. *Contemporary Economics, 9*(4), 90–96. https://doi.org/10.5709/ce.1897-9254.182

Salamaga, M. (2010). Miernik podobieństwa grupowania obiektów. *Wiadomości Statystyczne, 55*(6), 1–11.

Sánchez-Martínez, M. T., Sanchez-Campillo, J., & Moreno-Herrero, D. (2016). Mortgage debt and household vulnerability: Evidence from Spain before and during the global financial crisis. *International Journal of Housing Markets and Analysis*, *9*(3), 400–420. https://doi.org/10.1108/IJHMA-07-2015-0038

Schicks, J. (2014). Over-indebtedness in microfinance – an empirical analysis of related factors on the borrower level. *World Development*, *54*, 301–324. https://doi.org/10.1016/j.worlddev.2013.08.009

Yilmazer, T., & DeVaney, S. A. (2005). Household debt over the life cycle. *Financial Services Review*, *14*, 285–304.

5 Household over-indebtedness and well-being

5.1 Evolution of the concept of well-being

Though it may seem that ideas such as well-being or quality of life are straightforward and can be grasped intuitively, they prove in the course of research to be far more complicated. This is no doubt due to the complexity of the phenomena they are employed to describe (Gasper, 2007). What is more, the question of need satisfaction is not addressed solely by economists, but also by sociologists, psychologists, doctors, and educators. As a result, different research categories, whose scope of meaning varies according to the academic discipline concerned, are deployed to analyse the extent to which the needs and wants of a population are satisfied. That these concepts are encountered in both academic and colloquial discourse only compounds the terminological, and also methodological, diversity (Sointu, 2005). The fact that only some authors define the ideas used in their research (or refer to the earlier formulations of other scholars), and some go no further than outlining the indicators (variables) that describe a given category, represents a further difficulty (Barcaccia et al., 2013; Dodge et al., 2012). The divergent understanding of different categories also results from the fact that they are correlated at various levels of aggregation.

Given these obstacles and the lack of coherent, universally applied definitions of the categories studied, it is necessary before assessing the economic well-being of over-indebted households to review the commonest concepts that refer to need satisfaction and to well-being. First of all, a review of the subject literature is presented that also takes into account the achievements of Polish researchers in recent years. However, a warning note must be sounded: the sheer number of academic works and the profusion of approaches mean the literature must be examined very selectively. Hence, rather than aspiring to a comprehensive treatment of the category in question (this could be the subject of a separate study), the review is intended to provide a theoretical platform for arguments introduced later in the book and for decisions regarding the terminology it employs.

Two spheres of human existence can be assessed within the broad concept of well-being (material and non-material) and two ways of evaluating each can be employed (objective and subjective). Research into well-being can, of course,

DOI: 10.4324/9781003254706-6

be restricted solely to material issues, but it can also – and today this is much more frequent – extend far beyond the purely material or economic realms, and, irrespective of the analytical field already adopted, refer to objective and subjective measures. Undoubtedly, the more diverse the set of (inevitably interpenetrating) variables used to assess a household's situation, the fuller and truer the picture of its well-being will be.

In the narrowest terms, well-being can be defined by objective measures of wealth, material possessions, and income. The contemporary notions closest in meaning to this interpretation are living conditions and standard of living. Indeed, well-being has historically been viewed primarily through the lens of income and consumption (Ackerman et al., 1997; Bywalec, 2007; Paim, 1995; Panek, 2015c). Even leaving aside the difficulties connected with the correct conceptualisation of income (current income is not the best research category if only because income fluctuates, while the categories of permanent income and earning capacity are problematic on account of the difficulty in accessing appropriate datasets), such a narrow approach to the well-being of households would today appear far from satisfactory. It ignores relational issues (reference to other individuals and to feelings associated with the resources possessed). To expand the research spectrum by taking them into account makes it possible to analyse economic well-being (also: material well-being) or financial well-being,[1] and marks a departure from the concept of 'living conditions' as simply a field for evaluating the economic domain of well-being.

The concept of economic well-being therefore comprises a number of more specific dimensions. These include the perceived adequacy of income measured by respondents' responses to questions about whether their current level of income is (was) sufficient to cover their expenditure. In accordance with the assumption of diminishing marginal utility, additional income has a non-linear influence on well-being, which means that well-being is much more strongly determined by income in poorer countries than it is in richer ones (Naess, 1999). Moreover, as David G. Myers and Ed Diener (1995) and Richard A. Easterlin (2001) state, people derive satisfaction not so much from wealth itself as from its relative size and from the ability to satisfy their own aspirations. Numerous studies have confirmed the major role played by the perceived adequacy of income (and not by income level as such) in the shaping of economic well-being (Burchardt, 2005; Cracolici et al., 2014; Grable et al., 2013; Plagnol & Easterlin, 2008; Zwierzchowski & Panek, 2020). The evaluation of economic well-being depends, then, not only on the extent to which needs have so far been satisfied but also on how this is perceived in relation to a reference group (social comparison gap, framing). Subjective assessment in this regard, which extends to cover overall well-being too, also depends on wealth at the macroeconomic level (Diener et al., 2010, 2013; Diener & Biswas-Diener, 2002; OECD, 2013; Veenhoven, 2007; Weimann et al., 2015).

Although it may seem that what matters for material well-being is not so much the objective situation in its individual dimensions but how they are evaluated – for example, satisfaction with standard of living (Sirgy, 2018), individual financial satisfaction (Vera-Toscano et al., 2006), or feelings of financial security (Howell et al., 2013; Sirgy, 2018) – this is a viewpoint that in its extreme form entails certain pitfalls. For it should not be forgotten that to use subjective indicators alone, which play an increasingly important role in studies of need satisfaction, including in Poland (Czapiński & Panek, 2015; GUS, 2014; Słaby, 2007), can lead to conclusions detached from the actual level of need satisfaction and from the level of real income an individual achieves. After all, it is possible to feel that one's needs are inadequately satisfied under objectively good conditions (and vice versa).

Regardless of whether in the assessment of material well-being the focus is on the objective or subjective dimension, it is not the most comprehensive category for describing the situation of households, which is also shaped by non-material aspects, such as interpersonal contacts (family, friends), health, and leisure time. To base the assessment on material factors alone can produce incorrect conclusions. An increase in income can, for example, be accompanied by fewer real opportunities to participate in social life, less leisure time, greater feelings of isolation and insecurity, or negative changes in consumption, such as compulsive (uncontrolled) shopping, alcohol, drugs, and gambling. The scholars who have addressed this in their work include Janusz Czapiński (2012), Des Gasper (2007), Urszula Grzega (2012), Bruce Headey and Mark Wooden (2004), Teresa Słaby (2011), and Ruut Veenhoven (2007). In taking the broadest view of the question of need satisfaction, which is one that analyses the non-material and non-economic dimensions of an individual's life situation, we begin to consider themes of quality of life and well-being[2] or, to be more precise, of overall well-being.

Economists did not begin to take a close interest in quality of life until the second half of the twentieth century (Dodge et al., 2012). Since then, though, both the concept and ways of measuring it have been in continuous development, and a number of research domains referring to *life satisfaction, subjective well-being,* and even the *economics of happiness* have sprung into being. Although studies often adopt a very broad range of understandings of well-being, so that analysis encompasses almost all aspects of human life (Betti et al., 2016; OECD, 2020), it is necessary to be aware that the imprecision of the concept, which de facto constitutes an umbrella term (Diener, 2009; Gasper, 2007), affords researchers considerable latitude of interpretation. Hence, emphasis is often distributed differently in respect of material and non-material aspects of life and of their investigation using objective and subjective measures. Furthermore, there is no uniform understanding of the different categories.

Instead of attempting to assess quality of life holistically, some scholars (Cracolici et al., 2014) adopt research designs that focus on its individual dimensions. The arguments in favour of this approach are that the selection of fields to be analysed can already be subject to arbitrariness and randomness (Ringen, 1995) and that the complexity of the phenomenon under investigation means that a piecemeal treatment of it is unavoidable. Although it would appear that basing analyses on factors of only one kind may place limits on a correct assessment of the actual situation, the legitimacy of the approach cannot be denied where there are objective difficulties in accessing extensive, comparable, and reliable datasets (Harkness, 2007).

Yet leaving aside the practical question of data availability, it should be made clear that quality of life should refer both to material well-being and to subjective well-being or happiness. Undoubtedly, one must agree with Angus Campbell (1976) that rather than depending exclusively on objective life circumstances, quality of life (as psychologists postulate) depends on individual life experiences and subjective assessments of them. Quality of life is not only, then, restricted to the material world (having), but also understood as the level of satisfaction of overall human needs, including spiritual needs (being) and social needs (doing and interacting). A similar approach to studying quality of life is presented by Walenty Ostasiewicz (2013) and Tomasz Zalega (2016), while Des Gasper (2010) conceives of well-being from the economic (utilitarian) perspective as a sequential story composed of three elements: from having resources and getting goods (inputs/resources), through to consumption (life content) and on to happiness (thoughts and feelings). At the same time, he points out that the terminology applied to levels of aggregation can be made more responsive to subtle variations by attributing the notion of well-being to individuals and of quality of life to societies.

Sarah White (2010) defines well-being in three dimensions (material, social, and relational) and investigates each in both subjective and objective terms. The material dimension is composed of objective categories, such as income, wealth, consumption, and employment, and subjective assessments of them. The social and relational dimensions, meanwhile, refer to objective and subjective aspects of education, capabilities, attitudes to life, cultural values, and health, as well as to personal, social, and political relationships, access to public goods, security, discrimination, and the quality of the natural environment. Well-being thus emerges as a combination of objective – external, observable, and independently verifiable – aspects of the environment in which individuals function and their subjective assessments and perceptions (Panek, 2015a). Similarly, Teresa Słaby (2011) argues that the mutual interaction of economic and psychological factors exerts an influence on quality of life, and that objective and subjective approaches complement each other. For his part, Tomasz Zalega (2016) takes the view that a complete picture of quality of life is only obtained by studying both its subjective and objective features. Tadeusz Borys (2015) is also an advocate of applying both of these dimensions to studies of quality of life (while also distinguishing them clearly for cognitive and analytical purposes). This is the approach taken, for example, in the *Diagnoza społeczna* (Social Diagnosis) panel study (Czapiński & Panek, 2015). The complementary, subjective-objective investigative apparatus is also apparent in research done by Statistics Poland (cf. GUS, 2014, 2020; Szukiełojć-Bieńkuńska, 2015) and the European Union Statistics on Income and Living Conditions (EU-SILC).

Stein Ringen (1995) proposes measuring well-being either directly or indirectly. Direct measurement is concerned with the effects of actions individuals take, such as expenditure, consumption, and lifestyle, while in indirect measurement the analysis is conducted from the perspective of income, resources, and capabilities, and the choices they enable. Elizabeth L. Pollard and Patrice D. Lee (2003) identify five dimensions of well-being – physical, psychological, cognitive, social, and economic – each of which is framed in terms of its positive and negative aspects. M. Joseph Sirgy (2018) proposes a different conceptualisation of the factors that shape quality of life by classifying them as either personal or contextual. The first group includes socio-demographic determinants (age, sex, education, marital status, household structure), financial resources (income, wealth, financial capabilities), personality traits (including self-esteem), aspirations and goals (including professional goals), social norms, values, beliefs, and mental associations (e.g. images of wealthy people: who is seen as being rich, the extent to which wealth is a condition for need satisfaction, attitude to materialism), and lifestyle and habits (including habits of consumption). In addition to those concerned with the economy (rate of unemployment, inflation, economic growth), the group of contextual factors includes the social context (households' assessment of their own standard of living compared to that of other households) and adaptation (how income expectations are adapted by changing circumstances). Tomasz Panek (2015a) also proposes examining subjective well-being from personal and social perspectives.

As stated earlier, the ambiguity of the notion of quality of life permits a great deal of arbitrariness in the selection of variables to describe it. Even if quality of life is accepted as the category that most completely describes the situation of a household or individual, to draw upon a shorter or longer list of both the objective and subjective elements that make up an overall concept of quality of life is not the only solution. Measuring it exclusively by means of objective indicators, most often in the form of natural measures of intensity (quantitative or evaluative), is characteristic, for example, of the Scandinavian approach (Panek, 2015b). Today, however, due to the limitations of the objective approach, a research current relating to subjective well-being is developing (Diener, 2009; OECD, 2020). In this approach, an individual's experience or perception of how well they live is taken as the criterion of quality of life. Given that experiences or perceptions are not directly observable, self-assessments of these unobserved categories are often used as substitutes. Subjective quality of life can be equated with what people feel, how they function (at the individual and social levels), and how they evaluate their lives overall (Panek, 2015c). This approach thus combines emotional experiences (happiness, anxiety, anger) with a sense of possessing certain skills and being able to use them, and with a sense of connectedness with the environment. Yet a person's overall assessment of their life is the result of comparing the life they live now with the best possible life they could live. At its core, subjective well-being is composed of various domains, including – in addition to material well-being – (self-)satisfaction with work, health, free time, family, and social relations (Sirgy, 2018; van Praag et al., 2003).

To summarise, the approaches to quality of life encountered in the literature can be classified as subjective, objective, and mixed – the last being an approach that combines subjective and objective elements (Naess, 1999; Veenhoven, 2007). The three approaches are linked by the fact that they all take account of both positive and negative aspects of life (Myers & Diener, 1995; Naess, 1999; Pollard & Lee, 2003). However, these approaches can be distinct (Headey & Wooden, 2004). If quality of life is considered holistically, then it is justified to refer to both positive (well-feeling) and negative (unhappiness, ill-being) feelings. Teresa Słaby (2011) draws attention to the need for research into quality of life to take account, for example, of poverty, deprivation, unemployment, loss of physical and mental health, detrimental demographic changes, the state of the natural and anthropogenic environments, and social exclusion. According to Petra Böhnke (2008), however, evaluation of life satisfaction should, in addition to individual living conditions, such as income, labour market issues, health, and social relations, also take into account the quality of the societies in which individuals live. In this respect, she indicates the need to consider individual trust in political institutions, evaluate the quality of public services, and take account of social capital.

The plethora of approaches to quality of life, which results from the sheer breadth of the category, is also reflected in the scope of the data acquired (of life domains assessed) by institutions tasked with the multifaceted evaluation of the situation of households in an international comparative perspective. The approaches applied under the auspices of the European System of Social Indicators (EUSI) and the European Statistical System (ESS), and by the Organisation for Economic Cooperation and Development (OECD), are worthy of special mention in this regard.

Regina Berger-Schmitt and Heinz-Herbert Noll (2000) presented their proposal for domains and sub-domains of the quality of life category in the form of the EUSI. Each domain is linked to social policy goals, and indicators that serve to measure their implementation are described in a number of sub-domains or goal dimensions. The first major category includes goals concerning social and economic progress and improvements in peoples' economic well-being and quality of life, including promoting a high level of employment and reducing unemployment, developing education and professional training, promoting research and technical development, strengthening healthcare and social protection systems, improving public safety and combatting crime, increasing the availability of public transport, and care for the natural environment. The second category is about strengthening economic and social cohesion, including reducing disparities and reinforcing social bonds between regions and social groups, while the third is connected with sustainability. Here, the notion of quality of life is understood in very broad terms and includes not only individuals' objective and subjective well-being but also the quality of life of society as defined by its social integration and sustainability (Panek, 2016).

The ESS approach to measuring quality of life, which is based on Regina Berger-Schmitt and Heinz-Herbert Noll's proposal mentioned earlier (Panek, 2015b), provides for nine domains (fields) of quality of life: (1) material living conditions (income, material conditions, consumption), (2) health, (3) education,

(4) productive or main activity, (5) leisure and social interactions, (6) economic security and physical safety, (7) governance and basic rights, (8) natural and living environment, and (9) overall experience of life (Eurostat, 2020).

For its part, the OECD (2011, 2020) proposed a system for measuring well-being and applied it in the comparative analysis of quality of life in the states that are its members. It specifies 11 domains of well-being, of which some define material living conditions (economic well-being): (1) income and wealth, (2) jobs and earnings, (3) housing, and some define quality of life (non-monetary attributes of individuals that shape their opportunities and life chances), (4) health, (5) work and life balance, (6) education and skills, (7) social connections, (8) civic engagement and governance, (9) environmental quality, (10) personal security, and (11) subjective well-being.

Concluding our deliberations on the conceptual scope and methodology of research into well-being, and given the diversity of existing approaches to this category, it is now necessary to clearly outline the research position taken in this book.

First, it is consistent with the position taken by Barbara Podolec (2014), who argues that well-being represents a multifaceted research category that encompasses the material sphere of the life of a population, the non-material spheres of life, and the degree of satisfaction and contentment with particular aspects of life. This approach differs from one in which well-being is reduced to the objective dimension (Borys, 2015; Pawełek, 2000; Słaby, 2007). For it would seem that to observe only through the lens of objective indicators means eliminating too many levels of analysis – especially when contemporary studies of well-being are strongly influenced by interpenetrating theories and findings derived from psychology and economics (Easterlin, 2006; Słaby, 2011). At the same time, the view that the disagreements over the concepts applied in a particular approach to analysing quality of life (subjective or objective) are largely illusory, since they concern semantics, is wholly to be commended (Bywalec, 1991; Howell & Howell, 2008).

Recognising the need to go far beyond the purely material and objective sphere when assessing the situation of individuals (households), this is the understanding of well-being adopted in the remainder of this book. In stating this, it should be noted that due to the subject matter and research purpose of this study, it was necessary to narrow the space for assessing the well-being of indebted households to the material and financial dimensions (in both subjective and objective terms), that is, to the perspective determined by the constituents of economic well-being.

5.2 Definition of economic well-being

Rather like other constructs associated with well-being, economic well-being (also financial well-being), has been investigated not only by economists but also by specialists in financial consulting, developmental psychology, consumer decision-making, and the marketing of services. And again, rather as in the case of quality of life, no uniform definition and means of measurement has yet been formulated for the category. Original and entirely new definitions, as well as modified definitions, of economic well-being have, however, appeared in some studies (Table 5.1), while in others, despite its use as one of the major variables, no direct definition of it has been provided (cf. Guo et al., 2013; O'Neill et al., 2005; Prawitz et al., 2006; Shim et al., 2009).

Among the approaches taken in investigations of financial well-being is to analyse it – either largely or exclusively – using objective indicators that refer to the financial situation of a person or a household (e.g. income or debt to income). In this understanding, financial indicators are thus objective measures of financial well-being and no account is taken of subjective variables (Greninger et al., 1996).

Given that objective indicators only measure aspects of a household's or individual's financial condition, which can produce a misleading picture as a result of overlooking the subjective assessment of the situation (Prawitz et al., 2006), many studies have placed emphasis on a subjective approach to defining financial well-being (Brüggen et al., 2017; Gutter & Copur, 2011; Kim et al., 2003; O'Neill et al., 2005; Vosloo et al., 2014). Subjective measures make it possible to examine the ways in which people perceive and react to their own financial situation, as well as to explore feelings of financial confidence and security (Norvilitis et al., 2003). In this case, subjective assessments of a household's or individual's financial condition, including assets, debt and savings (Xiao et al., 2014), or their financial literacy and inclination to plan, are taken into account (Lee et al., 2020). Subjective financial well-being is examined using questions concerning respondents' feelings about, and perceptions of, their own financial situation. It can also be defined by reference to the financial shocks households experience (Handayani et al., 2016).

Table 5.1 Selected definitions of economic well-being (financial well-being)

Brüggen et al. (2017)	Financial well-being is the perception of being able to sustain current and anticipated desired living standards and financial freedom
CFPB (2015)	Financial well-being implies having financial security and financial freedom of choice, in the present and in the future
Kempson and Poppe (2018)	The extent to which someone is able to meet all their current commitments and needs comfortably, and has the financial resilience to maintain this in the future
Kim et al. (2003)	Financial well-being is a function of individual characteristics, financial behaviours, and financial stressor events
Rath and Harter (2010)	Financial well-being is about effectively managing your economic life
Vosloo et al. (2014)	Financial well-being can be defined as objective and subjective aspects of a person's financial situation evaluated against standards of comparison to form a person's opinion of their financial situation

Financial well-being has also sometimes been treated as a concept that covers both objective and subjective fields of evaluation, which, however, different studies represent using different sets of indicators. Nancy M. Porter and E. Thomas Garman (1992), for example, employ quantitative indicators of financial situation (income level, stage in the financial life cycle, number of children, and selected financial behaviours) as objective measures of financial well-being, and perceive satisfaction with standard of living, savings, and investments (in respect of aspirations, expectations, reference group, and past experiences) as a subjective measure. For Ragna B. Garðarsdóttir and Helga Dittmar (2012), the objective aspects of financial well-being are income and amount of debt, and the subjective aspects are money management skills, tendency to spend, compulsive buying, and financial worry. Research into the financial well-being of young people undertaken by Soyeon Shim and her team (2009) employed amount of debt as an objective measure, and contentment with financial situation and coping with financial difficulties as subjective indicators.

On the basis of a review of more than 40 articles on the financial well-being of emerging adults (aged 18–29), Angela Sorgente and Margherita Lanz (2017) defined the notion as a good and positive financial condition that has an objective and a subjective side (Figure 5.1). The objective side (defined as economic well-being)[3] is specified by an individual's cash flow balance and by the resources they already possess, such as tangible assets, savings, health insurance, and employee benefits. Subjective financial well-being, on the other hand, is composed of individuals' experiences in respect of their financial condition and their assessments of it. These evaluations tend to be emotional when they concern positive feelings (security, control) or negative feelings (worry, distress) caused by personal financial experiences. Subjective financial well-being (experiences and assessments) is linked with both the past and the future.

A comprehensive approach to defining financial well-being was also proposed by Elaine Kempson and Christian Poppe (2018) in a study conducted on a group of almost 2,000 adult inhabitants of Norway. Three groups of variables, which include aspects of the socio-economic environment, financial confidence

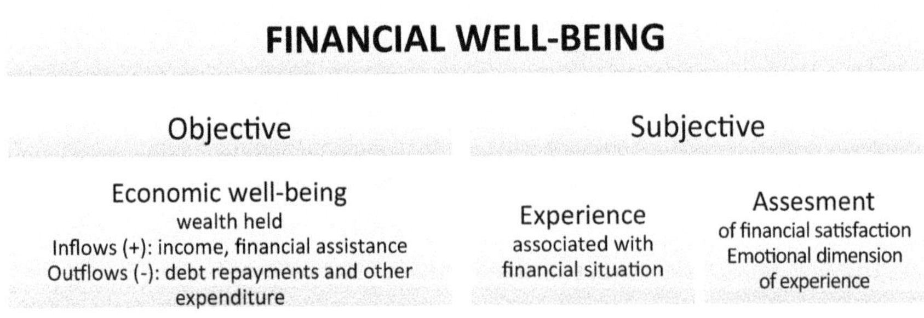

Figure 5.1 Elements of financial well-being

Source: after Sorgente and Lanz (2017).

and control, and money-use behaviours, exert the most significant and direct influence on financial well-being (Figure 5.2). Kempson and Poppe offer a broad definition of the socio-economic environment, which includes age, sex, income, changes in income and expenditure, labour market status, educational level, housing type, availability of family or friends able to help out financially if needed, and whether respondents talked to parents about managing money or saving when they were children. In their study, the money-use behaviours with the strongest impact on well-being are spending restraint, active saving for future financial resilience, and, primarily, restrained consumer borrowing. The latter behaviour involves financing current expenditure from loans, rolling over debts, and running an overdraft.

Money management behaviours, however, which include financial attitudes, financial knowledge and experience, and personality traits, exert only an indirect

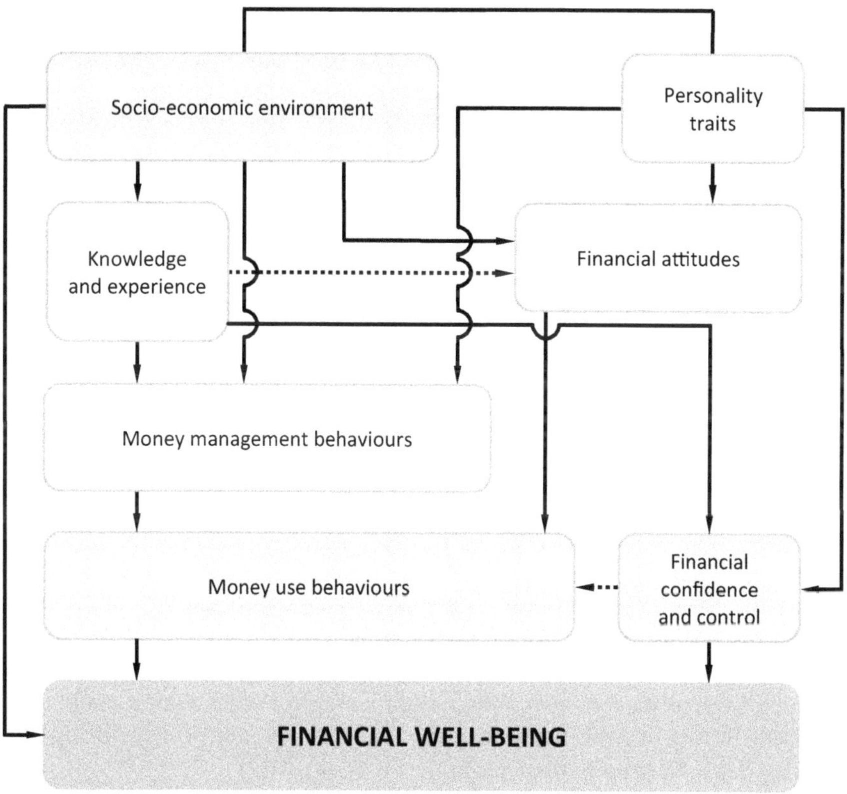

Figure 5.2 Financial well-being and its determinants

Note: the shaded blocks indicate groups of variables that have a direct influence on financial well-being, while the dotted lines indicate weak interactions between the blocks in the figure.

Source: Kempson and Poppe (2018).

influence on well-being. Such behaviours involve the ability to plan, analyse, and monitor financial flows and to take informed financial decisions based on the information gathered.

In summary, it would appear that if the aim is to achieve a comprehensive assessment of the financial (material) situation of an individual (household), it is most appropriate in the study of financial well-being to adopt an approach that incorporates both objective and subjective aspects. Not surprisingly, this conclusion is identical to that drawn in respect of research into quality of life. Subjective measures provide information that objective measures do not. They help the researcher to determine not only how the financial condition of a household is perceived but also how it affects individuals and families (Prawitz et al., 2006). The fact that people in similar financial situations according to objective measures such as wealth or income can have different impressions of their financial well-being is a further argument in support of taking subjective factors into consideration. Indeed, the majority of studies emphasise the importance of financial behaviours (cf. Joo & Grable, 2004) in influencing subjective assessments of financial well-being. Respondents may also have a different assessment of their financial situation on account of their family circumstances (Malone et al., 2010) or attitude to risk (Aboagye & Jung, 2018).

5.3 The impact of over-indebtedness on well-being: a theoretical framework

In the literature that analyses well-being, the prevailing focus of research is on the role played by income and wealth (Diener & Biswas-Diener, 2002; Howell & Howell, 2008; Kahneman et al., 1999). The impact of these factors has been widely discussed for many years at both the macroeconomic and microeconomic levels. Interestingly, some researchers take the position that indebtedness has a more powerful influence on well-being than income, which has traditionally been seen as the primary factor (Drentea & Lavrakas, 2000; Drentea & Reynolds, 2012).

The influence of indebtedness on well-being is multidimensional in the sense that it can be observed in connection with a number of its aspects, including those associated with economic and psychological well-being, with physical health, and with social relations – particularly family relations.

The general thrust of the findings available in the subject literature is that indebtedness has a powerful negative influence on quality of life. In fact, research suggests that the psychological dimension of indebtedness could have a greater impact on well-being than the objective amount of debt (Bridges & Disney, 2010; Selenko & Batinic, 2011; Tay et al., 2017).

This does not mean, of course, that indebtedness cannot have a positive effect on well-being. First, thanks to the increased purchasing power it affords, access to credit improves households' subjective financial well-being. With access to credit instruments, it is easier for households to limit the negative consequences of financial shocks in the short term (Clayton et al., 2015; Morse, 2011).

Second, borrowing enables households to finance the expenditure they regard as important. In this way, thanks to the faster realisation of goals (buying a flat or durable goods, education) and to spillover effects, it is possible to improve quality of life in other areas (Berger & Houle, 2016; Nissen et al., 2019; Tay et al., 2017). However, as Claudia Frade and Catarina Lopes (2009) contend, financial well-being and, in its wake, quality of life only improve up to a certain level of indebtedness. And, when the indebtedness grows too big, financial pressure and stress appear. Moreover, when high debt repayments place too great a burden on current consumption expenditure and impede need satisfaction, this has an economic dimension. Declan French and Donal McKillop (2017), for example, point to the deterioration in diet that results when credit obligations must be met. The subjective burden of debt is especially heavy when income is falling and a household takes a pessimistic view of its own financial situation (Brown et al., 2005; Drentea, 2000).

The positive effects of access to credit may, therefore, be attenuated by over-indebtedness. The appearance of problems in servicing debt consumes the attention of household members and leads to a decline in their quality of life. Yet this does not have to be connected with financial problems. For a household, debt is already a psychological burden in itself – one that definitely has a negative impact both on financial well-being and on quality of life. It should be noted, however, that the force of these dependencies is shaped by households' individual attitudes to borrowing and risk-taking, their patterns of financial behaviour, and how far they are satisfied with their own financial situation (Norvilitis et al., 2003; Rutherford & Fox, 2010; Selenko & Batinic, 2011). Furthermore, feedback effects, whereby the desire of households to take on debt diminishes when they take a positive view of their financial situation, cannot be ruled out in the relationships between financial well-being and indebtedness (Handayani et al., 2016).

Numerous studies have found that indebtedness has a negative impact on both mental and physical health (Blomgren et al., 2016; Drentea & Lavrakas, 2000; Richardson et al., 2013).[4] Members of indebted households are more likely to worry and feel anger and distress (Bridges & Disney, 2010; Drentea, 2000; Drentea & Reynolds, 2012; Hodson et al., 2014; Richardson et al., 2017; Selenko & Batinic, 2011) and to suffer from stress, depression (Gathergood, 2012; Hiilamo & Grundy, 2020; Hojman et al., 2016; Holmgren et al., 2019; Sweet et al., 2013; Zurlo et al., 2014), and mental illnesses in general (Dackehag et al., 2019). Furthermore, over-indebtedness also increases proneness to post-natal depression (Reading & Reynolds, 2001), and sometimes the mental stress associated with unpaid debt is so great that it leads to suicidal thoughts (Meltzer et al., 2011; Richardson et al., 2013; Turunen & Hiilamo, 2014).

A variety of studies have established that people who are over-indebted face problems with their health (Cannuscio et al., 2012), such as higher blood pressure (Sweet et al., 2013), headaches, and cardiovascular disease (Georgiades et al., 2009). They are also more likely to use stimulants such as cigarettes, alcohol, or drugs (Meltzer et al., 2013; Richardson et al., 2013, 2017). Yet work done by Carla Prentice and her associates (2017) indicates that financial difficulties can reduce disposable income and so lower demand for unhealthy goods of this kind. Meanwhile, Jacqueline Warth and her colleagues (2019) detected a significant correlation between over-indebtedness and sleep problems. For their part, Jenni Blomgren and her team (2017) demonstrated that over-indebtedness is associated with a higher risk of retiring on a disability pension due to chronic disease.

It should not be forgotten when analysing the relationships between objective indebtedness (expressed with the aid of a relative indicator) and quality of life that its level must be interpreted individually, since the subjective burden of indebtedness is conditioned by a variety of factors (cf. subsection 3.3). One of them is whether or not a household possesses financial assets (resources) that act as a kind of buffer to protect it against the excessive stress associated with holding debt (Garrett & James III, 2013). In addition to the nominal income level, moreover, which is also a factor mitigating the negative impact of debt on subjectively perceived financial well-being, the type of debt held is of great importance. A different kind of psychological burden is attached to each type of credit (mortgages, consumer credit, credit cards), and therefore the strength of its influence on households' quality of life depends indirectly on the reason for borrowing (Brown et al., 2005; Drentea, 2000; Georgarakos et al., 2010). Research shows that student loans (Aboagye & Jung, 2018), unsecured loans (Zurlo et al., 2014), and short-term loans (Berger et al., 2016) are particularly associated with reduced well-being and more acute symptoms of depression. The impact of indebtedness is not restricted to indebted parents; it also contributes to shaping the socio-emotional well-being of children (Berger & Houle, 2016).

Indebtedness, especially where it is excessive, has a negative impact on happiness and the way everyday life and the satisfaction to be derived from it are perceived (Białowolski et al., 2019). Besides this, the financial strain of servicing debt is a factor that reduces subjective quality of life in other areas, one of which is family relationships. Jeffrey Dew (2008), for example, found that indebtedness is a source of marital tension which, owing to frequent rows over financial matters, mutual accusations of irresponsible behaviour, and less free time spent together, reduces the satisfaction married couples derive from sharing their lives. The negative effect of indebtedness on depression among women caring for small children under 1 year old has been identified by Richard Reading and Shirley Reynolds (2001). The stress associated with over-indebtedness can disrupt the relaxed enjoyment of free time, especially vacations, gatherings with family or friends, and the pursuit of hobbies (Worthington, 2006).

As well as shaping quality of life in the economic realm, indebtedness also influences social well-being. Dimitris Georgarakos and his associates (2010) point out that debt repayment problems can lead to social stigmatisation. This is particularly evident in countries whose credit markets – and especially mortgage markets – are not strongly developed. Indebtedness also has a powerful impact on milestones in the family life cycle (Gicheva, 2016; Nissen et al., 2019), including on decisions to delay having children (Nau et al., 2015; Velez et al., 2019). Indeed, indebtedness is a significant determinant of subjective financial well-being among young people (Cherney et al., 2020). People entering adulthood with high levels of debt are more likely to delay buying a home (Mezza et al., 2016), and women heavily burdened by debt tend to postpone marriage and starting a family (Sieg & Wang, 2018).

5.4 Literature review of the well-being of households in Poland

The core concern of economics is the satisfaction of human needs and wants. Safeguarding standards of living and improving quality of life are regarded as the primary aims of social and economic policy at all levels of aggregation (Panek, 2015c). The great popularity of the quality of life question, which is measurable both by the large number of academic papers published on the subject and by the reports, briefings, and studies devoted to it by diverse institutions, derives from the strand of research that addresses the satisfaction of needs and wants and the safeguarding of standards of living.

With this in mind, reviewing research on quality of life is not easy – if only because an extensive body of work has been built up over the years that extends far beyond the bounds of economic science. Given that there is also a need to keep the book to manageable proportions, the review concentrates on work on well-being published after 2010 in relation to Poland.

The European Quality of Life Survey (EQLS) is one of the primary sources of data on the objective circumstances of the life of European citizens and how they feel about those circumstances themselves. Because it investigates a broad range of issues, including income and housing, and subjective questions, such as people's levels of happiness and how satisfied they are with their lives, it can be successfully employed as a source of data in other analyses of selected aspects of quality of life. Among the researchers to have drawn upon it are Tomasz Kwarciński and Paweł Ulman (2018, 2020). The European Social Survey (ESS) is a further Europe-wide study that makes it possible to track changes in social attitudes in regard to key issues, changes in value systems, and changes in behaviour. It consists of two parts: (1) a core section, in which information linked to the socio-demographic characteristics of respondents is gathered on, inter alia, subjective well-being, social exclusion, health, social trust, and personal safety, and (2) a rotating section – relating to specific topics. Data from the ESS have been used by Jadwiga Suchecka and Edyta Łaszkiewicz (2017).

Researchers also consult international databases, such as Passport – Euromonitor International's Global Market Information Database – and national aggregated databases published by Statistics Poland. Marta Kuc (2016) drew upon Passport to examine standards of living based on a composite indicator. Taking a broad approach to standards of living that, in addition to areas strictly related to households (income, expenditure), also covers areas linked to the environment (transport and communications) and non-economic fields (the state of the natural environment), she compared the situation of Polish households and assessed how far their position was convergent with that of households in the European Union in the period 1995–2012. Although there is no great variation in standards of living between countries as measured by the composite indicator, there is significant variation in individual areas. One of Kuc's interesting findings is that the opportunities to further improve standards of living through economic growth are limited in highly developed countries.

An interesting example of the work done on quality of life is provided by Tomasz Kwarciński and Paweł Ulman (2018, 2020), who studied the relationships between subjective and objective well-being. On the basis of an indicator of hybrid well-being, and employing a mobility index, a multidimensional approach, and fuzzy sets theory, they confirmed that assessments of quality of life do not accord with the objective conditions under which households operate.

Various dimensions of personal and social well-being have been analysed by Tomasz Panek (2015a) using a composite indicator and correspondence analysis. He found that Poland's level of subjective well-being is relatively low when compared to other European countries, but that it increases among the households he studied as income rises and as educational level rises.

Using multilevel modelling, Jadwiga Suchecka and Edyta Łaszkiewicz (2017) established that declared levels of life satisfaction depend on an individual's socio-economic and demographic profiles, their health, and factors such as levels of trust and civic and social engagement. They also found, however, that the strength of the individual variables differed according to the level of aggregation examined (micro, meso).

Ewa Sobolewska-Poniedziałek (2017) investigated the financial well-being of adult and senior citizens with the use of aggregated income data, including pension amounts. Her comparison of the material situation of senior citizens in selected European Union countries confirmed that a divide persists in this respect between the rich West and the poor East.

In their work, researchers also consult Polish sources of individual data, such as *Badania budżetów gospodarstw domowych GUS* (Statistics Poland Household Budget Surveys) (M. Cyrek & Cyrek, 2018; Czech, 2017; Dudek et al., 2012; Piekut, 2016, 2017; Utzig, 2018), *Diagnoza społeczna* (Social Diagnosis) (Czapiński, 2015; Dudek, 2017; Dudek & Szczesny, 2015, 2016; Growiec & Growiec, 2010; Murawska, 2012; Perera, 2014; Sompolska-Rzechuła, 2017), *EU-SILC Europejskie Badanie Warunków Życia Ludności* (European Union Statistics on Income and Living Conditions) (Panek, 2015c; Panek & Zwierzchowski, 2019; Zwierzchowski & Panek, 2020), and various surveys, such as those carried out by *Centrum Badania Opinii Społecznej* (Public Opinion Research Centre) (Włodarczyk, 2015a, 2015b). This cross-section of data sources enables diverse areas of the quality of life of Polish households to be studied.

Hanna Dudek and her associates (2012) investigated the influence of income on the structure of household expenditure and found that – in accordance with Engel's law – the living conditions of poor households differ from those of more affluent households, which is demonstrated by, among other things, the fact that, in the former group, basic needs account for a greater proportion of the expenditure.

Of the various areas of quality of life, Poles rate their social relationships and material conditions best, and questions concerning the environment they live in worst (Dudek & Szczesny, 2016). These issues were also addressed by Artur Czech (2017), who examined the impact of the degree of need satisfaction among selected groups of Polish households on their overall subjective assessment of their material situation as an element of quality of life. To that end, he employed a logistic regression model. Czech found that quality of life assessments are determined to the greatest extent by the satisfaction of needs associated with tourism and leisure outside the place of residence, clothing and footwear, and home furnishings. It is interesting to note that the impact of satisfying needs related to education and training and, to a certain extent (in some voivodships), of satisfying needs related to health and to settling housing costs on time, proved not to be statistically significant.

Numerous studies show that society is growing progressively happier and that the proportion of unhappy people is steadily decreasing. This trend is visible in terms of both Poles' overall satisfaction with life and their satisfaction with its various domains, of which living conditions (housing, home furnishings) and income have shown particular improvement (Włodarczyk, 2015a). As Katarzyna Włodarczyk concludes in her article on standards of living and quality of life in Polish towns (2015b), the major factor in quality of life is place of residence, and urban development has brought about positive changes in this respect over time.

Researchers have also given their attention to households outside the large urban centres. Here, it is worth mentioning Marlena Piekut's book on the consumption patterns of rural households (2017). Although it does not address quality of life directly, it does, in addition to consumption, discuss income, housing, and financial wealth. Even though the standards of living of rural households are lower than that of their urban counterparts, it is significant that their living conditions improved considerably in 2004–2014. This is demonstrated by convergence in the consumption patterns of poor and more affluent households and by the better (more modern) durables that households now have at their disposal. Although there have undoubtedly been many beneficial changes in the consumption of rural households, the proportion of their overall expenditure devoted to basic goods remains high, which effectively limits them to satisfying only essential needs. Similar conclusions concerning rural households can be found in the work of Magdalena Cyrek and Piotr Cyrek (2018) and Monika Utzig (2018), while Anna Murawska (2012) offers an alternative view of quality of life among rural populations. In analysing the technical infrastructure, households are equipped with, she stated, first, that its deficiencies negatively affect quality of life and, second, that underdeveloped technical infrastructure in rural areas does not correspond with positive, subjective assessments of satisfaction with housing and place of residence

Meanwhile, in another study, Marlena Piekut (2016) examined the situation in high-income households, that is, households whose per capita disposable income is at least PLN 5,000. It can be stated on the basis of the consumption trends of this group of households that their standards of living differ from those of other households due to the structure of their expenditure. A greater proportion of the budgets of wealthy households is made up of expenditure on services such as recreation, culture, restaurants, and accommodation, as well as expenditure on clothing and footwear.

Research done by Tomasz Panek (2015c) and Tomasz Panek and Jan Zwierzchowski (2019) has made a systematic contribution to identifying quality of life in households in Poland by voivodship. Collating and comparing data drawn from *Diagnoza społeczna* (Social Diagnosis) and from EU-SILC, Panek identified a number of domains and sub-domains of quality of life. In addition, he employed the *k*-means method to group voivodships separately according to objective and subjective perspectives. The dependence between these two dimensions of quality of life in Poland proved weak, although the divergence (differentiation) between groups of voivodships was significant. Panek's 2019 paper co-authored with Jan Zwierzchowski employed multiple indicators and multiple causes (MIMIC) models and the capability approach to investigate quality of life. The positive impact of material living conditions, which were identified as one of the domains of quality of life, is reflected in the growth of households' equivalent incomes, in their self-reported ability to 'make ends meet' with their current incomes, in the decline in monetary poverty and material deprivation, and in the diminished severity of problems associated with the quality of housing and how far the size of a home meets a household's needs. Further research by the same authors (Zwierzchowski & Panek, 2020), which also employed MIMIC models, identified characteristics (variables) that define the subjective well-being of households. The study established that the subjective well-being of households is primarily determined by better self-perceived health and higher income. By contrast, the variables that can be associated with lower subjective well-being included being elderly, living in a large city, being unemployed, being in arrears with debt repayments, and struggling with monetary poverty and material deprivation.

Agnieszka Sompolska-Rzechuła (2017) assessed the similarity of voivodships in terms of the quality of life of their inhabitants and defined typological classes of voivodships in terms of the analysed phenomenon. The analysis applied the fuzzy *c*-means classification method and was based on a wide range of indicators describing subjective and objective quality of life. The main finding was that there is considerable variation in quality of life between voivodships, which confirms the results of earlier research undertaken by Tomasz Panek (2015c) and Artur Czech (2017).

Hanna Dudek (2017) and Hanna Dudek and Wiesław Szczesny (2015, 2016) applied a different, broad approach (in the sense that it covers a large number of features or domains) to the analysis of quality of life. Using multivariate data analysis, they constructed a composite indicator of quality of life covering five dimensions, which consisted of the 16 sub-categories of life satisfaction (known as partial satisfactions) proposed by Janusz Czapiński (2015). They identified respondent characteristics, such as age, marital status, disability, and NGO membership, as well as household characteristics, such as socio-economic group, household type, and place of residence, as factors that influence life satisfaction.

In a study offering a more detailed interpretation of quality of life, Katarzyna Growiec and Jakub Growiec (2010) found that the subjective well-being of Poles is positively influenced not only by their earnings but also by the social capital they possess – especially that related to family and friends. As Diana Perera (2014) demonstrates, well-being is also strongly determined by various types of stressors. The results of analyses performed using a multinomial ordered probit model confirmed that stress linked to financial difficulties, in addition to stress associated with marital problems, health, and contact with the justice system, is one of the factors that has a negative impact on quality of life.

A separate group of studies on quality of life in Poland are those based on authors' own research using original methodologies and individually constructed research samples. It would seem that the large number of such studies stems from the demand for specialised, sectoral, and thematically focused research and from the paucity of nationwide projects that address multiple themes associated with households.

A wide-ranging study on the living standards of Polish households was produced by Urszula Grzega (2012). Using macro standard-of-living indicators (calculated on the basis of secondary data sources), partial indicators, and composite indicators, which, based on her own research, are combined with subjective standard-of-living indicators in the period covered by the analysis, Grzega argues that positive changes occurred in the first two decades of Poland's economic transformation. These were particularly prevalent in respect of satisfying nutritional, housing, and educational needs, and in respect of meeting material needs as well as safety and security. Standards of living vary depending on the socio-professional group. They are rated highest among the households of the self-employed and of white-collar employees doing hired work, and lowest by the households of disability pensioners and those living on unearned sources of income. No matter the domain of life under analysis, income was the most significant of the determinants identified as differentiating the capacity to satisfy needs. It was also the most significant factor influencing subjective assessments of standards of living. In turn, a household's self-reported evaluation of its income and also education are positively correlated with its assessment of its overall standard of living and the extent to which individual groups of needs are satisfied.

By means of a survey questionnaire, and with a sample of more than 1,900 people, Tomasz Zalega (2012) undertook a diagnosis of the material condition of Polish households during the financial and economic crisis. He discovered that people with disposable monthly incomes up to PLN 1,000, people aged 65 and over, people with a primary or basic vocational education, and unemployed people most often reported difficulties in satisfying current needs. The financial constraints that the households encountered influenced changes in their lifestyles and decisions connected with savings and working in the shadow economy. Their self-assessments of their financial situation were, moreover, found to be positively correlated with their levels of disposable income.

Sławomir Kalinowski (2015) conducted research into the living standards and conditions of a rural population with irregular incomes. What emerges from his analysis is that the income situation of the group of households surveyed is generally unfavourable, with an asymmetric, right-skewed income distribution and less income variation than in society as a whole. The low standard of living of this rural population with irregular incomes is also demonstrated by the high proportion – one-third – of its total expenditure accounted for by food, which is greater than the average value for households as a whole. Moreover, Kalinowski notes that satisfying nutritional needs often makes it necessary to forego other groups of needs, such as those connected with culture, education, health, and recreation, or means that these needs are insufficiently satisfied. He concludes on that basis that the group under examination is one of low affluence. Where material living conditions and home furnishings are concerned, the situation of the households examined is better. The majority own their own home. Kalinowski also notes that there is no shortage of durables in rural areas. Living conditions, meanwhile, are determined by household size, the age and education of the head of household, their place of residence, and their labour market position – including form of employment. Interestingly, there is a dichotomy among a significant proportion of this rural population between objective and subjective perceptions of living standards. Despite the relatively high level to which their needs are satisfied, some of the respondents are unsatisfied with their standard of living. At the same time, however, some of them lower their expectations and, despite their needs being satisfied to a relatively low degree, accept their economic situation. Kalinowski contends that poor standards of living do not result only from lower incomes, untypical forms of employment, or irregularity of earnings, but are also often the consequence of low aspirations.

It is not only the economically weakest households to which researchers have turned their attention. Households assigned to the 'economic elite' unsurprisingly enjoy higher levels of per capita income and are also characterised by a more modern consumption structure (Zalega, 2011), which is expressed in a lower proportion of overall expenditure devoted to food and in a higher proportion devoted to services, broadly understood.

Teresa Słaby (2014), in turn, analyses the quality of life of Poland's emerging upper class. She treats the ownership of material goods – which apart from their basic function (as a necessary part of life) can also be understood as an insurance policy, an investment, or a marker of prestige and prosperity – as a measure of perceived quality of life. Although material possessions were most important in determining their well-being, as the material position of the households studied improved, the strength of this factor declined in favour of non-material values, such as family and friends. The analyses performed by Marlena Piekut (2016), who found that basic goods and other goods – including gifts given by the households – stood at the top of the expenditure hierarchy in high-income households, would appear to confirm these findings.

Quality of life appears in a variety of spatial configurations in the literature on household well-being in Poland. Monika Mularska-Kucharek (2015), for example, investigated the relationships between quality of living and subjective quality of life among urban dwellers in the Łódzkie voivodship. The major conclusion she drew is that the characteristics of the broadly defined urban environment are important with respect to subjective quality of life. Earlier research by the same author (2013) confirmed the relationship between individual and family resources (social capital) and the subjective and objective dimensions of quality of life. It is possible when income variation is explained in this way to capture the relationships between the satisfaction of life needs in a variety of domains. At the same time – and this is a conclusion important to practical application – it is essential for social capital to remain cohesive and to be strengthened at both the individual and group levels.

Piotr Cyrek (2018) investigated subjective perceptions of changes in the material situation of households in Podkarpackie voivodship in the context of different types of consumption behaviour. In addition to differences in the types of purchases declared by urban and rural dwellers, he also established that the households of people in the older age ranges, and of those with the lowest levels of education, are more likely to report a need to take out loans.

Investigations of specific social groups represent a further type of research into quality of life. In this vein, Mirosława Janoś-Kresło (2017) and Joanna Dębicka and her associates (2017) undertook analyses of how people with disabilities perceive the quality of their lives. The studies demonstrated that the key determinants of life satisfaction for people with disabilities are assets and an improved material situation. In this type of household, deprivation is most keenly felt in respect of housing conditions, adult recreation, and clothing and footwear.

Teresa Słaby (2016) and Magdalena Kowalska (2019), on the other hand, selected research populations consisting of people aged 60 and above. The former studied quality of life among the native inhabitants of villages in the voivodships (provinces) of 'Poland B',[5] while the second pursued her investigations in the Małopolskie voivodship. Of the variables examined in Słaby's paper, age turned out to have a negative impact on quality of life (defined as social exclusion). Meanwhile, Kowalska concluded that the phenomenon of marginalisation in social life was not particularly prevalent among the respondents she studied.

Tomasz Zalega (2016), who drew his sample from among students of the University of the Third Age, also conducted research work on elderly people – in this case aged 65 and above. He found that, in general, their needs were adequately satisfied in respect of footwear, clothing, and home furnishings, but only averagely so in respect of food and housing. The respondents reserved their lowest ratings for healthcare, recreation, and culture. However, no major problems were detected in connection with the provision of durables. Nevertheless, almost half of the over 65s studied were unsatisfied with their current disposable income. Zalega contends that this has serious implications because the psychological well-being of elderly people is mainly determined by their material conditions and financial situation. In addition to income, the quality of life of elderly people is primarily determined by age, health, educational level, having a partner, and religiousness.

In her analysis of financial attitudes and behaviours, and of their influence on the life satisfaction of people aged 18–65, Dominika Maison (2019) placed emphasis on the subjective dimension of quality of life. The research found that life satisfaction is more strongly correlated with a person's perception, or subjective assessment, of their own financial situation than it is with objective indicators, such as income. What is more, psychological factors (sense of control, materialism, sense of injustice, and life satisfaction) are much stronger predictors of a person's perception of their financial situation than of its objective dimension (income).

5.5 Summary

The importance of household well-being is best demonstrated by the interest this issue has enjoyed for many years among economists and non-economists alike. As a result, the concept has evolved from being understood solely in terms of the material aspects of life, to being assessed from the perspective of economic well-being, and finally to being perceived in the light of a multifaceted quality of life. Despite many decades of effort, and thousands of analyses, devoted to achieving a profound grasp of the issue, to finding connections between the different dimensions of life, and to searching for appropriate research methods, the need for further investigation remains. Indeed, transformations in the economic system mean that new domains and determinants of quality of life are gaining in importance. They include financial well-being and the growing indebtedness of households.

The reviews carried out of the subject literature led to the adoption in this book of a broad definition of well-being, which combines objective and subjective approaches, and material and non-material dimensions, and refers to selected aspects of psychological well-being. By adopting this perspective, which breaks with a purely material approach, it is possible to provide a more complete depiction of the situation of households. Given the specificity of the research topic, attention is focused on financial well-being, which, as international studies indicate, is shaped by processes related to household indebtedness.

Two aspects of indebtedness, which are outlined above, exert an influence on well-being. On the one hand, indebtedness makes it possible to better manage consumption over the course of the life cycle and to satisfy needs, while on the other hand, the very fact of being indebted can in itself constitute a psychological burden that reduces people's well-being. The emergence of additional problems associated with indebtedness, which range from its crowding out of other expenditure – due to the need to make excessive repayments relative to income – to severe financial difficulties resulting in insolvency, reinforces its negative impact on quality of life. The consequences of over-indebtedness go beyond those described earlier and can also concern physical health, family relationships, and social bonds.

The conducted review of research on the quality of life of households in Poland shows that it varies greatly – not only in the terminology employed but also in respect of data sources and research methods. A significant number of analyses concern selected groups, or types, of households. This is an understandable approach given the vastness of the subject. Summarising the results presented by various authors, it may be concluded that from the macroeconomic viewpoint, when compared with developed countries, and despite the considerable progress made in recent years, standards of living in Poland remain low. And although consumption patterns are converging, there are still clear differences both spatially (rural–urban) and between households with different levels of wealth (rich–poor).

The satisfaction of higher order needs is of greater significance in the formation of individual evaluations of quality of life. To achieve this requires – first of all – an improvement in the areas rated as weakest. In many studies, education and health are indicated as significant determinants of the quality of life of Poles. Another interesting issue addressed in the research is the relationship between objective and subjective dimensions of well-being. In essence, there is a disjunction in the assessments of these two areas of well-being. For example, people's subjective evaluations of their financial situation have a stronger influence on overall well-being than do objective measurements of their financial situation. At any level of aggregation, the material conditions in which society functions are of the greatest importance. Just like that of individual incomes, the role of economic growth and infrastructure (both material and social) cannot be overestimated. It must not be forgotten, however, that the importance of living conditions in shaping overall life satisfaction undergoes re-evaluation as wealth increases at the micro- and macroeconomic levels. It would therefore seem necessary to take a wider view of the situation of households that takes into account their non-material and subjective dimensions. This is also the approach proposed in this book.

Notes

1 The notions of economic well-being, material well-being, and financial well-being are usually used synonymously in the literature (Cracolici et al., 2014; Joo, 2008; OECD, 2013; Sirgy, 2018; Sobolewska-Poniedziałek, 2017; Sorgente & Lanz, 2017; Xiao, 2013). They are also treated as such in this book.

2 Our approach, which is not original, is to treat quality of life and well-being as synonyms (Camfield et al., 2009; Dasgupta, 2001; McGillivray, 2005; Statham & Chase, 2010; van Praag & Frijters, 1999; Veenhoven, 2007). The categories of 'quality of life' and 'well-being' are therefore used interchangeably in this book. It should be acknowledged, however, that well-being can also be associated with a positive assessment of an individual's

overall quality of life or, simply, with happiness (Campbell, 1976; Veenhoven, 1991, 1996). The latter concept, which is as imprecise as the others, can be understood in a completely different way in the context of assessing the living conditions of individuals (households): as playing the role of a subjective indicator of quality of life (Easterlin, 2001).

3 By restricting economic well-being to the objective dimension, and treating it as an element of financial well-being, the authors take a different approach here to the one now dominant in the literature, whereby the notions of economic well-being and financial well-being are employed interchangeably.

4 It should be noted that even though they have been detected in a large number of studies, these dependencies can also operate in reverse. Poor mental health, and, particularly, depression, is a factor that increases the risk of falling into a toxic spiral of indebtedness and 'bad' debt. This is compounded by several factors, including a fall in income due to sickness absences or working fewer hours, and a decline in cognitive ability that leaves those affected particularly vulnerable to aggressive marketing strategies on the part of lenders (Autio et al., 2009; Hiilamo & Grundy, 2020; Meltzer et al., 2013).

5 [Translator's note:] 'Poland B' generally refers to the voivodships lying to the east of the Vistula River which have historically been less developed than the western parts of the country and which were controlled by the Austrian and Russian Empires from the late eighteenth century until 1918; its counterpart, 'Poland A', comprises the more prosperous voivodships lying to the west of the Vistula which were controlled by Prussia during the same period.

References

Aboagye, J., & Jung, J. Y. (2018). Debt holding, financial behavior, and financial satisfaction. *Journal of Financial Counseling and Planning, 29*(2), 208–218. https://doi.org/10.1891/1052-3073.29.2.208

Ackerman, F., Kiron, D., Goodwin, N. R., Harris, J. M., & Gallagher, K. (Eds.). (1997). *Human well-being and economic goals*. Washington, DC: Island Press.

Autio, M., Wilska, T.-A., Kaartinen, R., & Lähteenmaa, J. (2009). The use of small instant loans among young adults – A gateway to a consumer insolvency? *International Journal of Consumer Studies, 33*(4), 407–415. https://doi.org/10.1111/j.1470-6431.2009.00789.x

Barcaccia, B., Esposito, G., Matarese, M., Bertolaso, M., Elvira, M., & De Marinis, M. G. (2013). Defining quality of life: A wild-goose chase? *Europe's Journal of Psychology, 9*(1), 185–203. https://doi.org/10.5964/ejop.v9i1.484

Berger, L. M., Collins, J. M., & Cuesta, L. (2016). Household debt and adult depressive symptoms in the United States. *Journal of Family and Economic Issues, 37*(1), 42–57. https://doi.org/10.1007/s10834-015-9443-6

Berger, L. M., & Houle, J. N. (2016). Parental debt and children's socioemotional well-being. *Pediatrics, 137*(2), 1–8. https://doi.org/10.1542/peds.2015-3059

Berger-Schmitt, R., & Noll, H.-H. (2000). *Conceptual framework and structure of a European system of social indicators* (EuReporting Working Paper No. 9). Mannheim: Centre for Survey Research and Methodology (ZUMA).

Betti, G., Soldi, R., & Talev, I. (2016). Fuzzy multidimensional indicators of quality of life: The empirical case of Macedonia. *Social Indicators Research, 127*(1), 39–53. https://doi.org/10.1007/s11205-015-0965-y

Białowolski, P., Węziak-Białowolska, D., & VanderWeele, T. J. (2019). The impact of savings and credit on health and health behaviours: An outcome-wide longitudinal approach. *International Journal of Public Health, 64*(4), 573–584. https://doi.org/10.1007/s00038-019-01214-3

Blomgren, J., Maunula, N., & Hiilamo, H. (2016). Over-indebtedness and chronic disease: A linked register-based study of Finnish men and women during 1995–2010. *International Journal of Public Health, 61*(5), 535–544. https://doi.org/10.1007/s00038-015-0778-4

Blomgren, J., Maunula, N., & Hiilamo, H. (2017). Do debts lead to disability pension? Evidence from a 15-year follow-up of 54,000 Finnish men and women. *Journal of European Social Policy, 27*(2), 109–122. https://doi.org/10.1177/0958928716676548

Böhnke, P. (2008). Does society matter? Life satisfaction in the enlarged Europe. *Social Indicators Research, 87*(2), 189–210. https://doi.org/10.1007/s11205-007-9169-4

Borys, T. (2015). Typologia jakości życia i pomiar statystyczny. *Wiadomości Statystyczne, 60*(7), 1–18.

Bridges, S., & Disney, R. (2010). Debt and depression. *Journal of Health Economics, 29*(3), 388–403. https://doi.org/10.1016/j.jhealeco.2010.02.003

Brown, S., Taylor, K., & Wheatley Price, S. (2005). Debt and distress: Evaluating the psychological cost of credit. *Journal of Economic Psychology, 26*(5), 642–663. https://doi.org/10.1016/j.joep.2005.01.002

Brüggen, E. C., Hogreve, J., Holmlund, M., Kabadayi, S., & Löfgren, M. (2017). Financial well-being: A conceptualization and research agenda. *Journal of Business Research, 79*, 228–237. https://doi.org/10.1016/j.jbusres.2017.03.013

Burchardt, T. (2005). Are one man's rags another man's riches? Identifying adaptive expectations using panel data. *Social Indicators Research, 74*(1), 57–102. https://doi.org/10.1007/s11205-005-6519-y

Bywalec, C. (1991). *Wzrost gospodarczy a poziom życia społeczeństwa polskiego*. Warszawa: Instytut Rynku Wewnętrznego i Konsumpcji.

Bywalec, C. (2007). *Konsumpcja w teorii i praktyce gospodarowania*. Warszawa: Wydawnictwo Naukowe PWN.

Camfield, L., Crivello, G., & Woodhead, M. (2009). Wellbeing research in developing countries: Reviewing the role of qualitative methods. *Social Indicators Research, 90*(1), 5–31. https://doi.org/10.1007/s11205-008-9310-z

Campbell, A. (1976). Subjective measures of well-being. *American Psychologist, 31*(2), 117–124. https://doi.org/10.1037/0003-066X.31.2.117

Cannuscio, C. C., Alley, D. E., Pagán, J. A., Soldo, B., Krasny, S., Shardell, M., Asch, D. A., & Lipman, T. H. (2012). Housing strain, mortgage foreclosure, and health. *Nurs Outlook, 60*(3), 134–142.e1. https://doi.org/10.1016/j.outlook.2011.08.004

CFPB. (2015). *Measuring financial well-being: A guide to using the CFPB financial well-being scale*. Washington, DC: Consumer Financial Protection Bureau.

Cherney, K., Rothwell, D., Serido, J., & Shim, S. (2020). Subjective financial well-being during emerging adulthood: The role of student debt. *Emerging Adulthood, 8*(6), 485–495. https://doi.org/10.1177/2167696819879252

Clayton, M., Liñares-Zegarra, J., & Wilson, J. O. S. (2015). Does debt affect health? Cross country evidence on the debt-health nexus. *Social Science & Medicine, 130*, 51–58. https://doi.org/10.1016/j.socscimed.2015.02.002

Cracolici, M. F., Giambona, F., & Cuffaro, M. (2014). Family structure and subjective economic well-being: Some new evidence. *Social Indicators Research, 118*(1), 433–456. https://doi.org/10.1007/s11205-013-0425-5

Cyrek, M., & Cyrek, P. (2018). Difference in consumption between urban and rural households. In *Proceedings of the international scientific conference 'Economic Sciences for Agribusiness and Rural Economy' No 2, Warsaw, 7–8 June 2018* (pp. 68–74). Warsaw: Warsaw University of Life Sciences Press. https://doi.org/10.22630/ESARE.2018.2.7

Cyrek, P. (2018). Zmiany sytuacji materialnej i gospodarowanie dochodem w gospodarstwach domowych. *Marketing i Zarządzanie*, *2*(52), 17–27. https://doi.org/10.18276/miz.2018.52-02

Czapiński, J. (2012). Ekonomia szczęścia i psychologia bogactwa. *Nauka*, *1*, 51–88.

Czapiński, J. (2015). Indywidualna jakość i styl życia. Diagnoza Społeczna 2015. Warunki i jakość życia Polaków – Raport. *Contemporary Economics*, *9*(4), 200–331. https://doi.org/10.5709/ce.1897-9254.190

Czapiński, J., & Panek, T. (Eds.). (2015). Diagnoza społeczna 2015. Warunki i jakość życia Polaków – Raport. *Contemporary Economics*, *9*(4), 1–545.

Czech, A. (2017). Ocena jakości życia polskich gospodarstw domowych – ujęcie wojewódzkie. In E. Frątczak, T. Panek, & T. Słaby (Eds.), *Paradygmaty badawcze jakości życia w ekonomii, zarządzaniu i psychologii* (pp. 49–64). Wrocław: Wydawnictwo Uniwersytetu Ekonomicznego we Wrocławiu.

Dackehag, M., Ellegård, L.-M., Gerdtham, U.-G., & Nilsson, T. (2019). Debt and mental health: New insights about the relationship and the importance of the measure of mental health. *European Journal of Public Health*, *29*(3), 488–493. https://doi.org/10.1093/eurpub/ckz002

Dasgupta, P. (2001). *Human well-being and the natural environment*. Oxford: Oxford University Press.

Dębicka, J., Mazurek, E., & Szalonka, K. (2017). Postrzeganie jakości życia przez osoby niepełnosprawne. *Prace Naukowe Uniwersytetu Ekonomicznego We Wrocławiu*, *483*, 29–43. https://doi.org/10.15611/pn.2017.483.03

Dew, J. (2008). Debt change and marital satisfaction change in recently married couples. *Family Relations*, *57*(1), 60–71. https://doi.org/10.1111/j.1741-3729.2007.00483.x

Diener, E. (2009). Assessing subjective well-being: Progress and opportunities. In E. Diener (Ed.), *Assessing well-being: The collected works of Ed Diener* (Social Indicators Research Series, vol. 39, pp. 25–65). Dordrecht: Springer. https://doi.org/10.1007/978-90-481-2354-4_3

Diener, E., & Biswas-Diener, R. (2002). Will money increase subjective well-being? *Social Indicators Research*, *57*(2), 119–169. https://doi.org/10.1023/A:1014411319119

Diener, E., Ng, W., Harter, J., & Arora, R. (2010). Wealth and happiness across the world: Material prosperity predicts life evaluation, whereas psychosocial prosperity predicts positive feeling. *Journal of Personality and Social Psychology*, *99*(1), 52–61. https://doi.org/10.1037/a0018066

Diener, E., Tay, L., & Oishi, S. (2013). Rising income and the subjective well-being of nations. *Journal of Personality and Social Psychology*, *104*(2), 267–276. https://doi.org/10.1037/a0030487

Dodge, R., Daly, A., Huyton, J., & Sanders, L. (2012). The challenge of defining wellbeing. *International Journal of Wellbeing*, *2*(3), 222–235. https://doi.org/10.5502/ijw.v2i3.4

Drentea, P. (2000). Age, debt and anxiety. *Journal of Health and Social Behavior*, *41*(4), 437–450. https://doi.org/10.2307/2676296

Drentea, P., & Lavrakas, P. J. (2000). Over the limit: The association among health, race and debt. *Social Science & Medicine*, *50*(4), 517–529. https://doi.org/10.1016/S0277-9536(99)00298-1

Drentea, P., & Reynolds, J. R. (2012). Neither a borrower nor a lender be: The relative importance of debt and SES for mental health among older adults. *Journal of Aging and Health*, *24*(4), 673–695. https://doi.org/10.1177/0898264311431304

Dudek, H. (2017). Analiza zadowolenia z życia w ujęciu wielowymiarowym za pomocą modeli regresji typu FRM. In E. Frątczak, T. Panek, & T. Słaby (Eds.), *Paradygmaty badawcze jakości życia w ekonomii, zarządzaniu i psychologii* (pp. 65–79). Wrocław: Wydawnictwo Uniwersytetu Ekonomicznego we Wrocławiu.

Dudek, H., Koszela, G., & Landmesser, J. (2012). Wpływ sytuacji dochodowej na strukturę wydatków gospodarstw domowych. *Zeszyty Naukowe SGGW w Warszawie. Ekonomika i Organizacja Gospodarki Żywnościowej, 97*, 237–247.
Dudek, H., & Szczesny, W. (2015). Zastosowanie funkcji przynależności w analizie subiektywnego postrzegania jakości życia. *Ekonometria, 4*(50), 62–78. https://doi.org/10.15611/ekt.2015.4.04
Dudek, H., & Szczesny, W. (2016). Subjective perception of quality of life – multidimensional analysis based on fuzzy sets approach. *Research Papers of Wrocław University of Economics, 435*, 55–68. https://doi.org/10.15611/pn.2016.435.03
Easterlin, R. A. (2001). Income and happiness: Towards a unified theory. *The Economic Journal, 111*(473), 465–484. https://doi.org/10.1111/1468-0297.00646
Easterlin, R. A. (2006). Life cycle happiness and its sources: Intersections of psychology, economics, and demography. *Journal of Economic Psychology, 27*(4), 463–482. https://doi.org/10.1016/j.joep.2006.05.002
Eurostat. (2020). *Measuring progress*. https://ec.europa.eu/eurostat/web/ess/about-us/measuring-progress
Frade, C., & Lopes, C. A. (2009). Overindebtedness and financial stress: A comparative study in Europe. In J. Niemi, I. Ramsay, & W. C. Whitford (Eds.), *Consumer credit, debt and bankruptcy: Comparative and international perspectives* (pp. 249–272). Oxford: Hart Publishing.
French, D., & McKillop, D. (2017). The impact of debt and financial stress on health in Northern Irish households. *Journal of European Social Policy, 27*(5), 458–473. https://doi.org/10.1177/0958928717717657
Garðarsdóttir, R. B., & Dittmar, H. (2012). The relationship of materialism to debt and financial well-being: The case of Iceland's perceived prosperity. *Journal of Economic Psychology, 33*(3), 471–481. https://doi.org/10.1016/j.joep.2011.12.008
Garrett, S., & James III, R. N. (2013). Financial ratios and perceived household financial satisfaction. *Journal of Financial Therapy, 4*(1), 4. https://doi.org/10.4148/jft.v4i1.1839
Gasper, D. (2007). Human well-being: Concepts and conceptualizations. In M. McGillivray (Ed.), *Human well-being: Concept and measurement* (pp. 23–64). London: Palgrave Macmillan. https://doi.org/10.1057/9780230625600_2
Gasper, D. (2010). Understanding the diversity of conceptions of well-being and quality of life. *The Journal of Socio-Economics, 39*(3), 351–360. https://doi.org/10.1016/j.socec.2009.11.006
Gathergood, J. (2012). Debt and depression: Causal links and social norm effects. *The Economic Journal, 122*(563), 1094–1114. https://doi.org/10.1111/j.1468-0297.2012.02519.x
Georgarakos, D., Lojschova, A., & Ward-Warmedinger, M. E. (2010). *Mortgage indebtedness and household financial distress* (ECB Working Paper No. 1156). Frankfurt am Main: European Central Bank. http://doi.org/10.2139/ssrn.1456593
Georgiades, A., Janszky, I., Blom, M., László, K. D., & Ahnve, S. (2009). Financial strain predicts recurrent events among women with coronary artery disease. *International Journal of Cardiology, 135*(2), 175–183. https://doi.org/10.1016/j.ijcard.2008.03.093
Gicheva, D. (2016). Student loans or marriage? A look at the highly educated. *Economics of Education Review, 53*, 207–216. https://doi.org/10.1016/j.econedurev.2016.04.006
Grable, J. E., Cupples, S., Fernatt, F., & Anderson, N. (2013). Evaluating the link between perceived income adequacy and financial satisfaction: A resource deficit hypothesis approach. *Social Indicators Research, 114*(3), 1109–1124. https://doi.org/10.1007/s11205-012-0192-8
Greninger, S. A., Hampton, V. L., Kitt, K. A., & Achacoso, J. A. (1996). Ratios and benchmarks for measuring the financial well-being of families and individuals. *Financial Services Review, 5*(1), 57–70. https://doi.org/10.1016/S1057-0810(96)90027-X

Growiec, J., & Growiec, K. (2010). Social capital, well-being, and earnings. *European Societies, 12*(2), 231–255. https://doi.org/10.1080/14616690902718381

Grzega, U. (2012). *Poziom życia ludności w Polsce: Determinanty i zróżnicowania*. Katowice: Wydawnictwo Uniwersytetu Ekonomicznego w Katowicach.

Guo, L., Arnould, E. J., Gruen, T. W., & Tang, C. (2013). Socializing to co-produce: Pathways to consumers' financial well-being. *Journal of Service Research, 16*(4), 549–563. https://doi.org/10.1177/1094670513483904

GUS. (2014). *Warunki życia rodzin w Polsce*. Warszawa: Główny Urząd Statystyczny.

GUS. (2020). *Jakość życia i kapitał społeczny w Polsce. Wyniki badania spójności społecznej 2018*. Warszawa: Główny Urząd Statystyczny. https://stat.gov.pl/obszary-tematyczne/warunki-zycia/dochody-wydatki-i-warunki-zycia-ludnosci/jakosc-zycia-i-kapital-spoleczny-w-polsce-wyniki-badania-spojnosci-spolecznej-2018,4,3.html

Gutter, M., & Copur, Z. (2011). Financial behaviors and financial well-being of college students: Evidence from a national survey. *Journal of Family and Economic Issues, 32*(4), 699–714. https://doi.org/10.1007/s10834-011-9255-2

Handayani, D., Salamah, U., & Yusacc, R. N. (2016). Indebtedness and subjective financial wellbeing of households in Indonesia. *Economics and Finance in Indonesia, 62*(2), 78. https://doi.org/10.7454/efi.v62i2.549

Harkness, S. (2007). Social and political indicators of human well-being. In M. McGillivray (Ed.), *Human well-being: Concept and measurement* (pp. 88–112). London: Palgrave Macmillan. https://doi.org/10.1057/9780230625600_4

Headey, B., & Wooden, M. (2004). The effects of wealth and income on subjective well-being and ill-being. *Economic Record, 80*(s1), S24–S33. https://doi.org/10.1111/j.1475-4932.2004.00181.x

Hiilamo, A., & Grundy, E. (2020). Household debt and depressive symptoms among older adults in three continental European countries. *Ageing and Society, 40*(2), 412–438. https://doi.org/10.1017/S0144686X18001113

Hodson, R., Dwyer, R. E., & Neilson, L. A. (2014). Credit card blues: The middle class and the hidden costs of easy credit. *The Sociological Quarterly, 55*(2), 315–340. https://doi.org/10.1111/tsq.12059

Hojman, D. A., Miranda, Á., & Ruiz-Tagle, J. (2016). Debt trajectories and mental health. *Social Science & Medicine, 167*, 54–62. https://doi.org/10.1016/j.socscimed.2016.08.027

Holmgren, R., Nilsson Sundström, E., Levinsson, H., & Ahlström, R. (2019). Coping and financial strain as predictors of mental illness in over-indebted individuals in Sweden. *Scandinavian Journal of Psychology, 60*(1), 50–58. https://doi.org/10.1111/sjop.12511

Howell, R. T., & Howell, C. J. (2008). The relation of economic status to subjective well-being in developing countries: A meta-analysis. *Psychological Bulletin, 134*(4), 536–560. https://doi.org/10.1037/0033-2909.134.4.536

Howell, R. T., Kurai, M., & Tam, L. (2013). Money buys financial security and psychological need satisfaction: Testing need theory in affluence. *Social Indicators Research, 110*(1), 17–29. https://doi.org/10.1007/s11205-010-9774-5

Janoś-Kresło, M. (2017). Niedobory konsumpcji w gospodarstwach domowych z dziećmi z niepełnosprawnością. *Ekonomia – Wroclaw Economic Review, 23*(1), 23–34. https://doi.org/10.19195/2084-4093.23.1.3

Joo, S. (2008). Personal financial wellness. In J. J. Xiao (Ed.), *Handbook of consumer finance research* (pp. 21–33). New York: Springer. https://doi.org/10.1007/978-0-387-75734-6_2

Joo, S., & Grable, J. E. (2004). An exploratory framework of the determinants of financial satisfaction. *Journal of Family and Economic Issues, 25*(1), 25–50. https://doi.org/10.1023/B:JEEI.0000016722.37994.9f

Kahneman, D., Diener, E., & Schwarz, N. (1999). *Well-being: Foundations of hedonic psychology*. New York: Russell Sage Foundation.
Kalinowski, S. (2015). *Poziom życia ludności wiejskiej o niepewnych dochodach*. Warszawa: Wydawnictwo Naukowe PWN.
Kempson, E., & Poppe, C. (2018). *Understanding financial well-being and capability – A revised model and comprehensive analysis* (Professional Report No. 3). Oslo: Consumption Research Norway (SIFO).
Kim, J., Garman, E. T., & Sorhaindo, B. (2003). Relationships among credit counseling clients' financial wellbeing, financial behaviors, financial stressor events, and health. *Journal of Financial Counseling and Planning, 14*(2), 75–87.
Kowalska, M. (2019). Quality of elderly people's life in the region of Malopolskie Voivodship. *Acta Universitatis Lodziensis. Folia Oeconomica, 340*, 43–56. https://doi.org/10.18778/0208-6018.340.03
Kuc, M. (2016). *Przemiany w przestrzennym zróżnicowaniu poziomu życia ludności w państwach Unii Europejskiej*. Toruń: Wydawnictwo Naukowe Uniwersytetu Mikołaja Kopernika.
Kwarciński, T., & Ulman, P. (2018). A hybrid version of well-being: An attempt at operationalisation. *Zarządzanie Publiczne/Public Governance, 4*(46), 30–49. https://doi.org/10.15678/ZP.2018.46.4.03
Kwarciński, T., & Ulman, P. (2020). Quality of life paradox. Well-Being ranking of the selected European countries based on hybrid well-being approach. *Economics & Sociology, 13*(2), 160–180. https://doi.org/10.14254/2071-789X.2020/13-2/12
Lee, J. M., Lee, J., & Kim, K. T. (2020). Consumer financial well-being: Knowledge is not enough. *Journal of Family and Economic Issues, 41*(2), 218–228. https://doi.org/10.1007/s10834-019-09649-9
Maison, D. (2019). *The psychology of financial consumer behavior*. Cham: Springer International Publishing. https://doi.org/10.1007/978-3-030-10570-9
Malone, K., Stewart, S. D., Wilson, J., & Korsching, P. F. (2010). Perceptions of financial well-being among American women in diverse families. *Journal of Family and Economic Issues, 31*(1), 63–81. https://doi.org/10.1007/s10834-009-9176-5
McGillivray, M. (2005). Measuring non-economic well-being achievement. *Review of Income and Wealth, 51*(2), 337–364. https://doi.org/10.1111/j.1475-4991.2005.00157.x
Meltzer, H., Bebbington, P., Brugha, T., Farrell, M., & Jenkins, R. (2013). The relationship between personal debt and specific common mental disorders. *The European Journal of Public Health, 23*(1), 108–113. https://doi.org/10.1093/eurpub/cks021
Meltzer, H., Bebbington, P., Brugha, T., Jenkins, R., McManus, S., & Dennis, M. S. (2011). Personal debt and suicidal ideation. *Psychological Medicine, 41*(4), 771–778. https://doi.org/10.1017/S0033291710001261
Mezza, A. A., Ringo, D. R., Sherlund, S. M., & Sommer, K. (2016). *On the effect of student loans on access to homeownership* (Finance and Economics Discussion Series No. 2016–010). Washington, DC: Board of Governors of the Federal Reserve System. https://doi.org/10.17016/FEDS.2016.010
Morse, A. (2011). Payday lenders: Heroes or villains? *Journal of Financial Economics, 102*(1), 28–44. https://doi.org/10.1016/j.jfineco.2011.03.022
Mularska-Kucharek, M. (2013). *Kapitał społeczny a jakość życia na przykładzie zbiorowości wielkomiejskiej*. Łódź: Wydawnictwo Uniwersytetu Łódzkiego.
Mularska-Kucharek, M. (2015). O relacjach pomiędzy jakością zamieszkiwania a subiektywną jakością życia – na przykładzie mieszkańców miast. *Studia Miejskie, 19*, 131–145.
Murawska, A. (2012). Zmiany w poziomie i jakości życia ludności na obszarach wiejskich w Polsce. *Journal of Agribusiness and Rural Development, 3*(25), 169–180.

Myers, D. G., & Diener, E. (1995). Who is happy? *Psychological Science*, *6*(1), 10–19. https://doi.org/10.1111/j.1467-9280.1995.tb00298.x

Naess, S. (1999). Subjective approach to quality of life. *Feminist Economics*, *5*(2), 115–118. https://doi.org/10.1080/135457099338021

Nau, M., Dwyer, R. E., & Hodson, R. (2015). Can't afford a baby? Debt and young Americans. *Research in Social Stratification and Mobility*, *42*, 114–122. https://doi.org/10.1016/j.rssm.2015.05.003

Nissen, S., Hayward, B., & McManus, R. (2019). Student debt and wellbeing: A research agenda. *Kōtuitui: New Zealand Journal of Social Sciences Online*, *14*(2), 245–256. https://doi.org/10.1080/1177083X.2019.1614635

Norvilitis, J. M., Szablicki, P. B., & Wilson, S. D. (2003). Factors influencing levels of credit-card debt in college students. *Journal of Applied Social Psychology*, *33*(5), 935–947. https://doi.org/10.1111/j.1559-1816.2003.tb01932.x

OECD. (2011). *Compendium of OECD well-being indicators*. Paris: OECD Publishing.

OECD. (2013). *OECD guidelines on measuring subjective well-being*. Paris: OECD.

OECD. (2020). *How's life? 2020: Measuring well-being*. Paris: OECD Publishing. https://doi.org/10.1787/9870c393-en

O'Neill, B., Sorhaindo, B., Xiao, J. J., & Garman, E. T. (2005). Financially distressed consumers: Their financial practices, financial well-being, and health. *Journal of Financial Counseling and Planning*, *16*(1), 73–87.

Ostasiewicz, W. (2013). Dobrobyt i jakość życia: Badania w Polsce i za granicą. *Śląski Przegląd Statystyczny*, *17*(11), 229–243.

Paim, L. (1995). Definitions and measurements of well-being: A review of literature. *Journal of Economic and Social Measurement*, *21*(4), 297–309. https://doi.org/10.3233/JEM-1995-21403

Panek, T. (2015a). Analiza porównawcza subiektywnego dobrostanu w Europie. *Wiadomości Statystyczne*, *60*(2), 1–26.

Panek, T. (2015b). Hierarchiczny model pomiaru jakości życia. *Wiadomości Statystyczne*, *60*(6), 1–22.

Panek, T. (2015c). *Jakość życia gospodarstw domowych w Polsce w układzie wojewódzkim* (Zeszyty Naukowe No. 46). Warszawa: Instytutu Statystyki i Demografii SGH.

Panek, T. (2016). *Jakość życia: Od koncepcji do pomiaru*. Oficyna Wydawnicza SGH.

Panek, T., & Zwierzchowski, J. (2019). *Analiza porównawcza jakości życia w Polsce w układzie wojewódzkim w ramach podejścia możliwości* (Zeszyty Naukowe No. 51). Warszawa: Instytut Statystyki i Demografii SGH.

Pawełek, B. (2000). Poziom życia, jakość życia i warunki życia ludności. In A. Zeliaś (Ed.), *Taksonomiczna analiza przestrzennego zróżnicowania poziomu życia w Polsce w ujęciu dynamicznym* (pp. 12–23). Kraków: Akademia Ekonomiczna.

Perera, D. (2014). Wpływ stresu na jakość życia ludności w Polsce. *Wiadomości Statystyczne*, *1*, 38–50.

Piekut, M. (2016). Wydatki i trendy w konsumpcji w gospodarstwach domowych wysokodochodowych. *Problemy Zarządzania*, *14*(1(58), t. 2), 30–44. https://doi.org/10.7172/1644-9584.58.2

Piekut, M. (2017). *Wzorce konsumpcji według typów wiejskich gospodarstw domowych w latach 2004–2014*. Warszawa: Difin. https://depot.ceon.pl/handle/123456789/12809

Plagnol, A. C., & Easterlin, R. A. (2008). Aspirations, attainments, and satisfaction: Life cycle differences between American women and men. *Journal of Happiness Studies*, *9*(4), 601–619. https://doi.org/10.1007/s10902-008-9106-5

Podolec, B. (2014). *Wybrane aspekty analizy warunków życia ludności w Polsce. Metody ilościowe w badaniach empirycznych*. Kraków: Oficyna Wydawnicza AFM.

Pollard, E. L., & Lee, P. D. (2003). Child well-being: A systematic review of the literature. *Social Indicators Research, 61*(1), 59–78. https://doi.org/10.1023/A:1021284215801

Porter, N. M., & Garman, E. T. (1992). Money as part of a measure of financial well-being. *American Behavioral Scientist, 35*(6), 820–826. https://doi.org/10.1177/0002764292035006016

Prawitz, A. D., Garman, E. T., Sorhaindo, B., O'Neill, B., Kim, J., & Drentea, P. (2006). InCharge financial distress/financial well-being scale: Development, administration, and score interpretation. *Journal of Financial Counseling and Planning, 17*(1), 34–50. https://doi.org/10.1037/t60365-000

Prentice, C., McKillop, D., & French, D. (2017). How financial strain affects health: Evidence from the Dutch National Bank Household Survey. *Social Science & Medicine, 178*, 127–135. https://doi.org/10.1016/j.socscimed.2017.02.006

Rath, T., & Harter, J. (2010). *Wellbeing: The five essential elements*. New York: Gallup Press.

Reading, R., & Reynolds, S. (2001). Debt, social disadvantage and maternal depression. *Social Science & Medicine, 53*(4), 441–453. https://doi.org/10.1016/S0277-9536(00)00347-6

Richardson, T., Elliott, P., & Roberts, R. (2013). The relationship between personal unsecured debt and mental and physical health: A systematic review and meta-analysis. *Clinical Psychology Review, 33*(8), 1148–1162. https://doi.org/10.1016/j.cpr.2013.08.009

Richardson, T., Elliott, P., Roberts, R., & Jansen, M. (2017). A longitudinal study of financial difficulties and mental health in a national sample of British undergraduate students. *Community Mental Health Journal, 53*(3), 344–352. https://doi.org/10.1007/s10597-016-0052-0

Ringen, S. (1995). Well-being, measurement, and preferences. *Acta Sociologica, 38*(1), 3–15. https://doi.org/10.1177/000169939503800102

Rutherford, L. G., & Fox, W. S. (2010). Financial wellness of young adults age 18–30. *Family and Consumer Sciences Research Journal, 38*(4), 468–484. https://doi.org/10.1111/j.1552-3934.2010.00039.x

Selenko, E., & Batinic, B. (2011). Beyond debt. A moderator analysis of the relationship between perceived financial strain and mental health. *Social Science & Medicine, 73*(12), 1725–1732. https://doi.org/10.1016/j.socscimed.2011.09.022

Shim, S., Xiao, J. J., Barber, B. L., & Lyons, A. C. (2009). Pathways to life success: A conceptual model of financial well-being for young adults. *Journal of Applied Developmental Psychology, 30*(6), 708–723. https://doi.org/10.1016/j.appdev.2009.02.003

Sieg, H., & Wang, Y. (2018). The impact of student debt on education, career, and marriage choices of female lawyers. *European Economic Review, 109*, 124–147. https://doi.org/10.1016/j.euroecorev.2017.05.009

Sirgy, M. J. (2018). The psychology of material well-being. *Applied Research in Quality of Life, 13*(2), 273–301. https://doi.org/10.1007/s11482-017-9590-z

Słaby, T. (2007). Poziom i jakość życia. In T. Panek (Ed.), *Statystyka społeczna* (pp. 99–130). Warszawa: Polskie Wydawnictwo Ekonomiczne.

Słaby, T. (2011). Nowe propozycje w badaniach jakości życia. *Studia i Prace Kolegium Zarządzania i Finansów, 108*, 125–136.

Słaby, T. (2014). Merkantylizm psychiczny jako źródło jakości życia zalążkowej klasy wyższej w Polsce. *Zeszyty Naukowe Wyższej Szkoły Bankowej We Wrocławiu, 42*(4), 21–35.

Słaby, T. (2016). The quality of life of the aboriginal rural people 60+ in Poland. Selected research results, 2014. *Prace Naukowe Uniwersytetu Ekonomicznego We Wrocławiu, 435*, 84–97. https://doi.org/10.15611/pn.2016.435.05

Sobolewska-Poniedziałek, E. (2017). Dobrostan finansowy osób w dojrzałym i starszym wieku w wybranych krajach Unii Europejskiej. *Ekonomia – Wroclaw Economic Review, 23*(4), 95–109. https://doi.org/10.19195/2084-4093.23.4.8

Sointu, E. (2005). The rise of an ideal: Tracing changing discourses of wellbeing. *The Sociological Review, 53*(2), 255–274.

Sompolska-Rzechuła, A. (2017). Przestrzenne zróżnicowanie poziomu jakości życia w Polsce. *Wiadomości Statystyczne, 6*, 38–57.

Sorgente, A., & Lanz, M. (2017). Emerging adults' financial well-being: A scoping review. *Adolescent Research Review, 2*(4), 255–292. https://doi.org/10.1007/s40894-016-0052-x

Statham, J., & Chase, E. (2010). *Childhood wellbeing: A brief overview* [Briefing Paper 1]. Loughborough: Childhood Wellbeing Research Centre.

Suchecka, J., & Łaszkiewicz, E. (2017). Wykorzystanie modelowania wielopoziomowego w analizie jakości życia. *Studia Ekonomiczne. Zeszyty Naukowe Uniwersytetu Ekonomicznego w Katowicach, 344*, 133–144.

Sweet, E., Nandi, A., Adam, E. K., & McDade, T. W. (2013). The high price of debt: Household financial debt and its impact on mental and physical health. *Social Science & Medicine, 91*, 94–100. https://doi.org/10.1016/j.socscimed.2013.05.009

Szukiełojć-Bieńkuńska, A. (2015). Pomiar jakości życia w statystyce publicznej. *Wiadomości Statystyczne*, 7, 19–32.

Tay, L., Batz, C., Parrigon, S., & Kuykendall, L. (2017). Debt and subjective well-being: The other side of the income-happiness coin. *Journal of Happiness Studies, 18*(3), 903–937. https://doi.org/10.1007/s10902-016-9758-5

Turunen, E., & Hiilamo, H. (2014). Health effects of indebtedness: A systematic review. *BMC Public Health, 14*(1), 489. https://doi.org/10.1186/1471-2458-14-489

Utzig, M. (2018). Wydatki konsumpcyjne w wiejskich i miejskich gospodarstwach domowych jako miara ich poziomu życia. *Roczniki Naukowe Stowarzyszenia Ekonomistów Rolnictwa i Agrobiznesu, 20*(4), 195–199. https://doi.org/10.5604/01.3001.0012.3061

van Praag, B. M. S., & Frijters, P. (1999). The measurement of welfare and well-being: The Leyden approach. In D. Kahneman, E. Diener, & N. Schwarz (Eds.), *Well-being: The foundations of hedonic psychology* (pp. 413–432). New York: Russell Sage Foundation.

van Praag, B. M. S., Frijters, P., & Ferrer-i-Carbonell, A. (2003). The anatomy of subjective well-being. *Journal of Economic Behavior & Organization, 51*(1), 29–49. https://doi.org/10.1016/S0167-2681(02)00140-3

Veenhoven, R. (1991). Is happiness relative? *Social Indicators Research, 24*(1), 1–34. https://doi.org/10.1007/BF00292648

Veenhoven, R. (1996). Happy life-expectancy. *Social Indicators Research, 39*(1), 1–58. https://doi.org/10.1007/BF00300831

Veenhoven, R. (2007). Subjective measures of well-being. In M. McGillivray (Ed.), *Human well-being: Concept and measurement* (pp. 214–239). London: Palgrave Macmillan. https://doi.org/10.1057/9780230625600_9

Velez, E., Cominole, M., & Bentz, A. (2019). Debt burden after college: The effect of student loan debt on graduates' employment, additional schooling, family formation, and home ownership. *Education Economics, 27*(2), 186–206. https://doi.org/10.1080/09645292.2018.1541167

Vera-Toscano, E., Ateca-Amestoy, V., & Serrano-Del-Rosal, R. (2006). Building financial satisfaction. *Social Indicators Research,* 77(2), 211–243. https://doi.org/10.1007/s11205-005-2614-3

Vosloo, W., Fouché, J., & Barnard, J. (2014). The relationship between financial efficacy, satisfaction with remuneration and personal financial well-being. *International Business & Economics Research Journal, 13*(6), 1455–1470. https://doi.org/10.19030/iber.v13i6.8934

Warth, J., Puth, M.-T., Tillmann, J., Porz, J., Zier, U., Weckbecker, K., & Münster, E. (2019). Over-indebtedness and its association with sleep and sleep medication use. *BMC Public Health, 19*(1), 957. https://doi.org/10.1186/s12889-019-7231-1

Weimann, J., Knabe, A., & Schöb, R. (2015). *Measuring happiness: The economics of well-being*. Cambridge, MA: The MIT Press.

White, S. C. (2010). Analysing wellbeing: A framework for development practice. *Development in Practice, 20*(2), 158–172. https://doi.org/10.1080/09614520903564199

Włodarczyk, K. (2015a). Jakość życia postrzegana przez Polaków w XXI wieku. *Konsumpcja i Rozwój, 1*, 3–16.

Włodarczyk, K. (2015b). Quality of urban life in Poland. *Journal of International Studies, 8*(2), 155–163. https://doi.org/10.14254/2071-8330.2015/8-2/13

Worthington, A. C. (2006). Debt as a source of financial stress in Australian households. *International Journal of Consumer Studies, 30*(1), 2–15. https://doi.org/10.1111/j.1470-6431.2005.00420.x

Xiao, J. J. (2013). Family economic well-being. In G. W. Peterson & K. R. Bush (Eds.), *Handbook of marriage and the family* (pp. 573–611). Boston: Springer. https://doi.org/10.1007/978-1-4614-3987-5_24

Xiao, J. J., Chen, C., & Chen, F. (2014). Consumer financial capability and financial satisfaction. *Social Indicators Research, 118*(1), 415–432. https://doi.org/10.1007/s11205-013-0414-8

Zalega, T. (2011). Wpływ kryzysu na postawy i zachowania konsumpcyjne elit ekonomicznych. *Problemy Zarządzania, 9*(1 (31)), 186–202.

Zalega, T. (2012). Diagnoza sytuacji materialnej polskich gospodarstw domowych w okresie kryzysu finansowo-ekonomicznego. *Management and Business Administration. Central Europe, 20*(5), 50–82. https://doi.org/10.7206/mba.ce.2084-3356.29

Zalega, T. (2016). *Segment osób w wieku 65+ w Polsce. Jakość życia – Konsumpcja – Zachowania konsumenckie*. Warszawa: Wydawnictwo Naukowe Wydziału Zarządzania Uniwersytetu Warszawskiego.

Zurlo, K. A., Yoon, W., & Kim, H. (2014). Unsecured consumer debt and mental health outcomes in middle-aged and older Americans. *The Journals of Gerontology Series B: Psychological Sciences and Social Sciences, 69*(3), 461–469. https://doi.org/10.1093/geronb/gbu020

Zwierzchowski, J., & Panek, T. (2020). Measurement of subjective well-being under capability approach in Poland. *Polish Sociological Review, 2*, 157–178. https://doi.org/10.26412/psr210.02

6 The economic well-being of over-indebted households

Own research

6.1 A cross-sectional analysis of the economic well-being of over-indebted households

As stated in previous chapters, analysis of the economic well-being of households is conducted here by reference to two dimensions of need satisfaction: material and financial. In this subsection, we focus on a cross-sectional approach to the phenomenon under investigation, while in the following one we employ an aggregate measure – in the form of a composite indicator – to attempt to assess the significance of selected factors in the shaping of the economic well-being of over-indebted and not-over-indebted households.

Income level is one of the core economic categories considered when evaluating economic well-being. Table 6.1 presents the distribution of the monthly income of over-indebted (OI) and not-over-indebted households (NOI). Among the objectively over-indebted households, those with incomes of up to PLN 4,000 predominate. This means close to two-thirds of households over-indebted according to DSTI30 (debt service to income) and more than 86% of households whose per capita income after credit and loan repayments is below the poverty line. The income distribution is flatter in the case of subjectively over-indebted households than it is for households that are over-indebted according to the objective measures. It is also noticeable that the group of the wealthiest over-indebted households (with an income over PLN 6,000) is approximately one-and-a-half to two times larger when measured by subjective burden of debt (SB) than when measured by DSTI30. The income distribution of households that are not over-indebted has a shape similar to a normal distribution, with every third such household having an income of over PLN 6,000.

Alongside income, households' own perceptions of their financial state also play a role in their economic well-being. The distribution of subjectively assessed financial state is skewed rightwards for both over-indebted and not-over-indebted households (Table 6.2), and the distribution is almost identical in the case of households over-indebted according to objective measures (DSTI30 and BPL). Assessments of their own financial state made by subjectively over-indebted households are worse than the assessments made by objectively over-indebted households. This is particularly true of households that live well and

DOI: 10.4324/9781003254706-7

Table 6.1 Distribution of the monthly income of over-indebted and not-over-indebted households (%)

Item	*Monthly income of household (PLN)*				
	up to 2,000	*(2,000–4,000]*	*(4,000–6,000]*	*(6,000–8,000]*	*over 8,000*
DSTI30	33.33	32.14	23.21	5.36	5.95
BPL	38.86	47.89	12.05	0.60	0.60
SB	21.71	34.86	22.29	11.43	9.71
NOI	3.23	26.62	36.12	15.59	18.44

Table 6.2 Over-indebted and not-over-indebted households' subjective assessments of their financial state (%)

Item	*Subjective assessment of financial situation*				
	1	*2*	*3*	*4*	*5*
DSTI30	1.19	10.12	36.31	29.17	23.21
BPL	0.90	8.43	33.73	32.83	24.10
SB	1.60	17.02	39.36	29.79	12.23
NOI	0.00	1.71	19.81	42.67	35.81

Note: (1) We lack money for even basic, everyday expenditure. (2) We have enough money for our basic needs and nothing more. (3) We live frugally in order to meet at least our basic needs, and sometimes we succeed in putting some money aside for larger purchases. (4) We have enough to satisfy all of our needs. (5) We live very well and we can satisfy all of our needs – however sophisticated.

can satisfy all of their needs, even the most sophisticated needs (Assessment 5). It is also significant that a little over 10% of households whose debt repayments exceed 30% of income have enough money for basic needs and nothing more (the proportion for SB is a little over 17%), while only 1.71% of not-over-indebted households have enough money for basic needs and nothing more.

Another category defining the economic well-being of households is objective housing conditions. One of their determinants is the size of the dwelling in square metres. The area of the dwellings occupied by the majority of both over-indebted and not-over-indebted households is below the average of 83.14 m^2, which produces a right-skewed distribution (Figure 6.1). Not-over-indebted households occupy flats or houses with an area above 150 m^2, and flats with an area of 60–80 m^2, more often than do over-indebted households, while households over-indebted according to subjective measures (SB) occupy flats with an area of 40–60 m^2 more often than the households in the remaining categories (DSTI, BPL, NOI). Regardless of the indicator considered, over-indebted households occupy small flats of 20–40 m^2, or flats or houses of 100–150 m^2, more often than not-over-indebted households.

Well-being is also influenced by households' satisfaction with the dwellings they inhabit (Christoph & Noll, 2003), which is decided not only by their

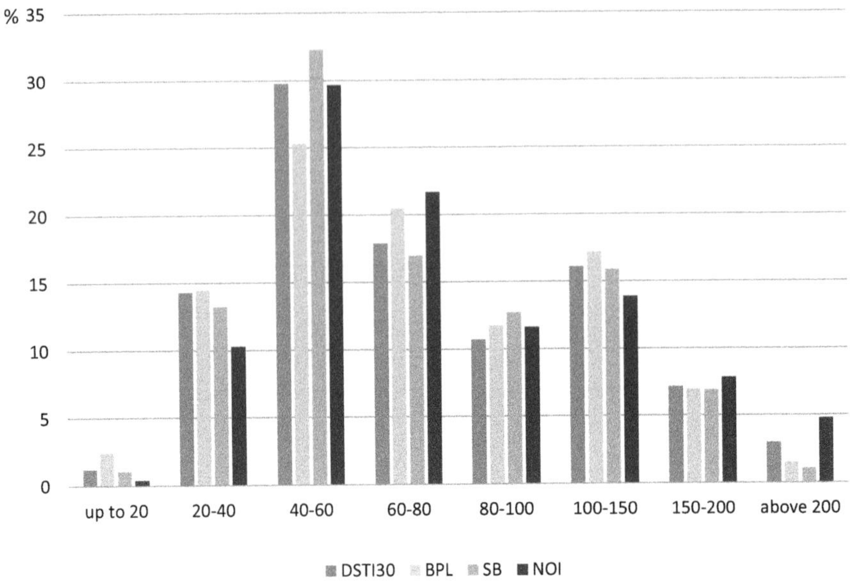

Figure 6.1 Size distribution of flats and houses occupied by over-indebted and not-over-indebted households (m^2)

size but also by whether or not they are overcrowded. Statistics Poland defines a dwelling as overcrowded when the ratio of people to rooms is 2:1 or above (GUS, 2013).[1] As the present research does not provide information on the number of rooms in an occupied dwelling, an overcrowded dwelling is assumed to be one in which the area available to each person is 28.2 m^2 or less, that is, below the average area of a dwelling in Poland in 2018 according to Statistics Poland.

In general, overcrowding of occupied dwellings is noticeable among households renting flats, or living with parents or friends, regardless of whether the household is over-indebted or not (Table 6.3). However, the proportion of such households is 9 to 18 percentage points higher among households over-indebted according to below the poverty line (BPL) and SB than among not-over-indebted households. There are similar disparities where the household owns the dwelling, although the differences are no greater than 14 percentage points. Households which own a house, which generally affords them more space, are best placed where overcrowding is concerned. When compared with not-over-indebted households, it is noticeable that of the households over-indebted according to DSTI30, the objective housing situation is better among those who own houses and worse among those who own flats. Yet even in relation to this indicator, the results do not support the conclusion that indebtedness is correlated with the size of the dwelling owned.

Table 6.3 Proportion of over-indebted and not-over-indebted households occupying overcrowded dwellings by form of ownership (%)

Item	*Form of ownership*					
	Owns flat		*Owns house*		*Renting or other*	
	Not overcrowded	*Overcrowded*	*Not overcrowded*	*Overcrowded*	*Not overcrowded*	*Overcrowded*
DSTI30	36.36	63.64	88.64	11.36	40.00	60.00
BPL	25.00	75.00	63.73	36.27	12.16	87.84
SB	28.42	71.58	75.44	24.56	21.62	78.38
NOI	38.62	61.38	85.71	14.29	30.34	69.66

Table 6.4 The subjectively perceived housing conditions of over-indebted and not-over-indebted households (%)

Item	*Housing conditions*				
	Poor	*Quite poor*	*Average*	*Quite good*	*Good*
DSTI30	0.00	0.00	22.62	17.86	59.52
BPL	1.21	0.60	23.49	23.80	50.90
SB	0.53	0.53	24.34	19.05	55.56
NOI	0.00	0.57	10.08	18.44	70.91

On the whole, there is no correspondence between subjective perceptions and objective measures of housing. This can be explained by history (the size of dwellings in Poland has tended to be small) and perhaps also by the point of reference (social norms) for the degree to which housing needs are satisfied.[2] Despite the fact that the majority of households occupy overcrowded dwellings (Table 6.3), they assess their housing conditions as either good or quite good (Table 6.4). Here, though, the highest ratings by far are given by not-over-indebted households, of which 90% assess their housing conditions as good or quite good. This contrasts with over-indebted households, which take a slightly more negative view of their housing conditions, with approximately 25% rating them as average at best. The lower ratings given by over-indebted households to their housing conditions are probably related to those conditions being objectively worse compared to not-over-indebted households, but it may also be connected with overly optimistic consumption plans. Households borrow to meet their housing needs, yet the clash between their awakened aspirations and the objective realities which – for reasons of income or creditworthiness – make those aspirations difficult or impossible to realise, leads them to view their situation as subjectively worse.

In respect of the satisfaction of consumption needs, the analysis of households' economic well-being is based on subjective assessments (declarations) regarding the main categories of expenditure (Table 6.5). The research supports the general observation that a greater proportion of respondents from over-indebted

Table 6.5 Levels of difficulty in satisfying selected consumption needs (%)

Item	*Great difficulty*	*Moderate difficulty*	*Little difficulty*	*No difficulty*
Food				
DSTI30	1.19	5.36	36.31	57.14
BPL	0.90	3.92	39.76	55.42
SB	2.12	6.35	42.86	48.68
NOI	0.57	2.09	17.11	80.23
Clothing and footwear				
DSTI30	4.22	12.05	45.78	37.95
BPL	3.33	12.12	50.91	33.64
SB	5.88	13.37	47.59	33.16
NOI	0.76	5.33	31.62	62.29
Utilities (water, gas, electricity)				
DSTI30	2.38	2.98	33.33	61.31
BPL	1.51	3.31	36.14	59.04
SB	1.06	3.17	39.68	56.08
NOI	0.38	1.71	18.63	79.28
Household furnishings and maintenance				
DSTI30	1.81	12.05	52.41	33.73
BPL	2.13	13.72	56.71	27.44
SB	3.19	18.62	54.79	23.40
NOI	0.57	8.37	47.15	43.92
Healthcare				
DSTI30	4.27	12.20	40.85	42.68
BPL	4.94	13.89	41.36	39.81
SB	7.45	14.89	45.21	32.45
NOI	2.29	8.02	37.40	52.29
Leisure time				
DSTI30	23.49	26.51	39.76	10.24
BPL	20.12	32.01	39.02	8.84
SB	23.78	35.14	36.76	4.32
NOI	6.68	18.89	49.81	24.62
Transport and communication (car, telephone, Internet)				
DSTI30	4.24	9.09	55.15	31.52
BPL	3.06	9.48	58.10	29.36
SB	4.32	14.59	57.84	23.24
NOI	1.72	4.77	38.17	55.34

households than from not-over-indebted households report difficulties in realising their consumption plans. This confirms the intuitive conclusion that the debt repayment burden has a negative impact on the satisfaction of needs.

More than 50% of over-indebted households find it at least moderately difficult to satisfy leisure-time needs, and almost 25% declare great difficulty in satisfying them. Where expenditure on healthcare and on household furnishings and maintenance is concerned, however, the proportion of over-indebted respondents declaring at least moderate difficulty is, depending on the indicator, 14 to 22%, and for transport and communication 13 to 19%. The least frequently reported problems, regardless of the degree of difficulty, were those related to the basic categories of expenditure, such as food and utilities (electricity, water, gas). It is striking, however, that the proportion of over-indebted households reporting great difficulty in satisfying selected consumption needs is considerably greater (in one extreme case, almost eight times greater) than among their not-over-indebted counterparts. Regardless of the degree of difficulty declared, it should be emphasised that – if the indications of not-over-indebted households are taken as the reference point – over-indebtedness restricts the satisfaction of the various consumption needs unevenly. This unfavourable situation is particularly evident in respect of satisfying basic needs (food, clothing and footwear, transport and communication). The proportion of households who have no difficulty in financing this type of expenditure is 26 to 27 percentage points higher among not-over-indebted households than among over-indebted ones.

For all of the above categories of consumption needs other than utilities, and against different types of indebtedness indicators, subjectively over-indebted households more often declare great or moderate difficulty in satisfying them than objectively over-indebted households. Households' views of their indebtedness, which can probably be at least partially explained by an examination of the individual characteristics and attitudes of the respondents, would therefore appear to be linked to assessments of the satisfaction of consumption needs.

It is puzzling that the proportion of over-indebted households driven below the poverty line by their debt burden and reporting difficulties is comparable to, and even in some cases lower than, that of households over-indebted according to DSTI30 and SB (especially where great difficulty is reported). Interestingly, this pattern is visible both for expenditure on basic goods (food) and on higher order goods (leisure time). These results suggest that an objectively difficult income situation shifts the reference point for consumption aspirations and modifies perceptions of the degree to which needs are satisfied (adaptive preferences are accordingly revealed) (cf. Kowalski & Kwarciński, 2016).

As expected, the financial security of over-indebted households as measured by the ability to repay debt from current income, or from savings, is far lower than that of not-over-indebted households (Table 6.6). While for the latter group, more than half of respondents are able to pay off their entire debt from current income or savings, in the case of over-indebted households this figure is, at best, less than 30% (BPL). The relatively high percentage of over-indebted

Table 6.6 The financial security of households and their budget management skills (%)

Item	*Ability to repay entire debt*		*Budget management*	
	From current income or savings	*By selling some or all assets*	*Timely debt repayment*	*Arrears in respect of various charges and payments*
DSTI30	21.43	79.17	97.02	2.98
BPL	29.82	83.18	96.99	2.11
SB	16.93	73.02	92.06	6.35
NOI	51.80	95.82	100.00	0.19

households returned by the BPL measure (when compared to over-indebted households distinguished using the SB and DSTI30 measures) could, it seems, result from the lower amounts of debt found in this group of households.

Only slightly more than 4% of not-over-indebted households are unable to cover their debt with proceeds from the sale of all of their assets. This confirms the general observation that, in relation to their assets and annual income, the debt level of Polish households is not high when compared to highly developed countries. Moreover, these households report no difficulty in repaying credit and loan instalments on time and are in arrears in other areas only sporadically. The situation of over-indebted households is in this respect worse and is especially disadvantageous in the case of the SB indicator. Almost 27% of subjectively over-indebted households are unable to repay their debt by selling all of their assets. These households are also far more likely to indicate difficulties in settling debt obligations on time (both loans and other liabilities). It may be assumed, therefore, that there are rational and objective grounds for the feeling of being overburdened with debt experienced by this group of households. An explanation for the greater difficulty subjectively over-indebted households encounter in managing their current budgets can also be sought in their specific financial attitudes (Kempson & Poppe, 2018). However, it may also be the case – as demonstrated by Sendhil Mullainathan and Eldar Shafir (2013) and Anuj K. Shah and his associates (2012) – that the psychological burden associated with debt monopolises the attention of borrowers and thereby reduces their ability to ensure that repayments are made on time.

Our research showed that over-indebtedness has a noticeable impact on the psychophysical condition of respondents (Table 6.7), and the first finding of the analysis in this respect is that debt has a stronger impact on mental health than on physical health. The second observable pattern is that the negative consequences of indebtedness for health are more evident in the group of households that feels subjectively over-indebted than in the group whose debt service-to-income ratio exceeds 30% or the group below the poverty line once repayments have been made. When compared to not-over-indebted households, the proportion of people in objectively over-indebted households (according to DSTI30) confirming the negative psychological consequences of indebtedness ranges

Table 6.7 The consequences of over-indebtedness: the health and psychological dimensions (%)

Item	*NOI*	*DSTI30*	*BPL*	*SB*
Debt is a source of health problems (high blood pressure, headaches, ulcers, and other problems)	2.85	20.83	13.86	31.75
Debt is sometimes a source of stress and worry	17.84	50.00	40.06	74.60
Debt is a severe mental burden	3.04	19.05	12.35	35.45
Debt is an unbearable mental burden	0.19	5.36	4.82	9.52

from almost three times higher (indebtedness is sometimes a source of stress and worry) to more than 28 times higher (indebtedness is an unbearable mental burden). Debt-related stress is declared by 50% of over-indebted households on the DSTI30 indicator and by as many as 75% of over-indebted households on the SB indicator. For declarations that debt represents a severe mental burden, the respective proportions are just over 19% and just over 35%. Indeed, the disproportions captured in the frequency of responses in the psychological and health dimensions are also characteristic of households over-indebted according to the other two indicators (SB and BPL).

To conclude this account of the economic well-being of households, it is worth briefly analysing their responses in respect of coping with financial difficulty. This allows for a more complete picture of the differences in attitudes (preferences) between over-indebted and not-over-indebted households and provides information – in this instance indirectly – on their economic well-being. Limiting expenditure is by far the most frequent means of coping with financial difficulty indicated by both over-indebted households (according to DSTI30, BPL, or SB) and households not classified as such by any of the indicators (DSTI30, BPL, A3, NL4, SB) (Table 6.8). No matter which indebtedness criterion is adopted, this choice – with indications of 'probably' and 'definitely' counted together – is made by approximately 80% of the households studied. The next two items in descending order of frequency, which were also selected far more often than the remaining options, are recourse to savings and taking additional work. While it appears that savings constitute a common and vital tool used in situations of financial difficulty, including in countries richer than Poland, it is interesting to note the high frequency with which taking more work is indicated in Poland in this context when compared with western countries (cf. Lusardi et al., 2011). There are at least two possible interpretations, which are not mutually exclusive and which would require in-depth research to confirm. One is connected with conditions in the labour market and the other with the specific limitations on the set of options available for coping with financial difficulty.

If we look for differences between not-over-indebted and over-indebted households in respect of the three basic means of coping with financial turmoil mentioned earlier, it should be stressed that the former indicate recourse to

Table 6.8 Methods used by over-indebted and not-over-indebted households to cope with financial difficulty (%)

Item	*NOI*		*DSTI30*		*BPL*		*SB*	
	Probably	*Definitely*	*Probably*	*Definitely*	*Probably*	*Definitely*	*Probably*	*Definitely*
Recourse to savings	47.42	25.05	42.51	19.76	48.48	19.70	36.90	17.11
Borrowing	19.12	3.63	24.10	7.83	20.06	5.17	26.34	8.06
Limiting current expenditure	48.47	27.67	49.70	33.94	53.35	24.70	50.53	31.91
Household members take additional work	35.50	19.47	34.34	25.30	32.22	23.10	32.09	29.41
Accepting help from relatives	22.43	5.51	21.43	8.93	25.60	9.04	26.06	10.64
Claiming welfare benefits	3.24	0.57	4.19	1.20	10.27	3.63	5.32	2.66
Non-payment of debt obligations and bills	0.95	0.76	3.57	3.57	5.42	1.51	6.88	2.12
Asset disposal	9.02	2.11	8.38	1.20	6.34	0.60	13.90	1.07

savings more often and limiting expenditure less often. This may indicate the existence of a kind of safety buffer in the form of savings that these households have accumulated with a view to maintaining their consumption levels and standards of living. By contrast, borrowing and non-payment – the latter being particularly characteristic of this group – are the coping strategies over-indebted households select more often than the others to remedy their financial troubles. This, in turn, could be dictated by the perception of credit as a last resort for solving the problem of repaying debt obligations and by psychological consent to the non-payment of bills resulting from personal experience of the speed, inevitability, and severity of the sanctions for falling into arrears (Wałęga, 2013, p. 153).

If the analysis is narrowed to over-indebted households only, and hence to the DSTI30, BPL, and SB indicators, two questions merit particular attention. First, the relatively low level of indications of the use of savings to cope with financial distress can be seen in the case of subjectively over-indebted households (when the 'probably' and 'definitely' answers are counted together the difference in respect of DSTI30 is above 8 percentage points and in respect of BPL above 14 percentage points). Moreover, given that this group of households is responsible for the highest proportion of indications for borrowing and asset disposal, two explanations for this circumstance emerge (which of course remain speculative in the absence of in-depth research). Either subjectively over-indebted households are particularly inclined to borrow and save simultaneously (cf. subsection 1.1) or the fact that they indicate asset disposal far more often than households over-indebted according to DSTI30 and BPL is simply due to their lack of savings. Second, households classified as over-indebted according to BPL select borrowing more rarely than the other two groups, while at the same time they select options for dealing with financial distress such as claiming welfare benefits far more often. It would appear that this can be explained by the nature of the indicator itself, which is intended to capture the households that have the greatest difficulties in satisfying basic needs and, being relatively poor, that have limited access, at least where the institutions of the banking system are concerned, to credit.

More than 90% of households (the sum of indications of 'probably' and 'definitely'), regardless of whether they are over-indebted or not, state that in the case of financial difficulties they would reduce spending on cigarettes, alcohol, and other stimulants (Table 6.9). In terms of frequency of indications, expenditure associated with leisure time (above 80%) and with household furnishings and maintenance (just under 80% in the case of all households – other than those classified as over-indebted on the BPL indicator, where the proportion is slightly above 80%) occupies second and third place, respectively. Such responses are not surprising given that these are not essential goods and some may even be perceived as luxuries and hence be foregone relatively easily. What makes these goods different from the respondents' point of view, however, is the ease with which they are willing to give them up (which can be measured by the distribution of indications of 'probably' and 'definitely'). When analysing the

Table 6.9 Expenditure foregone by over-indebted and not-over-indebted households when in financial difficulty (%)

Item	*NOI*		*DSTI30*		*BPL*		*SB*	
	Probably	*Definitely*	*Probably*	*Definitely*	*Probably*	*Definitely*	*Probably*	*Definitely*
Food	22.84	5.58	34.07	11.85	28.92	8.03	32.03	13.73
Alcohol, cigarettes, and other stimulants	12.05	80.00	12.69	78.36	15.79	76.11	11.41	79.87
Clothing and footwear	46.82	22.90	47.41	20.74	48.59	18.07	44.16	26.62
Utilities (saving on water, gas, or electricity)	16.28	16.28	38.52	20.74	41.60	20.00	43.87	16.77
Household furnishings and maintenance	52.67	25.95	43.70	34.07	50.80	29.60	41.18	37.25
Healthcare (medicines, dentistry, convalescence)	7.11	0.51	13.97	5.15	14.00	3.60	16.77	2.58
Leisure time (holidays, recreation, culture, sport)	48.35	36.39	42.22	40.74	40.96	43.78	37.50	48.68
Transport and communication (car, telephone, Internet)	42.35	15.82	43.70	17.04	43.78	16.87	40.79	20.39

most frequently indicated categories, which are (1) alcohol, cigarettes, and other stimulants, (2) leisure time, and (3) household furnishings and maintenance, we go from the overwhelming predominance of 'definitely' responses over 'probably' responses for all groups of households, through relative balance (the predominance of 'definitely' over 'probably' in the case of BPL and SB, and 'probably' over 'definitely' in the case of NOI and DSTI), to the predominance of 'probably' answers across all groups.

The convergence of households' preferred means of limiting expenditure applies to those indicated most rarely as well as to those indicated most often. Both over-indebted and not-over-indebted households were least inclined to save by cutting expenditure on food, and they were particularly averse to reducing consumption of goods and services relating to healthcare. Here again the pattern of consumption-reduction choices can be explained by the nature of the product categories examined, which are essential to human biological functioning.

Significant differences can be observed between over-indebted and not-over-indebted households in respect of three potential sources of 'savings' when in financial distress. Regardless of the criterion of indebtedness (DSTI30, BPL, or SB), the former are more often prepared to reduce expenditure on food, and far more often prepared to limit their outlay on utilities (almost twice as often) and on healthcare (more than twice as often). As in the case of coping with financial difficulty by not paying bills (Table 6.8), the explanation for these asymmetries may be sought in people's personal experiences. While for households that are not over-indebted, the question about their preferred means of limiting expenditure on particular categories of goods and services might have been hypothetical in nature, in the case of over-indebted households it was much more likely to concern concrete consumption choices made in the real world.

6.2 Measuring economic well-being: a composite indicator approach

As the discussions set out in subsection 5.1 demonstrate, the notion of well-being spans a number of dimensions of human activity. This is significant for analysis insofar as the existence of qualitatively and quantitatively construed categories requires the application of a different set of research methods adapted to the nature of the data held. However, no set of indicators offering a universal, multidimensional description of the well-being of all population groups and a platform for comparative analysis over time and space has yet been specified. With a broad range of indicators at their disposal, different authors have proposed a variety of methods for measuring quality of life. In the international and Polish literature, they include various types of composite indicators (Diener, 2000; Grzega, 2012; Kalinowski, 2015; McGillivray & Noorbakhsh, 2007; Michalos, 2014; Panek, 2015b, 2015a, 2017; Veenhoven, 2007; Zeliaś, 2000), including ones based on fuzzy sets theory (Betti, 2017; Betti et al., 2016; Dudek & Szczesny, 2016; Kwarciński & Ulman, 2020).

In this subsection, a fuzzy sets approach – first developed to analyse poverty – is used to evaluate the quality of life of over-indebted and not-over-indebted households from the perspective of financial well-being. It is based on the concept of fuzzy sets originally proposed by Lotfi Zadeh (1965) and used to study societal impoverishment by Andrea Cerioli and Sergio Zani (1990), Bruno Cheli and Achille Lemmi (1995), Gianni Betti and his team (2015), and Vijay Verma and his associates (2017).

Methods of assessing poverty in its non-monetary dimensions, which have also been employed by Gianni Betti and his associates (2015, 2016), Hanna Dudek and Wiesław Szczesny (2016), and Tomasz Kwarciński and Paweł Ulman (2020) as synthetic quality-of-life measures, have been adapted to investigate the economic well-being of over-indebted households. The signal advantage of this approach, which involves determining the degree to which each household analysed is a member of groups that are satisfied with particular life domains, is that it allows both quantitative and qualitative features to be included when estimating an indicator of well-being. The empirical values of the features under consideration are transformed as follows with the use of a membership function (cf. Panek, 2011):

$$e_{hji} = \frac{F\left(c_{hji}\right) - F(1)}{1 - F(1)}, h = 1,2,\ldots,m; j = 1,2,\ldots,k_h; i = 1,2,\ldots,n, \quad (1)$$

where

$F\left(c_{hji}\right)$ – the value of the distribution function of the distribution of ranks of a j-th variable (an element of well-being) from the h-th well-being domain for the i-th household,

$F(1)$ – the value of the distribution function of the distribution of ranks of a j-th variable from the h-th well-being domain for a rank equal to 1 (a variation of the j-th variable indicating the lowest level of well-being).

The values of this measure are obtained for each variable (indicator) and are in the interval [0, 1].

The higher the value of the indicator determined by equation (1), the better the well-being indicated by the relevant variable. In the next step, the scores, calculated using equation (1), are aggregated by calculating a weighted average for each dimension and the arithmetic average for the overall well-being score. The following equation is used to obtain an aggregated and normalised value of the well-being score for each domain:

$$e_{hi} = \frac{\sum_{j=1}^{k_h} w_{hj} \cdot e_{hji}}{\sum_{j=1}^{k_h} w_{hj}} \quad (2)$$

where

e_{hi} – the aggregated well-being score for the i-th household in domain h,

w_{hj} – weighting for variable j in domain h,

k_h – number of variables in domain h.

Within each domain, a variety of weighting systems can be used to aggregate the well-being indicators.[3] The method used here is that applied by Gianni Betti and Vijay Verma (1999):

$$w_{hj} = w_{hj}^{a} \cdot w_{hj}^{b}, h = 1,2,\ldots,m; j = 1,2,\ldots,k_h \tag{3}$$

where
w_{hj}^{a} – measure of the variation in variable *j* determining well-being in domain *h*,
w_{hj}^{b} – measure of the correlation of variable *j* with other elements of well-being from the *h*-th domain.

The measure of the differentiation of the variables is:

$$w_{hj}^{a} = \frac{S(e_{hj})}{\overline{e_{hj}}} \tag{4}$$

where
$S(e_{hj})$ – standard deviation of variable *j* determining well-being in domain *h*,
$\overline{e_{hj}}$ – average of variable *j* determining well-being in domain *h*.

The measure of correlation (Panek, 2011) can be expressed as follows:

$$w_{hj}^{b} = \left(\frac{1}{1+\sum_{j'=1}^{k_h}\left|r_{e_{hj},h_{j'}}\right| \mid r_{e_{hj},h_{j'}} < r_{e_{hj}}^{\star}}\right)\left(\frac{1}{\sum_{j'=1}^{k_h}\left|r_{e_{hj},h_{j'}}\right| \mid r_{e_{hj},h_{j'}} \geq r_{e_{hj}}^{\star}}\right), \tag{5}$$

$$j, j' = 1,2,\ldots,k_h; h = 1,2,\ldots,m$$

where
$r_{e_{hj},h_{j'}}$ – correlation coefficient of the variables *j* and *j'* determining well-being in domain *h*,
$r_{e_{hj}}^{\star}$ – threshold value of the correlation coefficient for variable *j* determining well-being in domain *h*.

The threshold value of the correlation coefficient can be determined by a minimax equation:

$$r_{e_{hj}}^{\star} = \min_{j} \max_{j'} \left|r_{e_{hj},h_{j'}}\right|, j, j' = 1,2,\ldots,k_h; j \neq j' \tag{6}$$

This weighting method possesses many advantages (Betti et al., 2015; Dudek & Szczesny, 2015):

- it assigns less weight to indicators of low variation;
- it accounts for redundancy and does not reproduce the same information contained in various partial indicators in a given domain;
- it was officially adopted by Eurostat (2002) in measurements of poverty and social exclusion.

Next, the well-being scores for the particular domains are aggregated as a single composite well-being indicator for each household:

$$e_i = \frac{\sum_{h=1}^{m} e_{hi}}{m}, i = 1,2,\ldots,n \quad (7)$$

where m – number of domains.

The values of the composite indicator (7) fall within the interval [0, 1]. The higher the value of the indicator, the better the well-being.

The variables displayed in Table 6.10 were used to construct a composite indicator of economic well-being. Assessment of the economic well-being of over-indebted households and those not classified as such was conducted in two dimensions:[4] financial and material.

Table 6.10 Baseline variables identifying economic well-being

Variable	*Description*
Financial dimension	
Objective	
Income (PLN)	Up to 2,000 (2,000–4,000] (4,000–6,000] (6,000–8,000] Above 8,000
Debt repayment	Impossible even by selling all assets or wealth Possible only by selling some or all assets or wealth Can be met in full from current income and savings
Timely debt repayment	Delayed – or payments discontinued Ahead of schedule or on schedule
Arrears in respect of various charges and payments	Yes No
Subjective	
Subjective assessment of financial situation	We lack money for even basic, everyday expenditure We have enough money for our basic needs and nothing more We live frugally in order to meet at least our basic needs, and sometimes we manage to put some money aside for larger purchases We have enough to satisfy all of our needs We live very well and we can satisfy all of our needs – however sophisticated
Indebtedness is a source of health problems	Yes No
Indebtedness is a source of stress or mental strain	Yes No

Variable	*Description*
Material dimension	
Objective	
Form of ownership of flat or house	Social housing, local authority housing, rented housing, other
	Privately owned flat, tenanted cooperative housing or housing association, or house/ part of a house
Area of flat or house in square metres	Area of flat or house in square metres per person
Subjective	
Assessment of housing conditions	Poor
	Quite poor
	Average
	Quite good
	Good
Satisfaction of household needs (ability to finance expenditure given financial situation):	No – definitely not No – not really Yes – but only partially
– food	Yes – definitely
– clothing and footwear	
– utilities (water, gas, electricity)	
– household furnishings and maintenance	
– healthcare (visits to doctor, medicines, treatment)	
– expenditure on leisure time (holidays, recreation, culture, sport)	
– transport and communication (car, telephone, Internet)	

Cronbach's alpha coefficient was employed to assess the reliability of the measurement scale for economic well-being (the consistency of the items included in the composite indicator). It evaluates how well a set of baseline indicators of economic well-being measures a single, unidimensional phenomenon described by a latent variable (measured by a composite indicator). Its values fall within the interval [0, 1]. In practice, measurement is assumed to be reliable when the value of the coefficient is greater than 0.7 (Panek, 2017).

For all variables (Table 6.10), the Cronbach alpha coefficient was 0.83, which shows that the baseline indicators measure economic well-being correctly, which is to say that the measurement is reliable. For the financial and material dimensions, the respective values of the coefficient were 0.62 and 0.82.

The distribution of composite indicator values displayed in Figure 6.2 and the information set out in Table 6.11 provide a platform for comparing the economic well-being of over-indebted and not-over-indebted households. It is generally the case that the situation of not-over-indebted households is better – regardless of whether it is gauged by the general indicator or by its individual

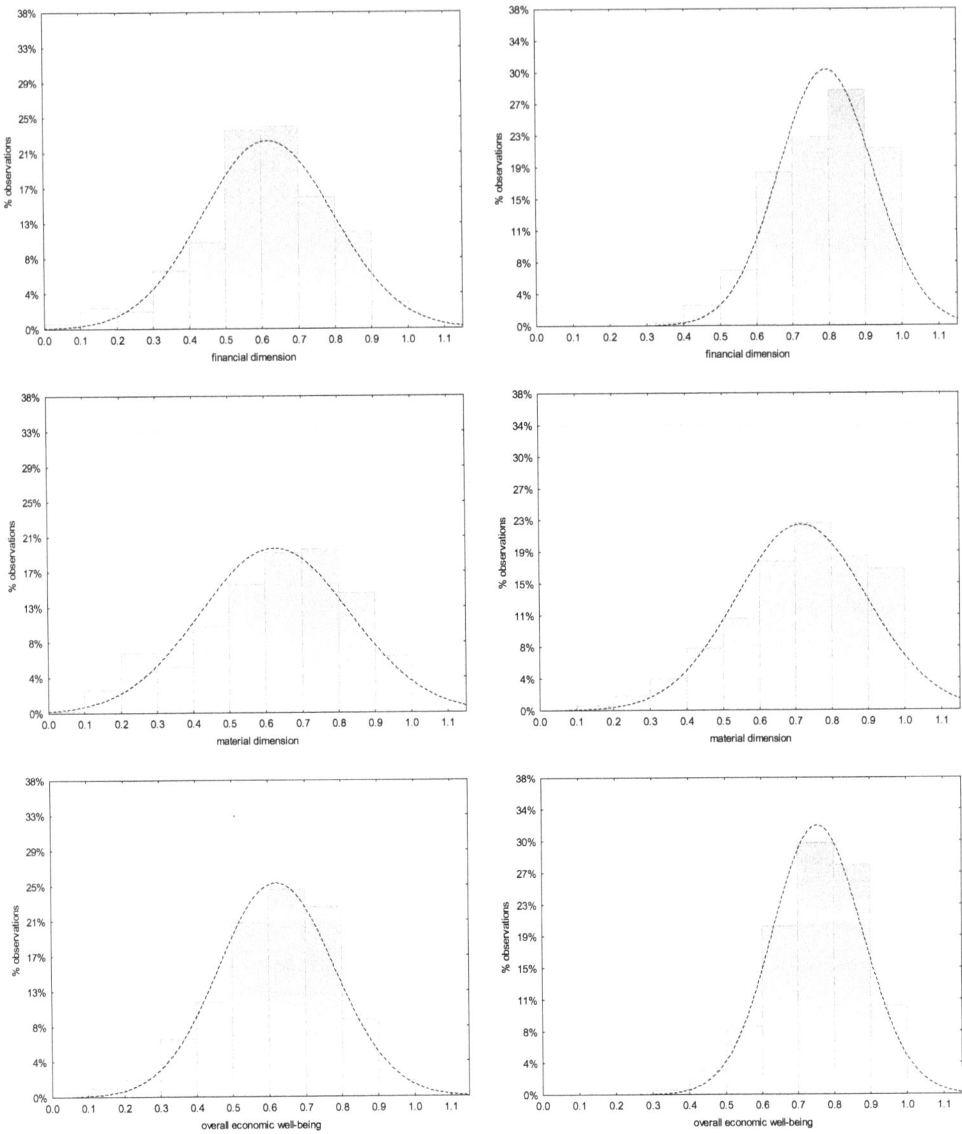

Over-indebted households

Not-over-indebted households

Figure 6.2 Distribution of indicator values for the overall well-being, and for financial and material dimensions of well-being of over-indebted households (left panel) and not-over-indebted households (right panel)

dimensions. This conclusion is supported not only by the average value of the indicators but also by the median. The distributions of the investigated indicators are skewed leftwards (this is confirmed by the skewness coefficient – Table 6.11), which signifies that the economic well-being of the majority of households is better than the average suggests.

Based on the distributions of the values of the economic well-being indicators, it may be stated that they are flatter for over-indebted households than they are for households for which over-indebtedness does not present a problem. This indicates greater differentiation (dispersion with respect to the average) in the economic well-being of over-indebted households, which is also confirmed by the coefficient of variation (Table 6.11). This group can therefore include both households of very high well-being and households of low well-being.

A more detailed analysis of economic well-being can be conducted by comparing it between different groups of households. Table 6.12 displays the values of the composite indicator for the economic well-being of over-indebted and not-over-indebted households (overall, and in the financial and material dimensions). The overall conclusion that the economic well-being of not-over-indebted households is better – regardless of the criterion used – than the well-being of over-indebted households was confirmed for all dimensions. The difference in the overall value of the composite indicator between not-over-indebted and over-indebted households ranges from 0.13 to 0.18 in favour of the former, although in individual dimensions the variance is 0.04 to 0.26. Generally, households over-indebted according to the SB indicator have the poorest well-being, largely as a result of considerably worse well-being in the financial

Table 6.11 Basic characteristics of the economic well-being indicator – overall, and in the financial and material dimensions – for over-indebted and not-over-indebted households

Item	*Average*	*Min*	*Max*	*CV*	*Skewness*	*Q25*	*Med*	*Q75*
Financial dimension								
OI	0.614	0.073	1.000	29.19	−0.560	0.505	0.605	0.753
NOI	0.789	0.352	1.000	16.48	−0.541	0.697	0.797	0.870
Overall	0.706	0.073	1.000	25.28	−0.742	0.595	0.728	0.844
Material dimension								
OI	0.622	0.094	0.993	32.94	−0.508	0.498	0.651	0.766
NOI	0.713	0.123	0.991	25.17	−0.687	0.607	0.734	0.859
Overall	0.670	0.094	0.993	29.46	−0.629	0.542	0.697	0.825
Overall economic well-being								
OI	0.618	0.119	0.961	25.47	−0.433	0.517	0.626	0.739
NOI	0.751	0.320	0.990	16.49	−0.437	0.662	0.763	0.844
Overall	0.688	0.119	0.990	22.64	−0.584	0.592	0.708	0.801

Note: CV – coefficient of variation; Med – median; OI – over-indebted; NOI – not-over-indebted.

Table 6.12 Values of the economic well-being indicator – overall, and in the financial and material dimensions – by socio-demographic, economic, and household indebtedness characteristics

Item	*DSTI30*			*BPL*			*SB*			*NOI*		
	FD	*MD*	*Overall*	*FD*	*MD*	*Overall*	*FD*	*MD*	*Overall*	*FD*	*MD*	*Overall*
Sex												
Woman	0.584	0.677	0.631	0.574	0.583	0.579	0.524	0.605	0.564	0.793	0.712	0.752
Man	0.582	0.663	0.623	0.598	0.594	0.596	0.528	0.626	0.577	0.786	0.714	0.750
Age ranges												
Up to 34	0.662	0.647	0.654	0.656	0.541	0.598	0.589	0.591	0.590	0.790	0.638	0.714
35–54	0.598	0.706	0.652	0.592	0.621	0.606	0.556	0.632	0.594	0.813	0.727	0.770
55+	0.502	0.624	0.563	0.486	0.600	0.543	0.433	0.608	0.521	0.748	0.778	0.763
Education												
Basic vocational or lower	0.461	0.582	0.521	0.541	0.564	0.552	0.410	0.528	0.469	0.742	0.640	0.691
Secondary	0.582	0.673	0.627	0.601	0.588	0.594	0.509	0.597	0.553	0.778	0.695	0.736
Tertiary	0.659	0.718	0.689	0.628	0.632	0.630	0.628	0.699	0.663	0.814	0.753	0.783
Number of people in household												
1	0.463	0.704	0.584	0.385	0.641	0.513	0,400	0.688	0.544	0.700	0.765	0.733
2	0.559	0.677	0.618	0.509	0.567	0.538	0.497	0.606	0.552	0.767	0.724	0.745
3	0.633	0.663	0.648	0.615	0.635	0.625	0.564	0.647	0.605	0.800	0.694	0.747
4	0.659	0.656	0.658	0.636	0.598	0.617	0.570	0.569	0.570	0.829	0.702	0.765
5+	0.585	0.600	0.592	0.633	0.532	0.583	0.547	0.546	0.546	0.886	0.685	0.785
Place of residence												
Rural	0.580	0.729	0.655	0.601	0.652	0.626	0.504	0.656	0.580	0.802	0.775	0.789
Small town	0.564	0.662	0.613	0.580	0.565	0.573	0.509	0.603	0.556	0.778	0.691	0.735
Large town	0.609	0.619	0.614	0.585	0.539	0.562	0.564	0.591	0.578	0.797	0.707	0.752

Income (PLN)												
Up to 2,000	0.414	0.618	0.516	0.487	0.570	0.528	0.320	0.591	0.456	0.523	0.639	0.581
(2,000–6,000]	0.653	0.691	0.672	0.653	0.602	0.627	0.556	0.600	0.578	0.759	0.692	0.726
Above 6,000	0.742	0.712	0.727	0.664	0.686	0.675	0.718	0.713	0.715	0.869	0.760	0.815
Debt type												
Bank	0.605	0.703	0.654	0.582	0.633	0.608	0.507	0.643	0.575	0.794	0.732	0.763
Non-bank	0.490	0.503	0.496	0.634	0.551	0.592	0.508	0.500	0.504	0.802	0.679	0.740
Mixed	0.568	0.652	0.610	0.523	0.562	0.543	0.559	0.628	0.594	0.741	0.733	0.737
Number of credits and loans												
1	0.604	0.707	0.655	0.621	0.610	0.615	0.512	0.621	0.567	0.797	0.719	0.758
2+	0.570	0.644	0.607	0.544	0.564	0.554	0.535	0.612	0.574	0.774	0.701	0.737
Overall	**0.583**	**0.669**	**0.626**	**0.589**	**0.590**	**0.590**	**0.526**	**0.616**	**0.571**	**0.789**	**0.713**	**0.751**

Note: FD – financial dimension; MD – material dimension; NOI – not-over-indebted.

dimension compared with households classified as over-indebted according to DSTI30 and BPL and with not-over-indebted households.

Households over-indebted according to the DSTI30 and SB indicators are generally characterised by better well-being in the material than in the financial dimension. By comparison, groups of households with a better situation in the financial dimension are far more frequent among those over-indebted according to the BPL indicator. That said, well-being in the material dimension is slightly better in the majority of groups. However, well-being is better in the financial dimension than in the material dimension for the majority of groups of households classified as not-over-indebted. The exceptions are households in the 55+ age range, one-person households, and households with the lowest monthly incomes. This is unsurprising, given that these are the very types of household which – regardless of the amount of debt they hold – are subject to strong pressure in the financial sphere (financial constraints).

It may be noted when analysing the importance of socio-demographic and economic features for the economic well-being of over-indebted households that well-being in the financial realm improves with educational level, the number of people in a household (with the exception of households of five people or more), and income. The results are consistent with expectations – better well-being in this dimension is obtained by households with socio-economic characteristics that tend to shape their economic situation positively. The age of a respondent has the opposite effect, however. The findings in respect of the relationship between household size and well-being are consistent with those of Maria Francesca Cracolici and her team (2014), who explained that low economic well-being exists among one-person households because they are unable to share running costs with a partner, which causes greater stress. But in the case of households with two or more children, they associated the lower well-being with difficulties in satisfying needs at an acceptable level.

Household size and place of residence have an adverse effect on well-being in the material dimension. On the other hand, in terms of age, households in the 35–54 range are marked by the best well-being in the material dimension, while those aged up to 34 are in the best situation in the financial dimension. These findings are consistent with those of Andrzej Cwynar (2020), who established that the level of financial well-being of Generation Y (millennials, that is, people born in the 1980s and 1990s) is significantly higher than that of other generations. The position of not-over-indebted households is a little different. Here, the best well-being in the financial dimension is found in the case of households in the 35–54 age range, and the best in the material dimension among households aged 55 and above.

Households with only bank debt are characterised by better economic well-being when compared with households that mix bank debt with other debt types – this is a pattern not observed only among households over-indebted according to SB. The worst ratings of economic well-being are recorded for over-indebted households (identified on the basis of DSTI30 and SB) whose credit is derived exclusively from non-bank lenders. This is not a surprising result – it can be surmised that in great measure these are households whose income situation makes bank loans unobtainable. Turning to the number of credits and loans, it can be seen that, in general (the exception once again being households over-indebted according to SB), households with one credit have better economic well-being – both overall and in individual dimensions.

Prompted by the observed disparities in economic well-being, the inequality of the distribution of the values of the composite indicator of economic well-being was investigated with the aid of the Gini coefficient.[5] This approach allowed the level of well-being of each surveyed household to be included in this measurement of inequality.

The values of the Gini coefficient indicate that the economic well-being (overall, and in the financial and material dimensions) of not-over-indebted households is closest to an egalitarian distribution. In turn, the greatest inequalities in well-being in the financial dimension are to be found among subjectively over-indebted households (SB) and in the material dimension among households over-indebted according to the BPL indicator. The Gini coefficient value for the former group of households is 0.230 and for the latter 0.205 (Table 6.13).

To analyse inequality with the aid of the decomposable Theil index[6] makes it possible to determine the proportion of a given subgroup (over-indebted or not-over-indebted) 'responsible' for overall inequality (Table 6.14). Regardless of the dimension, the over-indebted households contribute more

Table 6.13 Gini coefficient values representing the inequality of the distribution of the economic well-being of over-indebted and not-over-indebted households

Item	*FD*	*MD*	*Overall*
DSTI30	0.199	0.171	0.155
BPL	0.169	0.205	0.152
SB	0.230	0.193	0.178
OI	0.167	0.190	0.148
NOI	0.096	0.145	0.097

Note: FD – financial dimension; MD – material dimension; OI – over-indebted; NOI – not-over-indebted

Table 6.14 Theil index decomposition of the inequality of economic well-being

Item	*FD*	*MD*	*Overall*
Theil index	0.0359	0.0488	0.0277
OI (%)	55.31	55.36	54.01
NOI (%)	23.10	39.90	29.05
Intergroup inequality (%)	21.59	4.73	16.94

Note: FD – financial dimension; MD – material dimension; OI – over-indebted; NOI – not-over-indebted

to creating it. Inequalities of economic well-being among over-indebted households shape well-being in almost the same proportions in the financial and material dimensions (55.31% and 55.36%, respectively). Intergroup inequalities – between the economic well-being of over-indebted and not-over-indebted households – have the greatest influence on overall inequality in the financial dimension (21.59%). For its part, the relatively low intergroup inequality (4.73%) recorded in the material dimension could be the result of low differentiation in the housing conditions of over-indebted and not-over-indebted households.

6.3 The impact of over-indebtedness on economic well-being

In addition to conducting studies aimed at measuring well-being, it is also important to analyse its relationship with the demographic, economic, and sociological factors that shape it. Scholars have employed various methods to identify the determinants of quality of life, which include linear or linearised models (Łuszczyk, 2013), logistic regression (Czech, 2017; Dębicka et al., 2017; Rutherford & Fox, 2010; Słaby, 2016), fractional regression models (FRM) (Dudek, 2017), ordered logit or probit models (Brown & Gray, 2016; Perera, 2014), hierarchical models (Diener et al., 2013; Netemeyer et al., 2018), multilevel models (Suchecka & Łaszkiewicz, 2017), structural equation modelling (Llosada-Gistau et al., 2015; Zwierzchowski & Panek, 2020), and the classification and regression tree approach (CART) (Galletta, 2016).

Regression modelling was employed to analyse the influence of over-indebtedness on the economic well-being of households. Taking advantage of the classical least squares method, the parameters of a linear model were estimated[7] for a composite indicator of economic well-being (Table 6.15). The explanatory variables first proposed were those identifying over-indebted households based on the various indicators and, as in Table 4.7, the socio-demographic and economic characteristics of the households.[8] The independent variables also included respondents' psychological features as well as debt types – bank, non-bank, and mixed.

The variables in the estimated models were selected by the backward stepwise regression method. All of the parameter assessments proved to be statistically significantly different from zero. An F-test determined that the influence of all of the explanatory variables in explaining the variation of the dependent variable (the value of the economic well-being indicator) was significant and rejected the hypothesis that these variables have no combined effect on economic well-being. The value of the coefficient of determination (R^2) ranged from 34.2% (model 3) to 74.4% (model 2). These coefficients of determination values can be considered satisfactory in the case of individual data, as the statistical significance of the influence of the factors examined on economic well-being is vitally important to the present research.

Table 6.15 Parameter estimates for the linear model of the composite indicator of economic well-being

Item	*Overall (Model 1)*				*Financial dimension (Model 2)*				*Material dimension (Model 3)*			
	Coef.	*Stderr*	*t -statistic (987)*	*p-value*	*Coef.*	*Std err*	*t-statistic (991)*	*p-value*	*Coef.*	*Std err*	*t-statistic (995)*	*p-value*
Intercept	0.217	0.032	6.744	0.000	0.093	0.025	3.664	0.000	0.302	0.046	6.568	0.000
DSTI30	–	–	–	–	−0.020	0.009	−2.266	0.024	–	–	–	–
BPL	−0.026	0.010	−2.522	0.012	−0.055	0.010	−5.706	0.000	–	–	–	–
SB	−0.045	0.009	−4.966	0.000	−0.080	0.008	−9.377	0.000	–	–	–	–
A3	−0.133	0.024	−5.484	0.000	−0.181	0.022	−8.169	0.000	−0.090	0.039	−2.311	0.021
DT_2	–	–	–	–	0.026	0.007	3.940	0.000	−0.041	0.011	−3.620	0.000
NL	−0.013	0.004	−3.184	0.001	−0.013	0.004	−3.529	0.000	−0.012	0.006	−1.889	0.059
EDU	0.018	0.003	5.877	0.000	0.010	0.003	3.969	0.000	0.028	0.005	5.732	0.000
AGE	0.034	0.005	6.339	0.000	0.013	0.005	2.605	0.009	0.057	0.008	7.259	0.000
NUM	0.017	0.003	5.338	0.000	0.045	0.003	15.042	0.000	−0.010	0.005	−2.064	0.039
RESID	−0.024	0.003	−6.813	0.000	–	–	–	–	−0.048	0.006	−8.603	0.000
SAFS	0.068	0.004	16.794	0.000	0.090	0.004	24.579	0.000	0.048	0.006	7.533	0.000
QINC	0.038	0.004	9.877	0.000	0.040	0.004	11.399	0.000	0.036	0.005	7.763	0.000
SI_2	−0.045	0.010	−4.310	0.000	–	–	–	–	−0.048	0.012	−3.941	0.000
SI_3	−0.019	0.010	−1.900	0.058	–	–	–	–	–	–	–	–
SI_4	−0.030	0.014	−2.184	0.029	−0.023	0.010	−2.249	0.025	–	–	–	–
SI_5	−0.050	0.017	−2.921	0.004	−0.039	0.014	−2.792	0.005	–	–	–	–
BEH_2	−0.036	0.015	−2.378	0.018	−0.036	0.014	−2.654	0.008	–	–	–	–
BEH_5	0.027	0.010	2.812	0.005	–	–	–	–	0.049	0.016	3.105	0.002
Statistics of the model	$R^2 = 0.597$; $F(16.987) = 91.55$ ($p<0.001$); standard error of the estimation: 0.100				$R^2 = 0.744$; $F(14.991) = 205.79$ ($p<0.001$); standard error of the estimation: 0.091				$R^2 = 0.342$; $F(11.995) = 46.97$ ($p<0.001$); standard error of the estimation: 0.161			

Note: QINC – quintiles of per capita income; designation of remaining variables as in Table 4.7. Categorical variables are employed in the models, and dummy variables have been used in cases in which a digit appears in the designation of a variable.

It can be stated in analysing the influence of over-indebtedness on household economic well-being that – regardless of the indicator adopted – it has a negative influence on well-being in the financial dimension (model 2). The situation is similar in respect of overall economic well-being (model 1). The results of the estimations therefore fully confirm the findings set out in Table 6.12. Only over-indebtedness due to repayment arrears of 3 months or more (A3) (model 3) worsens well-being in the material dimension. This is the variable that has the most powerful impact on the value of the composite indicator in each model. The number of credits held also has a negative influence on economic well-being (models 1–3).

The determinants of well-being also include households' socio-demographic features. Both overall and in the two dimensions, economic well-being improves with the respondent's educational level, age, and the number of people in the household (although this does not apply to the latter variable in the material dimension). Maria Francesca Cracolici and her team (2014) demonstrated that in its interrelationships and interactions with economic factors (income) and personal factors, education has a positive influence on well-being. However, the results obtained in respect of age are not consistent with those of other authors (cf. Cwynar, 2020; Panek, 2015a; Włodarczyk, 2015). Income level (captured here as quintile groups – QINC) and households' subjective assessments of their financial situation have a positive influence on economic well-being too. In the models considered, these are among the variables that determine well-being most strongly. What is more, their direction of impact is consistent with expectations and with previous research (cf. Burchardt, 2005; Diener & Biswas-Diener, 2002; Zwierzchowski & Panek, 2020).

Place of residence, however, exerts a negative influence on economic well-being – both overall (model 1) and in the material dimension (model 3), the larger the locality in which a household resides, the poorer is its economic well-being. The well-being of blue-collar households and of those supporting themselves from other sources (model 1) is noticeably worse when compared to self-employed households. The households of retirement and disability pensioners, and of households supporting themselves from other sources (model 2) are in a worse situation in the financial dimension (model 2), while in the material dimension it is only blue-collar households that differ significantly statistically from self-employed households.

With respondents' behavioural features in mind, it is noticeable that people who are optimists (BEH_5) (models 1 and 3) have better well-being both overall and in the material dimension. Meanwhile, making purchases with the aim of emulating others (BEH_2) (models 1 and 2) worsens well-being. These results indicate that economic well-being depends not only on the socio-economic attributes of households but also on the individual characteristics of respondents – their attitudes, beliefs, and lifestyles. This accords with the findings of Judith Aboagye and Ji Young Jung (2018), who, using data from the American National Financial Capability Study, identified a negative relationship between the propensity to overspend and perceived satisfaction with one's financial situation.

With the influence of over-indebtedness on economic well-being confirmed (models 1–3), the next stage in the analysis was to identify the similarities and differences in the factors that influence the economic well-being of over-indebted and not-over-indebted households. For households over-indebted according to at least one of the indicators, and for not-over-indebted households, Table 6.16 presents the results of the parameter estimates for linear models of overall economic well-being. The estimated models explain 52% and 48% of the variation in economic well-being, respectively. For models 4 and 5, the result of the significance test for the distribution of regression coefficients allows us to reject the null hypothesis in favour of an alternative hypothesis: that there is a linear relationship between the explained variable (economic well-being) and at least one of the variables included in the model.

The majority of the proposed variables have a statistically significant influence on shaping the economic well-being of households. For both groups of households, well-being improves in line with per capita income and their subjective assessment of their financial situation. A similar relationship was shown

Table 6.16 Parameter estimates for the linear model of the composite indicator of overall economic well-being for over-indebted and not-over-indebted households

Item	*Over-indebted (model 4)*				*Not-over-indebted (model 5)*			
	Coef.	*Std err*	*t-statistic (467)*	*p-value*	*Coef.*	*Std err*	*t-statistic (514)*	*p-value*
Intercept	0.213	0.034	6.301	0.000	0.115	0.036	3.161	0.002
QINC	0.035	0.005	7.148	0.000	0.044	0.004	10.277	0.000
SAFS	0.078	0.006	13.821	0.000	0.065	0.005	12.479	0.000
SI_2	−0.047	0.012	−4.106	0.000	–	–	–	–
SI_5	−0.062	0.020	−3.076	0.002	–	–	–	–
NL	−0.016	0.006	−2.910	0.004	−0.014	0.007	−2.104	0.036
DT_2	−0.023	0.012	−1.923	0.055	–	–	–	–
NUM	0.012	0.005	2.490	0.013	0.023	0.004	5.794	0.000
RESID	−0.037	0.006	−6.596	0.000	−0.014	0.004	−3.332	0.001
EDU	0.020	0.005	4.315	0.000	0.020	0.004	5.488	0.000
AGE	–	–	–	–	0.046	0.006	8.091	0.000
BEH_2	–	–	–	–	−0.051	0.018	−2.807	0.005
BEH_5	0.046	0.014	3.242	0.001	–	–	–	–
BEH_7	–	–	–	–	0.027	0.013	2.051	0.041
BEH_8	0.030	0.015	1.953	0.051	–	–	–	–
Statistics of the model	$R^2 = 0.515$; $F(11.467) = 45.12$ ($p<0.001$); standard error of the estimation: 0.111				$R^2 = 0.480$; $F(9.514) = 52.70$ ($p<0.001$); standard error of the estimation: 0.090			

Note: QINC – quintiles of per capita income; designation of remaining variables as in Table 4.7. Categorical variables are employed in the models, and dummy variables have been used in cases in which a digit appears in the designation of a variable.

in studies by Richard Easterlin (2001), Maria Francesca Cracolici and her team (2014), and Nurul Shahnaz Mahdzan and his associates (2019). Economic well-being also improves the greater the number of people in a respondent's household and the higher their educational level. The positive impact of education on quality of life was confirmed in research carried out by Hanna Dudek and Wiesław Szczesny (2016). In not-over-indebted households, age too has a positive effect on economic well-being (model 5).

The size of the locality in which a household resides has a negative impact on economic well-being – the larger the locality, the poorer the well-being. Economic well-being also deteriorates as the number of credits held increases. In the case of over-indebted households (model 4), the type of debt held can worsen well-being, such that holding non-bank debt indicates poorer well-being when compared to other debt types. In addition, source of income has a negative impact on economic well-being (model 4) and, more precisely, it may be stated that households supporting themselves from blue-collar work, or from other sources of income such as farming and benefits, experience significantly worse well-being than self-employed households.

Economic well-being also turns out to be significantly determined by certain psychological characteristics of respondents. For over-indebted households (model 4), being an optimist (BEH_5) and making informed financial decisions (BEH_8) has a positive impact on well-being. Finally, for not-over-indebted households (model 5), having a basic knowledge of economics (BEH_7) increases well-being, while respondents who make purchases to emulate their friends and acquaintances (BEH_2) have poorer well-being.

6.4 Summary

The income situation of over-indebted households varies depending on the indicator applied to measure their indebtedness. Generally speaking, a greater proportion of households with higher income was noted among subjectively over-indebted households than among households objectively over-indebted according to the DSTI and BPL indicators. Regardless of which indicator of over-indebtedness is used, a pronounced rightward skew of the income distribution is noticeable when compared to not-over-indebted households. When assessing their own financial situation, over-indebted households take a far less favourable view than not-over-indebted households.

Economic well-being can be evaluated not only through the lens of income but also on the basis of housing conditions. The conducted research does not allow us to conclude unequivocally that the housing situation of over-indebted households (taking into account the size of the dwelling and the overcrowding rate) differs from that of not-over-indebted households. Yet in their subjective assessments of their housing situation, the former take a noticeably poorer view (on all indicators) compared to not-over-indebted households.

An important dimension in the evaluation of economic well-being is measuring how difficult it is for the studied households to realise their consumption plans. The subjective level of need satisfaction is generally lower among over-indebted households than among not-over-indebted households. Across product groups (needs), however, the impact of over-indebtedness is not uniform. While all households are least likely to report significant difficulties in meeting basic needs (such as food or utilities), it is in these areas that the greatest disparities between over-indebted and not-over-indebted households are visible. Another interesting conclusion is that in almost every cross section – if the analysis is restricted to great and moderate difficulty in meeting consumption needs – people who feel subjectively over-indebted rate their level of need satisfaction worse than do others.

Matters of financial security make up another dimension of financial well-being. It emerged from the analysis, which found that the proportion of over-indebted households unable to repay their entire debt even after selling all of their assets was greater by 13 to 23 percentage points than among not-over-indebted households, that, regardless of the indicator, to be classified as over-indebted lowers the level of financial well-being. On the other hand, the differences between the two groups of households are not so great where loan repayment arrears are concerned, and being in arrears is not in itself very common.

These questions of financial security are associated with non-economic consequences of indebtedness. In light of international research, it is indisputable that indebtedness powerfully determines the psychological and health aspects of well-being. Indeed, the impact of over-indebtedness on the studied households is felt first and foremost in the psychological dimension – three out of four people classified as over-indebted according to the SB indicator experience stress and worry associated with the debt they hold, while for nearly one in ten of them it represents an unbearable mental burden. The proportion of households declaring psychological problems of varying severity is smaller, though still significant, among households classified as over-indebted according to the other indicators. Over-indebted households also report physical health problems, such as high blood pressure and headaches, more frequently than not-over-indebted households.

In the case of financial difficulty, the effect of over-indebtedness on economic well-being is evident in a particular way because – depending on the counter-measures taken – its negative consequences can impact various dimensions of well-being. For over-indebted households, the emergence of financial difficulty makes restricting consumption (day-to-day spending) an immediate necessity more often than in the case of not-over-indebted households. Indeed, their limited safety buffer – in the form of accumulated savings – more often forces over-indebted households to resort to solutions that can be regarded as extreme, such as welfare benefits, taking out further loans and credits, or even ceasing debt repayment. In-depth research in this area, which would presumably include the nature of the over-indebtedness and the socio-economic profile of the households concerned, could help to identify the specific determinants of the solutions they choose.

When analysing the categories of expenditure that potential financial difficulties could force people to cut back on, it can be seen that over-indebted households are more likely to report cuts in expenditure on basic needs (food, utilities, health). The differences in the responses given by over-indebted and not-over-indebted households suggest that they could have been dictated – at least in part – by personal experiences of consumption deprivation. This prompts the general observation that the economic well-being of over-indebted households is worse than that of their not-indebted counterparts and is more evident in the subjective dimension of economic well-being, where it emerges from assessments of income and housing, of need satisfaction, of safety and security, and of psychophysical state.

The breadth of the research category at issue, that is, economic well-being, and its dual nature (quantitative and qualitative) necessitated the application of appropriate methods to obtain an aggregate measure of economic well-being, and the approach adopted to achieve this was based on fuzzy sets theory. Analysis of economic well-being was conducted using a composite indicator made up of two dimensions: material and financial. The former covers objective and subjective housing conditions and evaluates households' capacity for need satisfaction. The latter includes information on households' financial situation (income and its assessment, level of financial security, and timeliness of debt repayments) their attitudes towards their financial situation, and its impact on their psychophysical state.

The distribution of the indicator values for economic well-being overall and in the financial and material dimensions indicates that over-indebted households experience poorer well-being than not-over-indebted households. An analysis of partial well-being indicators in various cross sections of over-indebted households leads to the conclusion that better well-being in the financial dimension is accompanied by higher income, a higher level of education, and a greater number of people in the household (no greater than four). In the material dimension, by turn, improvement in well-being is noticeable as the number of people in the household and the size of the locality it resides in decreases. The economic well-being of households is differentiated by the number of loans they hold and their type. In general terms, the financial and material situation of people with a large number of loans, and of people who simultaneously access credit from banks and from loan companies, is worse than that of people who have only one credit or who borrow exclusively from banks. It was established using the Gini coefficient that the greatest differentiation in economic well-being in the material dimension is found among households over-indebted according to the BPL index, and in the financial dimension among subjectively over-indebted households (SB).

Econometric modelling was employed to determine the dependence of economic well-being on economic and socio-demographic features and on household debt characteristics. The estimated multiple linear regression models confirmed that over-indebtedness has a negative impact on economic well-being both overall and in the financial dimension. Furthermore, being in arrears with repayments has a negative influence on the material dimension of economic well-being. The negative influence of the number of credits on the economic well-being of households (in both dimensions) and of debts to loan companies (when compared with bank debts) on well-being in the material dimension is also noticeable. Household attributes such as level of education, age, number of people in the household (economic well-being overall and in the financial dimension), the quintile per capita income group, and subjective assessment of financial situation proved statistically significant, and their positive impact on economic well-being is consistent with expectations and with the results of other scholars' work. Of the behavioural features investigated (the attitudes of respondents), making purchases to emulate friends and acquaintances has a negative impact on the value of the composite indicator of economic well-being, while an optimistic outlook has a positive influence on it.

Notes

1 According to European Union standards, an overcrowded property is one in which the household does not have at its disposal a minimum number of rooms equal to one room for the household (implicitly a living room), one room (bedroom) per couple in the household, one room (bedroom) for each single person aged 18 or above, one room (bedroom) per pair of single people of the same sex aged 12–17, one room (bedroom) for each single person aged 12–17 and not included in the previous category, and one room (bedroom) per pair of children under 12 years of age (Eurostat, 2020a).

2 According to Eurostat data, 39.2% of households in Poland (compared to 15.5% in the EU-28) lived in overcrowded dwellings (more than one person per room) in 2018. In this respect, Poland is near the bottom of the ranking of EU countries. This situation is worse only in Bulgaria (41.6%), Latvia (43.4%), and Romania (46.3%) (Eurostat, 2020b).

3 A study by Hanna Dudek and Wiesław Szczesny (2015), in which the same method of composite indicator construction was used and different weighting systems were used to aggregate features, found that for the data analysed, the choice of weights had no significant impact on the distribution of composite indicators.

4 In the research, the domains or dimensions are adopted *a priori* based on consulting the subject literature and on the available data. It is also possible to employ factor analysis to specify domains or dimensions (Betti, 2017; Betti et al., 2016).

5 The Gini coefficient measures the degree to which an empirical distribution deviates from an egalitarian one. In the context of enquiry into the inequality of a distribution of well-being, an egalitarian distribution is one in which each respondent achieves the same level of well-being. The Gini coefficient assumes values in the range [0, 1]. The more unequal the distribution, the higher the value of the coefficient. Where a distribution is egalitarian, the Gini coefficient equals 0.

6 The Theil index, which makes it possible to determine the contribution to overall inequality of the subgroups studied, is one of a broader group of measures that share an important feature known as additive decomposability (Shorrocks, 1980; Ulman & Wałęga, 2006).

7 Because they provided the best results in the statistical sense, linear models were employed in the analysis. See Maddala (2001) for more on linear and linearised models, and also Ulman (2015), who also shows their application to individual data concerning households.

8 Quintile groups of per capita income (QINC) are included in the explanatory variables instead of household monthly income.

References

Aboagye, J., & Jung, J. Y. (2018). Debt holding, financial behavior, and financial satisfaction. *Journal of Financial Counseling and Planning*, *29*(2), 208–218. https://doi.org/10.1891/1052-3073.29.2.208

Betti, G. (2017). Fuzzy measures of quality of life in Germany: A multidimensional and comparative approach. *Quality & Quantity*, *51*(1), 23–34. https://doi.org/10.1007/s11135-015-0291-0

Betti, G., Gagliardi, F., Lemmi, A., & Verma, V. (2015). Comparative measures of multidimensional deprivation in the European Union. *Empirical Economics*, *49*(3), 1071–1100. https://doi.org/10.1007/s00181-014-0904-9

Betti, G., Soldi, R., & Talev, I. (2016). Fuzzy multidimensional indicators of quality of life: The empirical case of Macedonia. *Social Indicators Research*, *127*(1), 39–53. https://doi.org/10.1007/s11205-015-0965-y

Betti, G., & Verma, V. (1999). Measuring the degree of poverty in a dynamic and comparative context: A multi-dimensional approach using fuzzy set theory. *Proceedings, ICCS-VI, Lahore, Pakistan*, *11*, 289–301.

Brown, S., & Gray, D. (2016). Household finances and well-being in Australia: An empirical analysis of comparison effects. *Journal of Economic Psychology*, *53*, 17–36. https://doi.org/10.1016/j.joep.2015.12.006

Burchardt, T. (2005). Are one man's rags another man's riches? Identifying adaptive expectations using panel data. *Social Indicators Research*, *74*(1), 57–102. https://doi.org/10.1007/s11205-005-6519-y

Cerioli, A., & Zani, S. (1990). A fuzzy approach to the measurement of poverty. In C. Dagum & M. Zenga (Eds.), *Income and wealth distribution, inequality and poverty* (pp. 272–284). Berlin: Springer. https://doi.org/10.1007/978-3-642-84250-4_18

Cheli, B., & Lemmi, A. (1995). A "totally" fuzzy and relative approach to the multidimensional analysis of poverty. *Economic Notes*, *24*(1), 115–134.

Christoph, B., & Noll, H.-H. (2003). Subjective well-being in the European Union during the 90s. In J. Vogel (Ed.), *European welfare production: Institutional configuration and distributional outcome* (Social Indicators Research Series, Vol. 18, pp. 197–222). Dordrecht: Springer. https://doi.org/10.1007/978-94-007-0977-5_8

Cracolici, M. F., Giambona, F., & Cuffaro, M. (2014). Family structure and subjective economic well-being: Some new evidence. *Social Indicators Research*, *118*(1), 433–456. https://doi.org/10.1007/s11205-013-0425-5

Cwynar, A. (2020). Financial literacy, behaviour and well-being of millennials in Poland compared to previous generations: The insights from three large-scale surveys. *Review of Economic Perspectives*, *20*(3), 289–335. https://doi.org/10.2478/revecp-2020-0015

Czech, A. (2017). Ocena jakości życia polskich gospodarstw domowych – ujęcie wojewódzkie. In E. Frątczak, T. Panek, & T. Słaby (Eds.), *Paradygmaty badawcze jakości życia w ekonomii, zarządzaniu i psychologii* (pp. 49–64). Wrocław: Wydawnictwo Uniwersytetu Ekonomicznego we Wrocławiu.

Dębicka, J., Mazurek, E., & Szalonka, K. (2017). Postrzeganie jakości życia przez osoby niepełnosprawne. *Prace Naukowe Uniwersytetu Ekonomicznego We Wrocławiu*, *483*, 29–43. https://doi.org/10.15611/pn.2017.483.03

Diener, E. (2000). Subjective well-being: The science of happiness and a proposal for a national index. *American Psychologist*, *55*(1), 34–43. https://doi.org/10.1037/0003-066X.55.1.34

Diener, E., & Biswas-Diener, R. (2002). Will money increase subjective well-being? *Social Indicators Research*, *57*(2), 119–169. https://doi.org/10.1023/A:1014411319119

Diener, E., Tay, L., & Oishi, S. (2013). Rising income and the subjective well-being of nations. *Journal of Personality and Social Psychology, 104*(2), 267–276. https://doi.org/10.1037/a0030487

Dudek, H. (2017). Analiza zadowolenia z życia w ujęciu wielowymiarowym za pomocą modeli regresji typu FRM. In E. Frątczak, T. Panek, & T. Słaby (Eds.), *Paradygmaty badawcze jakości życia w ekonomii, zarządzaniu i psychologii* (pp. 65–79). Wrocław: Wydawnictwo Uniwersytetu Ekonomicznego we Wrocławiu.

Dudek, H., & Szczesny, W. (2015). Zastosowanie funkcji przynależności w analizie subiektywnego postrzegania jakości życia. *Ekonometria, 4*(50), 62–78. https://doi.org/10.15611/ekt.2015.4.04

Dudek, H., & Szczesny, W. (2016). Subjective perception of quality of life – multidimensional analysis based on fuzzy sets approach. *Research Papers of Wrocław University of Economics, 435*, 55–68. https://doi.org/10.15611/pn.2016.435.03

Easterlin, R. A. (2001). Income and happiness: Towards a unified theory. *The Economic Journal, 111*(473), 465–484. https://doi.org/10.1111/1468-0297.00646

Eurostat. (2002). *European social statistics. Income, poverty and social exclusion: 2nd report.* Luxembourg: Office for Official Publications of the European Communities.

Eurostat. (2020a). *Glossary: Overcrowding rate.* https://ec.europa.eu/eurostat/statistics-explained/index.php/Glossary:Overcrowding_rate

Eurostat. (2020b). *Overcrowding rate by age, sex and poverty status – Total population – EU-SILC survey.* https://ec.europa.eu/eurostat/web/products-datasets/-/ilc_lvho05a

Galletta, S. (2016). On the determinants of happiness: A classification and regression tree (CART) approach. *Applied Economics Letters, 23*(2), 121–125. https://doi.org/10.1080/13504851.2015.1054066

Grzega, U. (2012). *Poziom życia ludności w Polsce: Determinanty i zróżnicowania.* Katowice: Wydawnictwo Uniwersytetu Ekonomicznego w Katowicach.

GUS. (2013). *Mieszkania. Narodowy Spis Powszechny Ludności i Mieszkań 2011.* Warszawa: Główny Urząd Statystyczny.

Kalinowski, S. (2015). *Poziom życia ludności wiejskiej o niepewnych dochodach.* Warszawa: Wydawnictwo Naukowe PWN.

Kempson, E., & Poppe, C. (2018). *Understanding financial well-being and capability – A revised model and comprehensive analysis* (Professional Report No. 3). Oslo: Consumption Research Norway (SIFO).

Kowalski, R., & Kwarciński, T. (2016). Racjonalność, użyteczność, dobrobyt. In M. Gorazda, Ł. Hardt, & T. Kwarciński (Eds.), *Metaekonomia. Zagadnienia z filozofii ekonomii* (pp. 387–405). Kraków: Copernicus Center Press.

Kwarciński, T., & Ulman, P. (2020). Quality of life paradox. Well-Being ranking of the selected European countries based on hybrid well-being approach. *Economics & Sociology, 13*(2), 160–180. https://doi.org/10.14254/2071-789X.2020/13-2/12

Llosada-Gistau, J., Montserrat, C., & Casas, F. (2015). The subjective well-being of adolescents in residential care compared to that of the general population. *Children and Youth Services Review, 52*, 150–157. https://doi.org/10.1016/j.childyouth.2014.11.007

Lusardi, A., Schneider, D. J., & Tufano, P. (2011). *Financially fragile households: Evidence and implications* (NBER Working Paper No. 17072). Cambridge, MA: National Bureau of Economic Research. https://doi.org/10.3386/w17072

Łuszczyk, M. (2013). *Pomiar jakości życia w skali międzynarodowej.* Kraków: Fundacja Uniwersytetu Ekonomicznego w Krakowie.

Maddala, G. S. (2001). *Introduction to econometrics* (3rd ed.). Chichester: Wiley.

Mahdzan, N. S., Zainudin, R., Sukor, M. E. A., Zainir, F., & Ahmad, W. M. W. (2019). Determinants of subjective financial well-being across three different household income groups in Malaysia. *Social Indicators Research, 146*(3), 699–726. https://doi.org/10.1007/s11205-019-02138-4

McGillivray, M., & Noorbakhsh, F. (2007). Composite indexes of human well-being: Past, present and future. In M. McGillivray (Ed.), *Human well-being: Concept and measurement* (pp. 113–134). London: Palgrave Macmillan. https://doi.org/10.1057/9780230625600_5

Michalos, A. C. (Ed.). (2014). *Encyclopedia of quality of life and well-being research*. Dordrecht: Springer. https://doi.org/10.1007/978-94-007-0753-5

Mullainathan, S., & Shafir, E. (2013). *Scarcity: Why having too little means so much*. London: Allen Lane.

Netemeyer, R. G., Warmath, D., Fernandes, D., & Lynch Jr., J. G. (2018). How am I doing? Perceived financial well-being, its potential antecedents, and its relation to overall well-being. *Journal of Consumer Research, 45*(1), 68–89. https://doi.org/10.1093/jcr/ucx109

Panek, T. (2011). *Ubóstwo, wykluczenie spoleczne i nierownosci. Teoria i praktyka pomiaru*. Warszawa: Oficyna Wydawnicza SGH.

Panek, T. (2015a). Analiza porównawcza subiektywnego dobrostanu w Europie. *Wiadomości Statystyczne, 60*(2), 1–26.

Panek, T. (2015b). Hierarchiczny model pomiaru jakości życia. *Wiadomości Statystyczne, 60*(6), 1–22.

Panek, T. (2017). Model pomiaru jakości życia. In E. Frątczak, T. Panek, & T. Słaby (Eds.), *Paradygmaty badawcze jakości życia w ekonomii, zarządzaniu i psychologii* (pp. 11–38). Wrocław: Wydawnictwo Uniwersytetu Ekonomicznego we Wrocławiu.

Perera, D. (2014). Wpływ stresu na jakość życia ludności w Polsce. *Wiadomości Statystyczne, 1*, 38–50.

Rutherford, L. G., & Fox, W. S. (2010). Financial wellness of young adults age 18–30. *Family and Consumer Sciences Research Journal, 38*(4), 468–484. https://doi.org/10.1111/j.1552-3934.2010.00039.x

Shah, A. K., Mullainathan, S., & Shafir, E. (2012). Some consequences of having too little. *Science, 338*(6107), 682–685. https://doi.org/10.1126/science.1222426

Shorrocks, A. F. (1980). The class of additively decomposable inequality measures. *Econometrica, 48*(3), 613–625. https://doi.org/10.2307/1913126

Słaby, T. (2016). The quality of life of the aboriginal rural people 60+ in Poland. Selected research results, 2014. *Prace Naukowe Uniwersytetu Ekonomicznego We Wrocławiu, 435*, 84–97. https://doi.org/10.15611/pn.2016.435.05

Suchecka, J., & Łaszkiewicz, E. (2017). Wykorzystanie modelowania wielopoziomowego w analizie jakości życia. *Studia Ekonomiczne. Zeszyty Naukowe Uniwersytetu Ekonomicznego w Katowicach, 344*, 133–144.

Ulman, P. (2015). *Statystyka pracy: Wybrane zagadnienia*. Kraków: Wydawnictwo Uniwersytetu Ekonomicznego w Krakowie.

Ulman, P., & Wałęga, A. (2006). Nierówności dochodowe w Polsce i ich dekompozycja. *Zeszyty Naukowe Polskiego Towarzystwa Ekonomicznego, 4*, 77–96.

Veenhoven, R. (2007). Subjective measures of well-being. In M. McGillivray (Ed.), *Human well-being: Concept and measurement* (pp. 214–239). London: Palgrave Macmillan. https://doi.org/10.1057/9780230625600_9

Verma, V., Betti, G., & Gagliardi, F. (2017). Fuzzy measures of longitudinal poverty in a comparative perspective. *Social Indicators Research, 130*(2), 435–454. https://doi.org/10.1007/s11205-015-1194-0

Wałęga, G. (2013). *Kredytowanie gospodarstw domowych*. Warszawa: Polskie Wydawnictwo Ekonomiczne.

Włodarczyk, K. (2015). Jakość życia postrzegana przez Polaków w XXI wieku. *Konsumpcja i Rozwój, 1*, 3–16.

Zadeh, L. A. (1965). Fuzzy sets. *Information and Control, 8*(3), 338–353. https://doi.org/10.1016/S0019-9958(65)90241-X

Zeliaś, A. (2000). Niektóre sposoby konstruowania taksonomicznych mierników poziomu życia ludności. In A. Zeliaś (Ed.), *Taksonomiczna analiza przestrzennego zróżnicowania poziomu życia w Polsce w ujęciu dynamicznym* (pp. 86–95). Kraków: Akademia Ekonomiczna.

Zwierzchowski, J., & Panek, T. (2020). Measurement of subjective well-being under capability approach in Poland. *Polish Sociological Review, 2*, 157–178. https://doi.org/10.26412/psr210.02

Conclusion

The changing socio-economic context requires systematic research aimed at understanding and assessing household well-being. Its conclusions will not only make it possible to construct institutions and mechanisms to improve the well-being of individuals but also provide an opportunity to comprehend social processes within a broader frame of reference.[1]

One of the principal processes identified in many countries in recent years is the steady increase in household debt. It is a trend that affects Poland too. Given the value of the credits and loans granted by the banking system, it may be stated with confidence that they have become a permanent means of financing consumption. Thus, the issue of indebtedness is likely to appear and be addressed more broadly in academic discourse than hitherto. The research underlying the analyses presented in this book, which included 1,107 indebted households in Poland, is in line with this expectation.

As the most important detailed findings of the individual chapters are to be found in their summaries, this section presents only the general research conclusions accompanied by references to the hypotheses formulated in the introduction.

The conducted research made it possible to achieve the book's central aim and to test the research hypotheses. No previous study has taken such a comprehensive approach to the economic well-being of over-indebted households in Poland and its ramifications. The outcome of the analyses does not consist only in accomplishing the cognitive goals set out in the introduction but also in testing the possibilities for applying selected statistical tools and methods to the study of over-indebtedness.

In many studies of the economics of households – both theoretical and empirical – income is treated as the basic variable determining the indebtedness of households and economic well-being. This is reflected in the first of the detailed hypotheses formulated in the book. The results of the investigations confirm that an increase in income is accompanied by a lower probability that a household will be classified as over-indebted according to the DSTI30 indicator. Income growth also has a positive effect on the economic well-being of households, regardless of the extent of their debt obligations. While the empirically observed impact of income corresponds with the assumptions expressed

DOI: 10.4324/9781003254706-8

in the hypothesis mentioned earlier, to conclude that it is the most important determinant of over-indebtedness and economic well-being would overstate the case. Instead, it is one of the key variables, rather than the only one of such importance. Subjective elements in the form of respondents' assessment of their own financial situation are of equal importance to households' economic well-being, while the characteristics of the debt and behavioural factors are of equal importance to their over-indebtedness.

The cross-sectional analyses demonstrate that over-indebtedness has many aspects. This is because its magnitude – as captured by the different indicators – varies. While the value of the debt repayment burden indicator for all households is not high, and the extreme form of over-indebtedness – loss of liquidity – is an isolated occurrence, indebtedness still leads to poverty for nearly one in three of the households studied. What is more, the impact of debt repayments on households is not only confined to difficulties satisfying needs but also possesses a subjective dimension. Indeed, the psychological burden of debt, which can influence the non-economic aspects of their lives, is even felt by the households with the highest incomes. The research results therefore confirm that it is necessary to use diverse indicators when investigating over-indebted households. Only this approach allows us to capture the essence of over-indebtedness – especially since, as the research has established, a minority of objectively over-indebted households are at the same time subjectively over-indebted and vice versa. This confirms the aspect of one of the detailed hypotheses which states that there is limited overlap between the subjective and objective dimensions of over-indebtedness. At the same time, it cannot be concluded that subjective indebtedness is confirmed as more frequent than its objective counterpart in respect of Polish households. The proportion of households objectively over-indebted according to the DSTI30 indicator is almost identical to that of households which feel over-indebted, and this group of subjectively over-indebted households (SB) is far smaller than that of households identified as over-indebted by the second objective indicator: below the poverty line (BPL). This means that the nature of over-indebtedness is, despite everything, more an objective matter of economics than a subjective one of psychology.

Over-indebtedness does not occur with equal frequency among all household types. The cross-sectional analyses allowed us to identify the specificities of indebtedness in Poland, where it is households of low socio-economic status that are especially vulnerable to over-indebtedness. In their case, in particular, the need to cease measuring over-indebtedness by the standard, classical indicator of debt service to income (DSTI) became clear, for that indicator does not have to reach a high level in order to have a powerful impact on their economic well-being. With that in mind, this book proposes the use of an additional indicator, BPL, to investigate household indebtedness. To the best of the authors' knowledge, this is the first time the BPL indicator has been used to investigate the indebtedness and economic well-being of Polish households. It enjoys an advantage over other indicators in that it takes into account the social aspect of over-indebtedness and can identify households whose capacity to satisfy their needs can be seriously impaired by relatively small repayments.

The detailed hypothesis that objectively and subjectively over-indebted households borrow for different reasons should be rejected. Regardless of the size of their debt, the primary reason Polish households take on credits and loans is to finance their need for housing and durables. One might therefore be tempted to conclude that, in general, over-indebtedness is the product of deliberate consumption decisions. However, unrealistic consumption aspirations, which can lead to over-indebtedness where households are over-optimistic about their financial capabilities, can appear even in the case of needs as fundamental as housing. What is more, when attempting to identify the most important reasons for over-indebtedness, it might perhaps be necessary to examine the 'marginal' indebtedness that results in crossing the thin line between a heavy debt repayment burden and an excessive one. There is no doubt that further research – perhaps in the form of individual interviews rather than a closed-ended questionnaire – is required to better understand this issue.

If it is to be examined, the question of well-being must be operationalised. The multifaceted nature of the research made it necessary to employ a composite indicator to evaluate well-being. The fuzzy sets approach, developed primarily for the analysis of poverty, was successfully applied to evaluate economic well-being, which is a category hitherto absent from the Polish literature. It was assumed that to properly capture the role of over-indebtedness in shaping economic well-being, a combined analysis of material and financial matters, as well as subjective and objective ones, was needed. The approach taken here allowed for a holistic evaluation of well-being. Based on the results of the analysis, there are no grounds for rejecting the detailed hypothesis that over-indebtedness has a greater influence on economic well-being in the financial dimension than in the material dimension. According to all of the indicators applied, the variables identifying over-indebted households significantly determine well-being in the financial dimension. Repayment arrears, which are among the determinants of well-being in the material dimension, worsen well-being to a lesser degree there than in the financial dimension. The Gini coefficient, used to analyse the inequality of the distribution of the composite indicator of economic well-being, made it possible to draw additional conclusions concerning the two dimensions, while the Theil index was used for the decomposition of the inequality of economic well-being.

According to the final hypothesis, the detailed characteristics of the debt have a greater impact on the economic well-being of over-indebted households than of not-over-indebted households. The results of the parameter estimates for the multiple linear regression models do not offer unequivocal support for this supposition. Over-indebted and not-over-indebted households differ only slightly in terms of the negative impact of the number of loans held on economic well-being, while the impact of the variables describing debt type either proved statistically insignificant or significant at the level of 0.06.

Beyond the topics directly dictated by the need to test the hypotheses, the book assesses the spatial differentiation of over-indebtedness and characteristics of indebtedness (number of loans and debt type) and identifies the ways in which households cope with financial difficulties.

Three groups of voivodships (provinces) similar in terms of the variables adopted for analysis were extracted by Ward's method and then by the k-means method. However, the results of these operations did not support the conclusion that there exist regional specificities of over-indebtedness, that is, no clusters made up of adjacent voivodships were formed.

Over-indebted and not-over-indebted households proved remarkably consistent in their responses about their primary means of coping with financial difficulties. The method both groups indicated most frequently was limiting current expenditure, followed by recourse to savings and taking additional work. Over-indebted households were more likely than not-over-indebted households to favour borrowing and non-payment of debt when faced with financial shocks. There was similar agreement between the two groups of households in terms of their most frequent responses concerning the type of expenditure they limited – on stimulants, leisure activities, and home furnishings and maintenance. Where they differed sharply, however, was in the greater declared readiness of over-indebted households to limit expenditure on basic needs (food, utilities, healthcare).

To summarise, it may be stated that the main research hypothesis was confirmed in the course of the investigations. Irrespective of the criterion adopted to identify them, over-indebted households are characterised by poorer economic well-being than not-over-indebted households. That said, the variance in the values of the composite indicator of economic well-being between over-indebted and not-over-indebted households is smaller in respect of overall well-being than in respect of economic well-being in the financial and material dimensions. In general, the poorest well-being – in the financial dimension in particular – was characteristic of subjectively over-indebted households. In respect of economic well-being, households classified as over-indebted according to the DSTI30 indicator proved closest (but still not close) to not over-indebted households.

There is, however, variation in the strength of the impact of over-indebtedness captured by different indicators on the two dimensions (fields) of economic well-being. This could be accounted for by the fact that each of the indicators permits the identification of a group of over-indebted households specific to itself. All of the indicators analysed proved significant in the context of negative impact on the financial dimension of well-being and almost all (except DSTI30) proved significant in respect of overall well-being. Interestingly, the material dimension of well-being was influenced only by repayment arrears of more than 3 months (A3). This is the indicator, moreover, which had the most powerful impact on economic well-being – not only among all of the indicators adopted to analyse over-indebtedness but also among all of the variables analysed. Meanwhile, the indicator of the debt repayment burden in relation to income (DSTI30) proved to be the least significant in terms of impact on economic well-being. These findings lead to the conclusion that the choice of indicator is vitally important in studies devoted to assessing the well-being of over-indebted households and, perhaps, that it is necessary to adopt a set of indicators rather than only one for this purpose.

The research results and related conclusions can be used to create legal and institutional solutions to prevent the negative effects of an excessive debt burden. It would appear, however, that the multifaceted nature of over-indebtedness (even if only in terms of its causes and consequences) does not require the creation of separate regulatory arrangements to assist at-risk households, but rather points to the need to take over-indebtedness into consideration when undertaking measures in various areas of socio-economic life at the economic (income level, labour market), social (poverty and financial exclusion, social assistance), institutional (preventing usury, insolvency), and individual (promoting responsible social attitudes and mental health) levels. Monitoring over-indebtedness as part of a kind of early-warning system and taking preventive measures to limit the consequences of income shocks and their concomitant debt problems can protect against social and economic difficulties (financial crisis) that are far more serious than a temporary decline in well-being. Furthermore, issues associated with over-indebtedness should become a part of long-term initiatives designed to alleviate the detrimental consequences of this phenomenon, such as promoting good practices among lending institutions, establishing a system of financial education, and providing dedicated credit advice to groups vulnerable to over-indebtedness.

The authors are aware of the limitations of this research, which compel caution when considering the conclusions drawn from it. First, a major obstacle to designing a study of over-indebtedness was that the scale of this phenomenon among Polish households was essentially unknown, though intuitively estimated to be small. This issue affected the selection of the population studied – indebted households – and the sampling method used to guarantee the reliability of the research results in respect of over-indebted households. Second, it must be borne in mind that issues related to debt, just as issues related to income or wealth, are a sensitive matter for respondents. Third, it would appear that to some degree indebtedness continues to be negatively perceived in Poland, which means that respondents are reluctant to admit to taking out loans and credit. These difficulties are compounded by people's natural distrust of questionnaire surveys – especially those conducted by telephone. By avoiding this type of research, households often feel they are defending themselves against dishonest direct selling and an avalanche of unsolicited commercial information. What is more, given the data were collected by telephone, the level of detail obviously had to be restricted so that the survey could be conducted within a reasonable amount of time. Also, despite being based on a scrupulous review of the subject literature, the selection of research methods was likewise not devoid of subjectivity. Notwithstanding these reservations, however, the authors hope that the approach taken here will meet with approval and inspire further research into the well-being of over-indebted households.

The social aspects of indebtedness, and especially its consequences for economic and psychological well-being, point unequivocally to the need to carry out systematic research into over-indebted households. Given rapid technological progress and the swift development of the financial sector, resulting in still easier access to credits and loans, especially for households, this postulate assumes even greater significance. Changes in the economic, political, cultural, and social environment, both in Poland and worldwide, and the emergence of crisis phenomena, likewise justify further interest in research on the well-being of over-indebted households.

Note

1 One of the consequences of the social tensions brought about by the worsening well-being of some groups of households, by social inequalities, and by the excessive influence of financial institutions and large corporations is the popularity of Indignados in Spain and Occupy Wall Street in the United States.

Index

ability to make ends meet 64–65, 73, 77, 136
adaptive preferences 8, 157
anxiety 77, 124
arrears 13, 15, 17, 67, 71, 136, 161; budget management skills 158, 158; and concept of over-indebtedness 29, 65, 75; as variable of economic well-being indicator 166, 188; *see also* repayment arears (A) indicator
attitude to debt 16, 33, 72, 77, 131
attitude to risk 52, 66–67, 130
availability heuristic 8, 68

banking system 13, 22n12, 44, 66, 94, 161, 186
bankruptcy 64, 79–80; *see also* insolvency
basic goods 135, 139, 157
basic needs 53, 106, 110, 112, 135, 153, 153, 157, 161, 166, 189
behavioural biases 8, 21–22n3, 66, 68
behavioural economics 6–7, 21n3, 22n6, 68, 76
behavioural traits: as determinants of over-indebtedness 106–107, 108, 109, 110, 113, 115–116, 187; and economic well-being 175, 176, 177, 178
below poverty line (BPL) indicator: and economic well-being 152–154, 153, *154*, 155, 156, 158, 159, 160, 162, 157–163, 170, 171, 172–173, 173, 175, 187; as measure 17, 73, 75–76, 80; over-indebted households according to 88–105, *90*, *98*, 89, 91, 92, 95, 99, 101, *103*, 105, 108, 110, 109, 113, 116n4
biological needs 8
borrowing: and behavioural biases 8–9; and consumption smoothing 6–7; data sources in Poland on the extent of 11–15; as method to cope with financial difficulty 75, 160, 161; one-off studies in Poland on 15–20; and quality of life improvements 129, 131; reasons for 53–59, 67–68, 71, 98–99, 99, 132; stimulated by the social norms and consumption patterns 9–11
borrowing needs 10, 18
bounded rationality 6–7, 66, 113
BPL *see* below the poverty line (BPL) indicator
budget management 31, 129–130, 129; and education 68, 96; problems with 59, 68, 76; skills 128, 158, 158
buffer-stock savings 7

children 18, 33, 34, 133, 181n1; and indebtedness 14, 17–18, 132; and over-indebtedness 67, 93; and well-being 128–129, 132, 172
cognitive capacity 8, 67
composite index *see* composite well-being indicator
composite well-being indicator: inequality of the distribution of values of 173–174, 173; linear model of 174–177, 175, 177; as tool for comparative analysis 30, 152, 163, 165–167; well-being analysis by 133–134, 136–137, 169, 169, 170, 172–173, 188–190
conspicuous consumption 9
consumption: concept of well-being and 121–125, 131; cultural conditioning of 71; financial difficulties and reduction of expenditure on 156–157, 156, 163; financial margin indicator 75; satisfaction of consumption needs 152–153, 153; smoothing 5–7, 66, 91; social dimension of 8–10, 67, 93; types of needs financed by debt 53–59, 53, 54, 55, 98–99

credit cards 8, 14, 69–70, 132
credit market: developmental level 74, 76, 132; household behaviour on 66, 96–97, 113; in Poland 12–13, 19, 52; risk of over-indebtedness and 67, 69–71; as tool in consumption smoothing 6–11
credit unions 11, 70, 94; as source of loans 35–36, 37, 40–44, 41, 43, 45
creditworthiness 56, 67, 69, 97, 155
culture, as factor of over-indebtedness 67, 70–72
current consumption 14, 16, 53, 54, 55, 56–59, 98, 99, 131
current income 66, 92, 121, 136, 166; in life cycle models 6–7; and repayment capacity 35–36, 37, 39, 40, 41, 42, 43, 44, 45, 46, 157, 158; repayment capacity and indebtedness as threat to health 48; repayment capacity and safe levels of indebtedness 51

debt: psychological burden of 47, 48, 49, 77, 93, 96, 131–132, 158, 159, 161, 187; psychological dimension of 47, 64, 78, 130
debt service-to-income (DSTI) ratio: in different types of indebted households of 35–46, 37, 39, 41, 43, 45; and economic well-being 152–154, 153, *154*, 155, 156, 157–159, 158, 159, 160, 161, 162, 163, 170, 172, 173, 175, 186–187, 189–190; indebtedness as threat to health 48, 49; as measure 17–18, 73, 74–75, 78; motives for indebtedness by 55, 58–59; over-indebted households according to 88–105, 89, *90*, 91, 92, 95, *98*, 99, 101, *102*, 105, 108, 109, 110, 113, 116n4; quality of the loan portfolio of banks 13; safe levels of indebtedness 49, 51, 52; and type of loans 14
debt-to-assets (DTA) ratio 14, 36, 73, 74, 113
debt-to-income (DTI) ratio 8, 13–14, 68, 73–74, 73, 78, 127
debt-to-wealth (DTW) ratio 73, 73
decision-makers 6–7
depression 47, 131–132, 142n4
disability pensioners *see* pensioners
disposable income 5–6, *12*, 18, 75, 132, 136–138, 140
DSTI *see* debt service-to-income (DSTI) ratio
DTA *see* debt-to-assets (DTA) ratio
DTI *see* debt-to-income (DTI) ratio
DTW *see* debt-to-wealth (DTW) ratio
durable goods 13, 15, 131, 135, 138, 140; as a borrowing motive 53, 54, 55, 99; *see also* non-durable goods

economic system: structural changes 10–11, 70
economic well-being: composite indicator of 166, 167–169, 188, 189; concept of 120–121, 125–126; determinants of 174–178, 175, 177, 187–188; material and financial dimensions 152, 166–176, 167, *168*, 169, 170, 173, 175; method of evaluation 29–31, 152; relation to financial well-being 126–128, 127, 141n1, 141n3
ethnic minorities 69
European Commission 63–64
European Quality of Life Survey (EQLS) 133
European Social Survey (ESS) 133
European System of Social Indicators (EUSI) 125
European Union 71, 134, 181n1
European Union Statistics on Income and Living Conditions (EU-SILC) 33, 77, 123, 134, 136
expenditure cascades hypothesis 9
experimental economics 21, 68

falling wages hypothesis 9
family: family structure and model as determinant of over-indebtedness 66–67, 70; life cycle of 92, 132–133; relation to well-being 122, 124, 130, 132, 137, 139; as source of loan 35–36, 40, 129
financial attitudes 129, 140, 158
financial behaviour 127, 128, 130, 131
financial buffer 14, 93, 132, 161, 179; *see also* financial margin (FM) indicator
financial capabilities 7, 123–124, 188
financial conditions 22n11, 127–128, 130
financial decisions 8, 18, 21n3, *98*, 107, 109, 130, 178
financial difficulties 76–78; coping with 128, 159–163, 160, 162, 189; and over-indebtedness concept 65; risk of 70–71; *see also* repayment difficulties
financial freedom 127
financial literacy 16, 113, 127, 129, *129*
financial margin (FM) indicator 73, 75, 80
financial resources 124, 128, 132
financial satisfaction 122, *128*
financial security: of over-indebted households 157–158, 158; and well-being 122, 127–128, 127, 179–180

financial shocks 65–66, 127, 130, 189
financial well-being 121, 126, 134, 164, 141n1, 142n3, 172; and debt 130–133; objective and subjective aspects 127–129, 127, *128*, *129*, 130; *see also* economic well-being
fuzzy sets 30, 134, 163–164, 180, 188

Gini coefficient 30, 173, 173, 180, 181n5, 188

happiness 122–124, 132–133, 142n2
healthcare 125, 139, 156, 157, 162, 163, 167, 189
health problems 47, 49, 131–132, 159, 166, 179
hire purchase 35–36, 37, 38, 40, 41, 42, 43, 59, 77
Household Budget Survey 11, 13–14, 17–19, 32–33, 34, 35, 134
housing conditions 13, 31, 139, 153, 155, 155, 167, 174
housing loans 11–15, 19
housing needs 54, 57, 60, 71, 155, 188
hybrid well-being 134
hyperbolic discounting 8, 68

income buffer 18–19
income distribution 138, 152, 153
inequality: of economic well-being 30, 173, 173–174, 181n5, 181n6, 188, 191n1; impact on indebtedness 9–10, 71; income dispersion and deregulation 10; *see also* Gini coefficient; Theil index
insolvency 64, 190; as an indicator/measure of over-indebtedness 70–71, 73, 78; of Polish households 15–16; *see also* bankruptcy
interest rates 8, 20, 65–67, 69–71, 74–75
intertemporal choice 5, 7, 63, 66–67
irregular income 138

life cycle 92, 128, 132; motives for borrowing 52–53, 56; over-indebtedness 20, 66, 68, 74
life-cycle models 5–6, 18; behavioural economics perspective on 6–9; liquidity constraints 6–7; uncertainty 7
life needs 17, 139
life satisfaction: and over-indebtedness 20, 132; and well-being 122, 124–126; of Polish households 134–135, 137, 139–140
lifestyle 9, 67, 71, 124, 138, 176
liquidity: constraints of 6–7, 10; loss of 63–64, 68, 78, 187
living conditions 64, 121, 125, 134–135, 142n2; material 57, 125–126, 136, 138; *see also* European Union Statistics on Income and Living Conditions (EU-SILC)
loan companies 13, 15–16, 52, 94, 97, 171; and risk of over-indebtedness 67, 70; structure of indebted households and debt types 35–44, 37, 38, 41, 43, 45

macroeconomic shocks 70, 77
marginal utility 121
material deprivation 92, 136, 139, 180
material well-being 120–124, 126, 141n1; *see also* economic well-being
medical treatment 53, 53, 54, 55, 56–59, 99
mental accounting 8
mental health: impact of debt on 20, 47, 47, 48, 49, 64, 131, 158–159, 159; as indebtedness factor 142n4; as quality of life category 125
mortgages 56, 67, 69–70, 94, 132; data on 14–15; financial difficulties and 77, 94; in Poland 18–20, 116n3

National Bank of Poland (NBP) 11–12, 14, 56
need satisfaction 8; and over-indebtedness 64, 71, 131, 156–157, 156; studies on Polish households 133, 135–139; and well-being 120–124, 152–153, 156
new consumerism 9
NL *see* number of credits or loans (NL) indicator
non-bank lenders 15–16, 18, 22n12, 40, 49, 52, 94, 97, 172
non-bank loans: data on repayment of 14; and economic well-being 171, 172–174, 175, 177, 178; and over-indebtedness 92, 94, 95, 97, 106, 108, 109, 110, 112; safe levels of indebtedness 51, 52; spatial differentiation of 99–100, *100*, 103–105, 105; as threat to health 48, 49
non-durable goods 75
not-over-indebted (NOI) 17, 152–155, 153, *154*, 155, 159; composite indicator of well-being 167–174, 169, 170, 173, 177–178, 177, 188; coping with financial difficulties 159–163, 160, 162, 163, 188; financial security of 157–158, 158; level of satisfying of consumption needs 156–157, 156

number of credits or loans (NL) indicator: characteristics of over-indebted households broken down by 92, 94, 95, 97; in different types of indebted households 35–46, 37, 38, 41, 43, 45; as measure of over-indebtedness 73, 76, 88; and safe levels of debt 49–52, 50, 51; and subjective burden of debt 48, 49; as variable of model for over-indebtedness 106, 109, 112; and well-being 171, 173, 176, 178, 188

OECD 125–126
over-indebtedness: assessment based on mix indicators 88–90, 89, *90*, 94–98, 95; concept of 63–65; and coping with financial difficulty 159–163, 160, 162; factors determining 66–72; and financial security 157–158, 158; non-economic consequences of 158–159, 159; objective indicators of 73, 73–76, 78; and satisfying consumption needs 155–157, 156; studies on Polish households 17–20; subjective indicators of 73, 77

parents 67, 129, 132, 154
payday loans 36, 37, 38, 40, 41, 43, 44, 45, 70
pensioners 15, 35; characteristics of indebted 44, 45, 46; over-indebtedness of 91, 94, 95, 97, 112, 132; as vulnerable group 17; well-being of 134, 137, 176
permanent income 5–6
personality traits 92, 124, 129, 129
poverty: method of analysis 164–165; and over-indebtedness 67, 89, 93–94, 96–97, 187; and quality of life 125, 136; *see also* poverty line
poverty line 73, 75–76, 88–90, 114, 152; *see also* below poverty line (BPL) indicator
precautionary motive 7
preferences 6, 66, 77, 159; interdependency of 22n6; time inconsistency of 8, 68
provinces *see* voivodships
psychological well-being 20, 77, 78, 124, 130, 132, 140

quality of life: concept of 120, 122–126, 130, 141n2; influence of debt on 130–132; method of measure 163–164, 174; and over-indebtedness 64, 93, 178; of Polish households 15, 133–140

relative income hypothesis 9
religion 72, 140
repayment arears (A) indicator: and economic well-being 175, 176; as measure of over-indebtedness 73, 76; over-indebted households according to 88, 89, 116n3, 189
repayment capacity: by age 36, 37; as approach to define over-indebtedness 63–64, 74, 77; by educational level 39, 40; by household size 41, 42; indebtedness as threat to health 48, 49; of over-indebted and not-over-indebted households 157–158, 158; by place of residence 43, 44; safe levels of indebtedness 51; by source of income/maintenance 45, 46
retirement pensioners *see* pensioners
rural households: and indebtedness 34, 42, 43, 44, 48, 50; and motives for borrowing 54, 57; and over-indebtedness 91, 95, 106, 113; and well-being 135, 138–139, 170

SAFS *see* subjective assessment of financial situation
savings 20, 31, 72, 189; and financial-well-being 127–129; and indebtedness of households 35–46, 37, 39, 41, 43, 45, 48, 51; indicator of debt to 72–75, 73; and life cycle 5–7, 10, 21n3; and over-indebtedness 157–163, 158, 160, 162, 166; in Poland 14–15
SB *see* subjective debt burden (SB) indicator
self-control problem 8, 22n5, 68, 76
sex 31, 33, 34, 124, 129, 170; debt and health problems by 47; as determinant of over-indebtedness 106, 108, 110; safe level of debt by 49, 50; structure of over-indebted households by 91, 92, 95, 96
social capital 72, 125, 137, 139
Social Diagnosis 13, 15, 18–20, 56, 123, 134, 136
social exclusion 125, 133, 139, 165
social norms 8–9, 124, 155
social relations 124–125, 130, 135
standard of living: impact of debt on 66, 71, 75, 161; as part of well-being 121, 124, 127, 128; of Polish households 133–138; relationship with concept of over-indebtedness 63–64
Statistics Poland 13–14, 22n10, 32–33, 35, 123, 133–134, 154
stress 64, 137; as consequence of indebtedness 47–49, 47, 48, 77, 131, 159, 159; as psychological burden of debt 96, 131–132, 166; well-being 132, 172

student loans 132
subjective assessment of financial situation 138, 140, 176, 187; and financial well-being 127–128, 130; and level of household indebtedness 17, 19, 77–78; of over-indebted households 112, 152–153, 153, 175, 177; as variable 106, 108, 109, 110, 166
subjective debt burden (SB) indicator: determinants of over-indebtedness 105–113, 106, 108, 110; and economic well-being 152–163, 153, *154*, 155, 156, 158, 159, 160, 162, 169–173, 170, 173, 175, 187; as measure 73, 77; over-indebted households according to 88–99, 89, *90*, 91, 92, 95, 98, 99, 116n4; over-indebted household by voivodships 99–105, 101, *102*, *103*, 105
subjective well-being 122–126; of Polish households 133–134, 136–137

Theil index 30, 173, 173, 181n6, 188

unemployment 116n3, 124–125; unemployed people 15, 67, 136–138

unsecured loans 67, 75, 132
utilities 116n3, 156, 157, 162, 163, 167, 179–180, 189
utility 5, 9

voivodships 142n5; indebtedness in 13, 15; over-indebtedness in/by 99–105; quality of life in 135–136, 139; sample structure by 31–33, *33*
vulnerable groups 17, 65–69, 96, 142n4, 187

wealth 5, 11, 65; as determinant of debt 7–8; and motives for indebtedness 56–58; and over-indebtedness 92, 96, 152–153, 153; ratio of debt to 73–75, 73; and well-being 121, 123–124, 126, 128, 130, 135–136, 141, 166
welfare benefits 160, 161
welfare state 10, 71
well-being 11; composite indicator of 163–166, 181n5; concept of 121–126; and debt 130–132; of Polish households 133, 138–139
workplace loans 35–36, 37, 38, 40, 41, 43, 44, 45

For Product Safety Concerns and Information please contact our EU representative GPSR@taylorandfrancis.com
Taylor & Francis Verlag GmbH, Kaufingerstraße 24, 80331 München, Germany

www.ingramcontent.com/pod-product-compliance
Ingram Content Group UK Ltd.
Pitfield, Milton Keynes, MK11 3LW, UK
UKHW020005200926
475702UK00015B/2484
* 9 7 8 1 0 3 2 1 8 4 7 2 2 *